# BIOGRAPHICAL STUDIES

# BIOGRAPHICAL STUDIES

## WALTER BAGEHOT

M.A. AND FELLOW OF UNIVERSITY COLLEGE, LONDON

EDITED BY

## RICHARD HOLT HUTTON

AMS PRESS
NEW YORK

Reprinted from the edition of 1881, London
First AMS EDITION published 1970
Manufactured in the United States of America


Library of Congress Catalog Card Number: 75-111469
SBN: 404-00445-8

AMS PRESS, INC.
New York, N. Y. 10003

# PREFACE.

The interest with which Mr. Bagehot's 'Literary Studies' appear to have been received by the public, encourages me to collect and republish his Studies in Political Biography, most of them from the 'National Review,' and two—that on Adam Smith and that on Lord Althorp—from the 'Fortnightly Review,' which I do with the permission of the proprietors. These essays are, I think, valuable, not only as acute criticisms on the statesmen reviewed, but also, in no small degree, as expressing in some detail and with a good deal of vivacity the political mind of one of the shrewdest and most separate of the politicians of this generation. It will be seen, I think, that the late Sir George Cornewall Lewis comes very near to being, in Mr. Bagehot's mind, the ideal English statesman—indeed, that Sir George Lewis, with a little political ozone infused into him, would have been quite that ideal. I have, of course, altered and omitted nothing, even where the particular opinion expressed has not been verified but rather discredited by the course of subsequent events— for example, in relation to the general adhesion given by Mr. Bagehot (p. 333) to Sir George Lewis's scornful estimate of that 'village lawyer' Lincoln's Unionist policy. If there ever were overhaste or a touch of passion in either Sir George Lewis or his critic, it was apt to be shown in their condemnation of political measures recommended by deep popular emotions and convictions. But the reader of these pages will find, I think, a great deal more to surprise him in the shrewdness of the forecasts than in their occasional miscarriage.

I have added to the longer studies some pages consisting of a few shorter papers of the same kind taken from the ' Economist ' newspaper, which may be found, I hope, not the least interesting in this volume.

R. H. H.

ENGLEFIELD GREEN, *Dec.* 21, 1880.

# CONTENTS.

# BIOGRAPHICAL STUDIES.

## THE CHARACTER OF SIR ROBERT PEEL.[1]

### (1856.)

MOST people have looked over old letters. They have been
struck with the change of life, with the doubt on things now
certain, the belief in things now incredible, the oblivion of what
now seems most important, the strained attention to departed
detail, which characterise the mouldering leaves. Something
like this is the feeling with which we read Sir Robert Peel's
Memoirs. Who now doubts on the Catholic Question? It is
no longer a 'question.' A younger generation has come into
vigorous, perhaps into insolent life, who regard the doubts that
were formerly entertained as absurd, pernicious, delusive. To
revive the controversy was an error. The accusations which
are brought against a public man in his own age are rarely
those echoed in after times. Posterity sees less or sees more.
A few points stand forth in distinct rigidity; there is no idea of
the countless accumulation, the collision of action, the web of
human feeling, with which, in the day of their life, they were
encompassed. Time changes much. The points of controversy
seem clear; the assumed premises uncertain. The difficulty is
to comprehend 'the difficulty.' Sir Robert Peel will have to
answer to posterity, not for having passed Catholic emancipation
when he did, but for having opposed it before; not for having

[1] *Memoirs*, by the Right Hon. Sir Robert Peel, Bart., M.P., &c. Published
by the Trustees of his Papers, Lord Mahon (now Lord Stanhope) and the
Right Hon. Edward Cardwell, M.P. Part I. 'The Roman Catholic Question,'
1828-9.

B

been precipitate, but for having been slow; not for having taken 'insufficient securities' for the Irish Protestant Church, but for having endeavoured to take security for an institution too unjust to be secured by laws or lawgivers.

This memoir has, however, a deeper aim. Its end is rather personal than national. It is designed to show, not that Sir Robert did what was externally expedient—this was probably too plain—but that he himself really believed what he did to be right. The scene is laid not in Ireland, not in the county of Clare, not amid the gross triumphs of O'Connell, or the outrageous bogs of Tipperary, but in the Home Office, among files of papers, among the most correctly-docketed memoranda, beside the minute which shows that Justice A. should be dismissed, that Malefactor O. ought not to be reprieved. It is labelled 'My Conscience,' and is designed to show that 'my conscience' was sincere.

Seriously, and apart from jesting, this is no light matter. Not only does the great space which Sir Robert Peel occupied during many years in the history of the country entitle his character to the anxious attention of historical critics, but the very nature of that character itself, its traits, its deficiencies, its merits, are so congenial to the tendencies of our time and government, that to be unjust to him is to be unjust to all probable statesmen. We design to show concisely how this is.

A constitutional statesman is in general a man of common opinions and uncommon abilities. The reason is obvious. When we speak of a free government, we mean a government in which the sovereign power is divided, in which a single decision is not absolute, where argument has an office. The essence of the *gouvernement des avocats*, as the Emperor Nicholas called it, is that you must persuade so many persons. The appeal is not to the solitary decision of a single statesman; not to Richelieu or Nesselrode alone in his closet; but to the jangled mass of men, with a thousand pursuits, a thousand interests, a thousand various habits. Public opinion, as it is said, rules; and public opinion is the opinion of the average man. Fox used to say of Burke: 'Burke is a wise man; but he is wise too soon.' The average man will not bear this. He is a cool, common person, with a considerate air, with figures in his mind, with his own business to attend to, with a set of ordinary opinions arising from and suited to ordinary life. He can't bear novelty or originalities. He says: 'Sir, I never heard such a thing *before* in my life;' and he thinks this a *reductio ad absurdum.* You may see his taste by the reading of which he approves. Is there a more splendid monument of talent and industry than 'The Times'? No wonder that the average man—that any one—believes in it. As Carlyle observes: 'Let the highest intellect able to write epics try to write such a leader for the morning newspapers, it cannot do it; the highest intellect will fail.' But did you ever see anything there you had never seen before? Out of the million articles that everybody has read, can any one person trace a single marked idea to a single article? Where are the deep theories, and the wise axioms, and the everlasting sentiments which the writers of the most influential publication in the world have been the first to communicate to an ignorant species? Such writers are far too shrewd. The two million, or whatever number of copies it may be, they publish, are not purchased because the buyers wish to know new truth. The purchaser desires an article which he can appreciate at sight; which he can lay down and say, 'An excellent article, very excellent; exactly my own sentiments.' Original theories give trouble; besides, a grave man on the Coal Exchange does not desire to be an apostle of novelties among the contemporaneous dealers in fuel;—he wants to be provided with remarks he can make on the topics of the day which will not be known *not* to be his; that are not too profound; which he can fancy the paper only reminded him of. And just in the same way, precisely as the most popular political paper is not that which is abstractedly the best or most instructive, but that which most exactly takes up the minds of men where it finds them, catches the floating sentiment of society, puts it in such a form as society can fancy would convince another society which did not believe—so the most influential of constitutional statesmen is the one who most felicitously expresses the creed of the moment, who administers it, who embodies it in laws and institutions, who gives it the highest life it is capable of, who induces the average man to think, ' I could not have done it any better if I had had time myself.'

It might be said, that this is only one of the results of that tyranny of commonplace which seems to accompany civilisation. You may talk of the tyranny of Nero and Tiberius; but the real tyranny is the tyranny of your next-door neighbour. What law is so cruel as the law of doing what he does ? What yoke is so galling as the necessity of being like him ? What *espionnage* of despotism comes to your door so effectually as the eye of the man who lives at your door ? Public opinion is a permeating influence, and it exacts obedience to itself; it requires us to think other men's thoughts, to speak other men's words, to follow other men's habits. Of course, if we do not, no formal ban issues, no corporeal pain, no coarse penalty of a barbarous society is inflicted on the offender; but we are called ' eccentric;' there is a gentle murmur of ' most unfortunate ideas,' ' singular young man,' ' well-intentioned, I dare say; but unsafe, sir, quite unsafe.' The prudent, of course, conform. The place of nearly everybody depends on the opinion of everyone else. There is nothing like Swift's precept to attain the repute of a sensible man, ' Be of the opinion of the person with whom, at the time, you are conversing.' This world is given to those whom this world can trust. Our very conversation is infected. Where is now the bold humour, the explicit statement, the grasping dogmatism of former days ? They have departed, and you read in the orthodox works dreary regrets that the *art* of conversation has passed away. It would be as reasonable to expect the art of walking to pass away. People talk well enough when they know to whom they are speaking. We might even say that the art of conversation was improved by an application to new circumstances. 'Secrete your intellect, use common words, say what you are expected to say,' and you shall be at peace. The secret of prosperity in common life is to be commonplace on principle.

Whatever truth there may be in these splenetic observations, might be expected to show itself more particularly in the world of politics. People dread to be thought unsafe in proportion as they get their living by being thought to be safe. 'Literary men,' it has been said, 'are outcasts;' and they are eminent in a certain way notwithstanding. 'They can say strong things of their age; for no one expects they will go out and act on them.' They are a kind of ticket-of-leave lunatics, from whom no harm is for the moment expected; who seem quiet, but on whose vagaries a practical public must have its eye. For statesmen it is different—they must be thought men of judgment. The most morbidly agricultural counties were aggrieved when Mr. Disraeli was made Chancellor of the Exchequer. They could not believe he was a man of solidity; and they could not comprehend taxes by the author of 'Coningsby,' or sums by an adherent of the Caucasus. 'There is,' said Sir Walter Scott, 'a certain hypocrisy of action, which, however it is despised by persons intrinsically excellent, will nevertheless be cultivated by those who desire the good repute of men.' Politicians, as has been said, live in the repute of the commonalty. They may appeal to posterity; but of what use is posterity? Years before that tribunal comes into life, your life will be extinct. It is like a moth going into Chancery. Those who desire a public career, must look to the views of the living public; an immediate exterior influence is essential to the exertion of their faculties. The confidence of others is your *fulcrum.* You cannot, many people wish you could, go into parliament to represent yourself. You must conform to the opinions of the electors; and they, depend on it, will not be original. In a word, as has been most wisely

observed, ' under free institutions it is necessary occasionally to
defer to the opinions of other people ; and as other people are
obviously in the wrong, this is a great hindrance to the improvement of our political system and the progress of our species.'

Seriously, it is a calamity that this is so. Occasions arise in
which a different sort of statesman is required. A year or two
ago we had one of these. If any politician had come forward in
this country, on the topic of the war, with prepared intelligence,
distinct views, strong will, commanding mastery, it would have
brought support to anxious intellects, and comfort to a thousand
homes. None such came. Our people would have statesmen
who thought as they thought, believed as they believed, acted as
they would have acted. They had desired to see their own will
executed. There came a time when they had no clear will, no
definite opinion. They reaped as they had sown. As they had
selected an administrative tool, of course it did not turn out an
heroic leader.

If we wanted to choose an illustration of these remarks out
of all the world, it would be Sir Robert Peel. No man has
come so near our definition of a constitutional statesman—the
powers of a first-rate man and the creed of a second-rate man.
From a certain peculiarity of intellect and fortune, he was never
in advance of his time. Of almost all the great measures with
which his name is associated, he attained great eminence as an
opponent before he attained even greater eminence as their advocate. On the corn-laws, on the currency, on the amelioration
of the criminal code, on Catholic emancipation—the subject of
the memoir before us—he was not one of the earliest labourers
or quickest converts. He did not bear the burden and heat of
the day ; other men laboured, and he entered into their labours.
As long as these questions remained the property of first-class
intellects, as long as they were confined to philanthropists or
speculators, as long as they were only advocated by austere, in-
tangible Whigs, Sir Robert Peel was against them. So soon as
these same measures, by the progress of time, the striving of

understanding, the conversion of receptive minds, became the property of second-class intellects, Sir Robert Peel became possessed of them also. He was converted at the conversion of the average man. His creed was, as it had ever been, ordinary; but his extraordinary abilities never showed themselves so much. He forthwith wrote his name on each of those questions, so that it will be remembered as long as they are remembered.

Nor is it merely on these few measures that Sir Robert Peel's mind must undoubtedly have undergone a change. The lifetime of few Englishmen has been more exactly commensurate with a change of public opinion—a total revolution of political thought. Hardly any fact in history is so incredible as that forty and a few years ago England was ruled by Mr. Perceval. It seems almost the same as being ruled by the 'Record' newspaper. He had the same poorness of thought, the same petty Conservatism, the same dark and narrow superstition. His quibbling mode of oratory seems to have been scarcely agreeable to his friends; his impotence in political speculation moves the wrath—destroys the patience—of the quietest reader now. Other ministers have had great connections, or great estates, to compensate for the contractedness of their minds. Mr. Perceval was only a poorish *nisi prius* lawyer, and there is no kind of human being so disagreeable, so teasing, to the gross Tory nature. He is not entitled to any glory for our warlike successes: on the contrary, he did his best to obtain failure by starving the Duke of Wellington, and plaguing him with petty vexations. His views in religion inclined to that Sabbatarian superstition which is of all creeds the most alien to the firm and genial English nature. The mere fact of such a premier being endured shows how deeply the whole national spirit and interest was absorbed in the contest with Napoleon, how little we understood the sort of man who should regulate its conduct—'in the crisis of Europe,' as Sydney Smith said, 'he safely brought the Curates' Salaries Improvement Bill to a hearing'—and it still more shows the horror of all innovation which the recent events of French history had impressed on our

wealthy and comfortable classes. They were afraid of catching
revolution, as old women of catching cold. Sir Archibald
Alison to this day holds that revolution is an infectious disease,
beginning no one knows how, and going no one knows where.
There is but one rule of escape, explains the great historian,
' Stay still, don't move; do what you have been accustomed to
do, and consult your grandmother on everything.' In 1812
the English people were all persuaded of this theory. Mr.
Perceval was the most narrow-minded and unaltering man they
could find : he therefore represented their spirit, and they put
him at the head of the state.

Such was the state of political questions. How little of
real thoughtfulness was then applied to what we now call social
questions cannot be better illustrated than by the proceedings
on the occasion of Mr. Perceval's death. Bellingham, who
killed him, was, whether punishable or not, as clearly insane as
a lunatic can be who offends against the laws of his country.
He had no idea of killing Mr. Perceval particularly. His only
idea was, that he had lost some property in Russia ; that the
English government would never repay him his loss in Russia ;
and he endeavoured to find some cabinet minister to shoot as
a compensation. Lord Eldon lived under the belief that he
had nearly been the victim himself, and told some story of a
borrowed hat and an assistant's greatcoat to which he ascribed
his preservation. The whole affair was a monomaniac's delusion.
Bellingham had no ground for expecting any repayment. There
was no reason for ascribing his pecuniary ruin to the government of that day, any more than to the government of this
day. Indeed, if he had been alive now, it would have been
agreed that he was a particularly estimable man. Medical
gentlemen would have been examined for days on the doctrine
of ' irresistible impulse,' ' moral insanity,' ' instinctive pistol-
discharges,' and every respectful sympathy would have been
shown to so curious an offender. Whether he was punishable or not may be a question ; but all will now agree, that it

was not a case for the punishment of death. In that day there was no more doubt that he ought to be hanged, than there would now be that he ought on no account to be hanged. The serious reasons, of which the scientific theories above alluded to are but the exaggerated resemblance, which indicate the horrible cruelty of inflicting on those who do not know what they do the extreme penalty of suffering meant for those who perpetrate the worst they can conceive, are in these years so familiar that we can hardly conceive their being unknown. Yet the Tory historian has to regret 'that the motion, so earnestly insisted on by his counsel, to have the trial postponed for some days, to obtain evidence to establish his insanity, was not acceded to; that a judicial proceeding, requiring beyond all others the most calm and deliberate consideration, should have been hurried over with a precipitation which, if not illegal, was at least unusual;' and a noble lord 'improved' the moment of the assassination by exclaiming to the peers in opposition, 'You see, my lords, the consequence of your agitating the question of *Catholic emancipation.*' To those who now know England, it seems scarcely possible that this could have occurred here only forty-four years since. It was in such a world that Sir Robert Peel commenced his career. He was Under-Secretary of State for the Colonies at the time of Mr. Perceval's assassination.

It is not, however, to be imagined that, even if Mr. Perceval had lived, his power would have very long endured. It passed to milder and quieter men. It passed to such men as Lord Liverpool and Mr. Peel. The ruling power at that time in England, as for many years before, as even in some measure, though far less, now, was the class of aristocratic gentry; by which we do not mean to denote only the aristocracy, and do not mean to exclude the aristocracy, but to indicate the great class of hereditary landed proprietors, who are in sympathy with the House of Lords on cardinal points, yet breathe a somewhat freer air, are more readily acted on by the opinion of the community, more contradictable by the lower herd, and less removed from their prejudices by a refined and regulated education. From the time of the Revolution, more or less, this has been the ruling class in the community; the close-borough system and the county system giving them mainly the control of the House of Commons, and their feeling being in general, as it were, a mean term between those of the higher nobility and the trading public of what were then the few large towns. The rule of the House of Lords was rather mediate than direct. By those various means of influence and social patronage and oppression which are familiar to a wealthy and high-bred aristocracy, the highest members of it, of course, did exercise over all below them a sure and continual influence: it worked silently and commonly on ordinary questions and in quiet times; yet it was liable to be overborne by a harsher and ruder power when stormy passions arose, in the days of wars and tumults. So far as the actual selection of visible rulers goes, the largest amount of administrative power has rarely been in the hands of the highest aristocracy, and in a great measure for a peculiar reason : that aristocracy rarely will do the work, and rarely can do the work. The enormous pressure of daily-growing business, which besets the governors of a busy and complicated community, is too much for the refined habits, delicate discrimination, anxious judgment, which the course of their life develops in the highest classes, and with which it nourishes the indolence natural to those who have this world to enjoy. The real strain of the necessary labour has generally been borne by men of a somewhat lower grade, trained by an early ambition, a native aptitude, a hardy competition, to perform its copious tasks. Such men are partakers of two benefits. They are rough and ready enough to accomplish the coarse, enormous daily work; they have lived with men of higher rank enough to know and feel what such persons think and want. Sir Robert Walpole is the type of this class. He was a Norfolk squire, and not a nobleman ; he was bred a gentleman, and yet was quite coarse enough for any business: his career was what you would expect. For very many years he administered the government much as the aristocracy wished and desired. *They* were, so to speak, the directors of the company which is called the English nation; they met a little and talked a little: but Sir Robert was the manager, who knew all the facts, came every day, saw everybody, and was everything.

Passing over the time of Lord Liverpool, of whom this is not now the place to speak, some such destiny as this would, in his first political life, have appeared likely to be that of Sir Robert Peel. If an acute master of the betting art had been asked the 'favourite' statesman who was likely to rule in that generation, he would undoubtedly have selected Sir Robert. He was rich, decorous, laborious, and had devoted himself regularly to the task. There was no other such man. It was likely, at least to superficial observers, that his name would descend to posterity as the 'Sir Robert' of a new time;—a time changed, indeed, from that of Walpole, but resembling it in its desire to be ruled by a great administrator, skilful in all kinds of business transactions, yet associated with the aristocracy; by one unremarkable in his opinions, but remarkable in his powers. The fates, however, designed Peel for a very different destiny; and to a really close observer there were signs in his horoscope which should have clearly revealed it. Sir Robert's father and grandfather were two of the men who created Lancashire. No sooner did the requisite machinery issue from the brain of the inventor, than its capabilities were seized on by strong, ready, bold men of business, who erected it, used it, devised a factory system, combined a factory population—created, in a word, that black industrial region, of whose augmenting wealth and horrid labour tales are daily borne to the genial and lazy south. Of course, it cannot be said that mill-makers invented the middle classes. The history of England perhaps shows, that it has not for centuries been without an unusual number of persons with comfortable and mode-

rate means.   But though this class has ever been found among
us, and has ever been more active than in any other similar
country, yet to a great extent it was scattered, headless, motion-
less.   Small rural out-of-the-way towns, country factories few
and far between, concealed and divided this great and mixed
mass of petty means and steady intelligence.   The huge heaps
of manufacturing wealth were not to be concealed.   They at
once placed on a level with the highest in the land—in matters
of expenditure, and in those countless social relations which
depend upon expenditure—men sprung from the body of the
people, unmistakably speaking its language, inevitably thinking
its thoughts.   It is true that the first manufacturers were not
democratic.   Sir Robert Peel, the statesman's father—a type
of the class—was a firm, honest, domineering Conservative ;
but, however on such topics they may so think, however on
other topics they may try to catch the language of the class to
which they rise, the grain of the middle class will surely show
itself in those who have risen from the middle class.   If Mr.
Cobden were to go over to the enemy, if he were to offer to serve
Lord Derby *vice* Disraeli disconcerted, it would not be possible
for him to speak as the hereditary landowner speaks.   It is not
that the hereditary landowner knows more ;— indeed, either in
book-learning or in matters of observation, in acquaintance with
what has been, or is going to be, or what now is, the owners of
rent are not superior to the receivers of profits ; yet their
dialect is different—the one speaks the language of years of
toil, and the other of years of indolence.   A harsh laborious-
ness characterises the one, a pleasant geniality the other.   The
habit of industry is ingrained in those who have risen by it ; it
modifies every word and qualifies every notion.   They are the
βάναυσοι of work.   Vainly, therefore, did the first manufacturers
struggle to be Conservatives, to be baronets, to be peers.
The titles they might obtain, their outward existence they
might change, themselves in a manner they might alter ; but a
surer force was dragging them and those who resembled them

into another region, filling them with other thoughts, making them express what people of the middle classes had always obscurely felt, pushing forward this new industrial order by the side, or even in front, of the old aristocratic order. The new class have not, indeed, shown themselves republican. They have not especially cared to influence the machinery of government. Their peculiarity has been, that they wished to see the government administered according to the notions familiar to them in their business life. They have no belief in mystery or magic ; probably they have never appreciated the political influence of the imagination ; they wish to see plain sense applied to the most prominent part of practical life. In his later career, the second Sir Robert Peel was the statesman who most completely and thoroughly expressed the sentiments of this new dynasty ;—instead of being the nominee of a nobility, he became the representative of a transacting and trading multitude.

Both of these two classes were, however, equally possessed by the vice or tendency we commented on at the outset. They each of them desired to see the government carried on exactly according to their own views. The idea on which seems to rest our only chance of again seeing great statesmen, of placing deep deferential trust in those who have given real proofs of comprehensive sagacity, had scarcely dawned on either. The average man had, so to say, varied ; he was no longer of the one order, but of an inferior ; but he was not at all less exacting or tyrannical. Perhaps he was even more so ; for the indolent gentleman is less absolute and domineering than the active man of business. However that may be, it was the fate of Sir Robert Peel, in the two phases of his career, to take a leading share in carrying out the views, in administering the creed, first of one and then of the other.

Perhaps, in our habitual estimate of Peel we hardly enough bear this in mind. We remember him as the guiding chief of the most intelligent Conservative government that this country has ever seen. We remember the great legislative acts which

we owe to his trained capacity, every detail of which bears the
impress of his practised hand; we know that his name is pronounced with applause in the great marts of trade and seats of
industry; that even yet it is muttered with reproach in the
obscure abodes of squires and rectors.   We forget that his name
was once the power of the Protestant interest, the shibboleth by
which squires and rectors distinguished those whom they loved
from those whom they hated; we forget that he defended the
Manchester Massacre, the Six Acts, the Imposition of Tests,
the rule of Orangemen.   We remember Peel as the proper head
of a moderate, intelligent, half-commercial community; we
forget that he once was the chosen representative of a gentry
untrained to great affairs, absorbed in a great war, only just re-
covering from the horror of a great revolution.

In truth, the character of Sir Robert Peel happily fitted
him both to be the chosen head of a popular community,
imperiously bent on its own ideas, and to be the head of that
community in shifting and changing times.   Sir Robert was at
Harrow with Lord Byron, who has left the characteristic
reminiscence : ' I was always in scrapes, Peel never.'   And
opposed as they were in their fortunes as boys and men, they
were at least equally contrasted in the habit and kind of action
of their minds.   Lord Byron's mind gained everything it was
to gain by one intense, striking effort.   By a blow of the
imagination he elicited a single bright spark of light on
every subject, and that was all.   And this he never lost.
The intensity of the thinking seemed to burn it on the
memory, there to remain alone.   But he made no second
effort; he gained no more.   He always avowed his incapability
of continuous application: he could not, he said, learn the
grammar of any language.   In later life he showed considerable
talent for action; but those who had to act with him observed
that, versatile as were his talents, and mutable as his convictions had always seemed to be, in reality he was the most
stubborn of men.   He heard what you had to say; assented to

all you had to say; and the next morning returned to his original opinion. No amount of ordinary argumentative resistance
was so hopeless as that facile acquiescence and instantaneous
recurrence. The truth was, that he was—and some others are
similarly constituted—unable to retain anything which he did
not at any rate *seem* to gain by the unaided single rush of his
own mind. The ideas of such minds are often not new, very
often they are hardly in the strictest sense original; they really
were very much suggested from without, and preserved in some
obscure corner of memory, out of the way and unknown; but it
remains their characteristic, that they seem to the mind of the
thinker to be born from its own depths, to be the product of
its latent forces. There is a kind of eruption of ideas from a
subter conscious world. The whole mental action is volcanic;
the lava flood glows in 'Childe Harold;' all the thoughts are
intense, flung forth vivid. The day after the eruption the
mind is calm; it seems as if it could not again do the like; the
product only remains, distinct, peculiar, indestructible. The
mind of Peel was the exact opposite of this. His opinions far
more resembled the daily accumulating insensible deposits of
a rich alluvial soil. The great stream of time flows on with
all things on its surface; and slowly, grain by grain, a mould
of wise experience is unconsciously left on the still, extended
intellect. You scarcely think of such a mind as acting; it
seems always acted upon. There is no trace of gushing, overpowering, spontaneous impulse; everything seems acquired.
The thoughts are calm. In Lord Byron, the very style—
dashing, free, incisive—shows the bold impulse from which it
came. The stealthy accumulating words of Peel seem like
the quiet leavings of an outward tendency, which brought
these, but might as well have brought others. There is no
peculiar stamp either in the ideas. They might have been
anyone's ideas. They belong to the general diffused stock of
observations which are to be found in the civilised world. They
are not native to the particular mind, nor 'to the manner

born.' Like a science, they are credible or incredible by all men equally. This *secondary* order, as we may call it, of intellect, is evidently most useful to a statesman of the constitutional class, such as we have described him. He insensibly and inevitably takes in and imbibes, by means of it, the ideas of those around him. If he were left in a vacuum, he would have no ideas. The primary class of mind that strikes out its own belief would here be utterly at fault. It would want something which other men had; it would discover something which other men would not understand. Sir Robert Peel was a statesman for forty years; under our constitution, Lord Byron, eminent as was his insight into men, and remarkable as was his power, at least for short periods of dealing with them, would not have been a statesman for forty days.

It is very likely that many people may not think Sir Robert Peel's mind so interesting as Lord Byron's. They may prefer the self-originating intellect, which invents and retains its own ideas, to the calm receptive intellect which acquires its belief from without. The answer lies in what has been said—a constitutional statesman must sympathise in the ideas of the many. As the many change, it will be his good fortune if he can contrive to change with them. It is to be remembered, that statesmen do not live under hermetical seals. Like other men, they are influenced by the opinions of other men. How potent is this influence, those best know who have tried to hold ideas different from the ideas of those around.

In another point of view also Sir Robert Peel's character was exactly fitted to the position we have delineated. He was a great administrator. Civilisation requires this. In a simple age work may be difficult, but it is scarce. There are fewer people, and everybody wants fewer things. The mere tools of civilisation seem in some sort to augment work. In early times, when a despot wishes to govern a distant province, he sends down a satrap on a grand horse, with other people on little horses; and very little is heard of the satrap again unless he send back some of the little people to tell what he has been doing. No great labour of superintendence is possible. Common rumour and casual complaints are the sources of intelligence. If it seems certain that the province is in a bad state, satrap No. 1 is recalled, and satrap No. 2 is sent out in his stead. In civilised countries the whole thing is different. You erect a *bureau* in the province you want to govern ; you make it write letters and copy letters ; it sends home eight reports per diem to the head *bureau* in St. Petersburg. Nobody does a sum in the province without somebody doing the same sum in the capital, to ' check him,' and see that he does it correctly. The consequence of this is, to throw on the heads of departments an amount of reading and labour which can only be accomplished by the greatest natural aptitude, the most efficient training, the most firm and regular industry. Under a free government it is by no means better, perhaps in some respects it is worse. It is true that many questions which, under the French despotism, are referred to Paris, are settled in England on the very spot where they are to be done, without reference to London at all. But as a set-off, a constitutional administrator has to be always consulting others, finding out what this man or that man chooses to think ; learning which form of error is believed by Lord B., which by Lord C. ; adding up the errors of the alphabet, and seeing what portion of what he thinks he ought to do, they will all of them together allow him to do. Likewise, though the personal freedom and individual discretion which free governments allow to their subjects seem at first likely to diminish the work which those governments have to do, it may be doubted whether it does so really and in the end. Individual discretion strikes out so many more pursuits, and some supervision must be maintained over each of those pursuits. No despotic government would consider the police force of London enough to keep down, watch, and superintend such a population ; but then no despotic government would have such a city as London to keep down.

C

The freedom of growth allows the possibility of growth ; and though liberal governments take so much less in proportion upon them, yet the scale of operations is so much enlarged by the continual exercise of civil liberty, that the real work is ultimately perhaps as immense.   While a despotic government is regulating ten per cent. of ten men's actions, a free government has to regulate one per cent. of a hundred men's actions.   The difficulty, too, increases.   Anybody can understand a rough despotic community ;—a small buying class of nobles, a small selling class of traders, a large producing class of serfs, are much the same in all quarters of the globe ; but a free intellectual community is a complicated network of ramified relations, interlacing and passing hither and thither, old and new—some of fine city weaving, others of gross agricultural construction. You are never sure what effect any force or any change may produce on a framework so exquisite and so involved.   Govern it as you may, it will be a work of great difficulty, labour, and responsibility ; and no man who is thus occupied ought ever to go to bed without reflecting, that from the difficulty of his employment he may, probably enough, have that day done more evil than good.   What view Sir Robert Peel took of these duties, he has himself informed us.

'Take the case of the Prime Minister.   You must presume that he reads every important despatch from every foreign court. He cannot consult with the Secretary of State for Foreign Affairs, and exercise the influence which he ought to have with respect to the conduct of foreign affairs, unless he be master of everything of real importance passing in that department.   It is the same with respect to other departments ; India, for instance : how can the Prime Minister be able to judge of the course of policy with regard to India, unless he be cognisant of all the current important correspondence ?   In the case of Ireland and the Home Department it is the same.   Then the Prime Minister has the patronage of the Crown to exercise, which you say, and justly say, is of so much importance and of

so much value ; he has to make inquiries into the qualifications
of the persons who are candidates ; he has to conduct the whole
of the communications with the Sovereign ; he has to write,
probably with his own hand, the letters in reply to all persons
of station who address themselves to him ; he has to receive
deputations on public business ; during the sitting of Parliament he is expected to attend six or seven hours a day, while
Parliament is sitting, for four or five days in the week ; at least
he is blamed if he is absent.'

The necessary effect of all this labour is, that those subject
to it have no opinions. It requires a great deal of time to have
opinions. Belief is a slow process. That leisure which the
poets say is necessary to be good, or to be wise, is needful for
the humbler task of allowing respectable maxims to take root
respectably. The 'wise passiveness' of Mr. Wordsworth is
necessary in very ordinary matters. If you chain a man's head
to a ledger, and keep him constantly adding up, and take a
pound off his salary whenever he stops, you can't expect him to
have a sound conviction on Catholic emancipation or tithes, and
original ideas on the Transcaucasian provinces. Our system,
indeed, seems expressly provided to make it unlikely. The
most benumbing thing to the intellect is routine ; the most
bewildering is distraction : our system is a distracting routine.
You see this in the description just given, which is not exhaustive. Sir Robert Peel once requested to have a number of questions carefully written down which they asked him one day in
succession in the House of Commons. They seemed a list of
everything that could occur in the British Empire, or to the
brain of a member of parliament. A premier's whole life is a
series of such transitions. It is wonderful that our public
men have any minds left, rather than that a certain unfixity of
opinion seems growing upon them.

We may go further on this subject. A great administrator
is not a man likely to desire to have fixed opinions. His
natural bent and tendency is to immediate action. The existing

and pressing circumstances of the case fill up his mind. The letters to be answered, the documents to be filed, the memoranda to be made, engross his attention. He is angry if you distract him. A bold person who suggests a matter of principle, or a difficulty of thought, or an abstract result that seems improbable in the case 'before the board,' will be set down as a speculator, a theorist, a troubler of practical life. To expect to hear from such men profound views of future policy, digested plans of distant action, is to mistake their genius entirely. It is like asking the broker of the Stock Exchange what will be the price of the funds this day six months? His whole soul is absorbed in thinking what that price will be in ten minutes. A momentary change of an eighth is more important to him than a distant change of a hundred eighths. So the brain of a great administrator is naturally occupied with the details of the day, the passing dust, the granules of that day's life; and his unforeseeing temperament turns away uninterested from reaching speculations, from vague thought, and from extensive and far-off plans. Of course, it is not meant that a great administrator has absolutely no general views; some indeed he must have. A man cannot conduct the detail of affairs without having some plan which regulates that detail. He cannot help having some idea, vague or accurate, indistinct or distinct, of the direction in which he is going, and the purpose for which he is travelling. But the difference is, that this plan is seldom his own, the offspring of his own brain, the result of his own mental contention; it is the plan of someone else. Providence generally bestows on the working adaptive man a quiet adoptive nature. He receives insensibly the suggestions of others; he hears them with willing ears; he accepts them with placid belief. An acquiescent credulity is a quality of such men's nature; they cannot help being sure that what everyone says must be true; the *vox populi* is a part of their natural religion. It has been made a matter of wonder that Peel should have belonged to the creed of Mr. Perceval and Lord Sidmouth. Perhaps, indeed, our existing psychology will hardly explain the process by which a decorous young man acquires the creed of his era. He assumes its belief as he assumes its costume. He imitates the respectable classes. He avoids an original opinion, like an *outré* coat ; a new idea, like an unknown tie. Especially he does so on matters of real concern to him, on those on which he knows he must act. He acquiesces in the creed of the orthodox agents. He scarcely considers for himself; he acknowledges the apparent authority of dignified experience. He is, he remembers, but the junior partner in the firm ; it does not occur to him to doubt that those were right who were occupied in its management years before him. In this way he acquires an experience which more independent and original minds are apt to want. There was a great cry when the Whigs came into office, at the time of the Reform Bill, that they were not men of business. Of course, after a very long absence from office, they could not possess a technical acquaintance with official forms, a trained facility in official action. This Sir Robert Peel acquired from his apprenticeship to Mr. Perceval. His early connection with the narrow Conservative party has been considered a disadvantage to him ; but it may well be doubted whether his peculiar mind was not more improved by the administrative training than impaired by the contact with prejudiced thoughts. He never could have been a great thinker ; he became what nature designed, a great agent.

In a third respect also Sir Robert Peel conformed to the type of a constitutional statesman ; and that third respect also seems naturally to lead to a want of defined principle, and to apparent fluctuation of opinion. He was a great debater ; and of all pursuits ever invented by man for separating the faculty of argument from the capacity of belief, the art of debating is probably the most effectual. Mr. Macaulay tells us that, in his opinion, this is 'the most serious of the evils which are to be set off against the many blessings of popular government. The keenest and most vigorous minds of every generation,

minds often admirably fitted for the investigation of truth, are
habitually employed in producing arguments such as no man
of sense would ever put into a treatise intended for publication—arguments which are just good enough to be used once,
when aided by fluent delivery and pointed language.  The habit
of discussing questions in this way necessarily reacts on the intellects of our ablest men, particularly of those who are introduced into parliament at a very early age, before their minds
have expanded to full maturity.  The talent for debate is
developed in such men to a degree which, to the multitude,
seems as marvellous as the performances of an Italian *impro-
visatore.*  But they are fortunate indeed if they retain unim-
paired the faculties which are required for close reasoning, or
for enlarged speculation.  Indeed, we should sooner expect a
great original work on political science—such a work, for
example, as the " Wealth of Nations "—from an apothecary in a
country town, or from a minister in the Hebrides, than from a
statesman who, ever since he was one-and-twenty, had been a
distinguished debater in the House of Commons.'  But it may
well be doubted whether there is not in the same pursuit a deeper
evil, hard to eradicate, and tending to corrupt and destroy the
minds of those who are beneath its influence.  Constitutional
statesmen are obliged, not only to employ arguments which
they do not think conclusive, but likewise to defend opinions
which they do not believe to be true.  Whether we approve it
or lament it, there is no question that our existing political
life is deeply marked by the habit of advocacy.  Perhaps fifteen
measures may annually, on an average, be brought in by a
cabinet government of fifteen persons.  It is impossible to
believe that all members of that cabinet agree in all those measures.  No two people agree in fifteen things; fifteen clever
men never yet agreed in anything; yet they all defend them,
argue for them, are responsible for them.  It is always quite
possible that the minister who is strenuously defending a bill in
the House of Commons may have used in the cabinet the very

arguments which the Opposition are using in the House ; he may have been overruled without being convinced ; he may still think the conclusions he opposes better than those which he inculcates. It is idle to say that he ought to go out ; at least it amounts to saying that government by means of a cabinet is impossible. The object of a committee of that kind is to agree on certain conclusions; if every member after the meeting were to start off according to the individual bent and bias of his mind, according to his own individual discretion or indiscretion, the previous concurrence would have become childish. Of course, the actual measure proposed by the collective voice of several persons is very different from what any one of these persons would of himself wish ; it is the result of a compromise between them. Each, perhaps, has obtained some concession ; each has given up something. Everyone sees in the actual proposal something of which he strongly disapproves ; everyone regrets the absence of something which he much desires. Yet, on the whole, perhaps, he thinks the measure better than no measure ; or at least he thinks that if he went out, it would break up the government ; and imagines it to be of more consequence that the government should be maintained than that the particular measure should be rejected. He concedes his individual judgment. No one has laid this down with more distinctness than Sir Robert Peel. 'Supposing a person at a dinner-table to express his private opinion of a measure originating with a party with whom he is united in public life, is he, in the event of giving up that private opinion out of deference to his party, to be exposed to a charge almost amounting to dishonesty ? The idea is absurd.—What is the every-day conduct of government itself ? Is there anyone in this House so ignorant as to suppose that on all questions cabinet ministers, who yield to the decision of their colleagues, speak and act in parliament in strict conformity with the opinions they have expressed in the cabinet ? If ministers are to be taunted on every occasion that they hold opinions in the

cabinet different from what they do in this House, and if
parliament is to be made the scene of these taunts, I believe I
should not be going too far in saying the House would have
time for little else. It is the uniform practice with all
governments, and I should be sorry to think the practice
carries any stain with it, for a member of the administration
who chances to entertain opinions differing from those of the
majority of his colleagues, rather than separate himself from
them, to submit to be overruled, and even though he do not
fully concur in their policy, to give his support to the measures
which, as an administration, they promulgate. I will give the
House an instance of this fact. It was very generally reported
on a late occasion, that upon the question of sending troops
to Portugal a strong difference of opinion took place in the
cabinet. Now would it, I ask, be either just or fair to call on
those who, in the discussion of the cabinet, had spoken in
favour of sending out troops to aid the cause of Donna Maria,
to come down, and in parliament advocate that measure in
opposition to the decision of their colleagues ? No one would
think of doing so.' It may not carry a stain ; but it is a painful idea.

It is evident, too, that this necessarily leads to great
apparent changes of opinion—to the professed belief of a
statesman at one moment being utterly different from what it
seems to be at another moment. When a government is
founded, questions A, B, C, D, E, F, are the great questions of
the day—the matters which are obvious, pressing—which the
public mind comprehends. X, Y, Z, are in the background,
little thought of, obscure. According to the received morality,
no statesman would hesitate to sacrifice the last to the first.
He might have a very strong personal opinion on X, but he
would surrender it to a colleague as the price of his co-operation
on A or B. A few years afterwards times change. Question A
is carried, B settles itself, E and F are forgotten, X becomes
the most important topic of the day. The statesman who con-

ceded **X** before, now feels that he no longer can concede it ; there is no equivalent. He has never in reality changed his opinion, yet he has to argue in favour of the very measures which he endeavoured before to argue against. Everybody thinks he has changed, and without going into details, the secrecy of which is esteemed essential to confidential co-operation, it is impossible that he can evince his consistency. It is impossible to doubt that this is a very serious evil, and it is plainly one consequent on, or much exaggerated by, a popular and argumentative government. It is very possible for a conscientious man, under a bureaucratic government, to co-operate with the rest of a council in the elaboration and execution of measures, many of which he thinks inexpedient. Nobody asks him his opinion ; he has not to argue, or defend, or persuade. But a free government boasts that it is carried on in the face of day. Its principle is discussion ; its habit is debate. The consequence is, that those who conduct it have to defend measures they disapprove, to object to measures they approve, to appear to have an accurate opinion on points on which they really have no opinion. The calling of a constitutional statesman is very much that of a political advocate ; he receives a new brief with the changing circumstances of each successive day. It is easy to conceive a cold, sardonic intellect, moved with contempt at such a life, casting aside the half-and-half pretences with which others partly deceive themselves, stating anything, preserving an intellectual preference for truth, but regarding any effort at its special advocacy as the weak aim of foolish men, striving for what they cannot attain. Lord Lyndhurst has shown us that it is possible to lead the life of Lord Lyndhurst. One can conceive, too, a cold and somewhat narrow intellect, capable of forming, in any untroubled scene, an accurate plain conviction, but without much power of entering into the varying views of others ; little skilled in diversified argument ; understanding its own opinion, and not understanding the opinions of others ;--one can imagine such a mind pained, and cracked, and shattered, by endeavouring to lead a life of ostentatious argument in favour of others' opinions, of half-concealment of its chill, unaltering essence. It will be for posterity to make due allowance for the variance between the character and the position of Lord John Russell.

Sir Robert Peel was exactly fit for this life. The word which exactly fits his oratory is—specious. He hardly ever said anything which struck you in a moment to be true; he never uttered a sentence which for a moment anybody could deny to be plausible. Once, when they were opposed on a railway bill, the keen irascibility of Lord Derby stimulated him to observe 'that *no one* knew like the right honourable baronet how to *dress up* a case for that House.' The art of statement, the power of detail, the watching for the weak points of an opponent, an average style adapting itself equally to what the speaker believed and what he disbelieved, a business air, a didactic precision for what it was convenient to make clear, an unctuous disguise of flowing periods, and 'a deep·sense of responsibility' for what it was convenient to conceal, an enormous facility, made Sir Robert Peel a nearly unequalled master of the art of political advocacy. For his times he was perhaps quite unequalled. He might have failed in times of deep, outpouring patriotic excitement; he had not nature enough to express it. He might have failed in an age when there was nothing to do, and when elegant personality and the *finesse* of artistic expression were of all things most required. But for an age of important business, when there were an unusual number of great topics to be discussed, but none great enough to hurry men away from their business habits, or awaken the most ardent passion or the highest imagination, there is nothing like the oratory of Peel—able but not aspiring, firm but not exalted, never great but ever adequate to great affairs. It is curious to know that he was trained to the trade.

'Soon after Peel was born, his father, the first baronet, finding himself rising daily in wealth and consequence, and believing that money in those peculiar days could always command a seat in Parliament, determined to bring up his son expressly for the House of Commons. When that son was quite a child, Sir Robert would frequently set him on the table, and say, " Now, Robin, make a speech, and I will give you this cherry." What few words the little fellow produced were applauded ; and applause stimulating exertion, produced such effects that, before Robin was ten years old, he could really address the company with some degree of eloquence. As he grew up, his father constantly took him every Sunday into his private room, and made him repeat, as well as he could, the sermon which had been preached. Little progress in effecting this was made, and little was expected *at first* ; but by steady perseverance the habit of attention grew powerful, and the sermon was repeated almost *verbatim*. When at a very distant day the senator, remembering accurately the speech of an opponent, answered his arguments in correct succession, it was little known that the power of so doing was originally acquired in Drayton Church.'

A mischievous observer might say, that something else had remained to Sir Robert Peel from these sermons. His tone is a trifle sermonic. He failed where perhaps alone Lord John Russell has succeeded—in the oratory of conviction.

If we bear in mind the whole of these circumstances ; if we picture in our minds a nature at once active and facile, easily acquiring its opinions from without, not easily devising them from within, a large placid adaptive intellect, devoid of irritable intense originality, prone to forget the ideas of yesterday, inclined to accept the ideas of to-day—if we imagine a man so formed cast early into absorbing, exhausting industry of detail, with work enough to fill up a life, with action of itself enough to render speculation almost impossible—placed too in a position unsuited to abstract thought, of which the conventions and rules require that a man should feign other men's thoughts, should impugn his own opinions—we shall begin to imagine a conscientious man destitute of convictions on the occupations of his life—to comprehend the character of Sir Robert Peel.

That Sir Robert was a very conscientious man is quite certain. It is even probable that he had a morbid sense of administrative responsibility. We do not say that he was so weighed down as Lord Liverpool, who is alleged never to have opened his letters without a pang of foreboding that something had miscarried somewhere; but every testimony agrees that Sir Robert had an anxious sense of duty in detail. Lord Wellesley, somewhere in this volume, on an occasion when it would have been at least equally natural to speak of administrative capacity and efficient co-operation, mentions only 'the real impressions which your kindness and high character have fixed in my mind.' The circumstances of his end naturally produced a crowd of tributes to his memory, and hardly any of them omit his deep sense of the obligations of action. The characteristic, too, is written conspicuously on every line of these memoirs. Disappointing and external as in some respects they seem, they all the more evidently bear witness to this trait. They read like the conscientious letters of an ordinary practical man; the great statesman has little other notion than that it is his duty to transact his business well. As a conspicuous merit, the Duke of Wellington, oddly enough according to some people's notions at the time, selected Peel's veracity. ' In the whole course of my communication with him I have never known an instance in which he did not show the strictest preference for truth. I never had, in the whole course of my life, the slightest reason for suspecting that he stated anything which he did not firmly believe to be the fact. I could not sit down without stating what I believe, after a long acquaintance, to have been his most striking characteristic.' Simple people in the country were a little astonished to hear so strong a eulogy on a man for not telling lies. They were under the impression that people in general did not. But those who have considered the tempting nature of a statesman's pursuits, the secrets of office, the inevitable complication of his personal relations, will not be surprised that many statesmen should be without veracity, or that one should be eulogised for possessing it. It is to be remarked, however, in mitigation of so awful an excellence, that Sir Robert was seldom 'in scrapes,' and that it is on those occasions that the virtue of veracity is apt to be most severely tested. The same remark is applicable to the well-praised truthfulness of the Duke himself.

In conjunction with the great soldier, Sir Robert Peel is entitled to the fame of a great act of administrative conscience. He purified the Tory party. There is little doubt that, during the long and secure reign which the Tories enjoyed about the beginning of the century, there was much of the corruption naturally incident to a strong party with many adherents to provide for, uncontrolled by an effective Opposition, unwatched by a great nation. Of course, too, any government remaining over from the last century would inevitably have adhering to it various *remanet* corruptions of that curious epoch. There flourished those mighty sinecures and reversions, a few of which still remain to be the wonder and envy of an unenjoying generation. The House of Commons was not difficult then to manage. There is a legend that a distinguished Treasury official of the last century, a very capable man, used to say of any case which was hopelessly and inevitably bad: 'Ah, we must apply our majority to this question;' and no argument is so effectual as the mechanical, calculable suffrage of a strong, unreasoning party. There were doubtless many excellent men in the Tory party, even in its least excellent days; but the two men to whom the party, as such, owes most of purification were the Duke of Wellington and Sir Robert Peel. From the time when they became responsible for the management of a Conservative government, there was no doubt, in office or in the nation, that the public money and patronage were administered by men whom no consideration would induce to use either for their personal benefit ; and who would, as far as their whole power lay, discourage and prevent the corrupt use of either by others. The process by which they succeeded in conveying this impression is illustrated by a chapter in the Dean of York's 'Memoir of Peel,' in which that well-known dignitary recounts the temptations which he applied to the political purity of his relative :—

While Peel was Secretary for Ireland, I asked him to give a very trifling situation, nominally in his gift, to a worthy person for whom I felt an interest. He wrote me word that he was really anxious to oblige me in this matter, but that a nobleman of much parliamentary interest, who supported the government, insisted upon his right to dispose of all patronage in his own neighbourhood. So anxious was Peel to show his good will towards me, that he prevailed upon the Lord-Lieutenant to ask as a favour from the aforesaid nobleman that the situation might be given to my nominee ; but the marquis replied, that the situation was of no value, yet, to prevent a dangerous precedent, he must refuse the application.

In times long after, when Sir Robert Peel became prime minister, I asked him often in the course of many years for situations for my sons, which situations were vacant and in his immediate gift. I subjoin three letters which I received from him on these subjects ; they were written after long intervals and at different periods, but they all speak the same language :—

Whitehall, December 20 (no date of year).

MY DEAR DEAN OF YORK,—I thank you for your consideration of what you deem the unrequited sacrifice which I make in the public service. But I beg to say that my chief consolation and reward is the *consciousness* that my exertions are disinterested—that I have considered official patronage as a public trust, to be applied to the reward and encouragement of public service, or to the less praiseworthy, but still necessary, purpose of promoting the general interests of the government. That patronage is so wholly inadequate to meet the fair claims of a public nature, that are daily presented for my consideration, and that constitute the chief torment of office, that I can only overcome the difficulties connected with the distribution by the utmost forbearance as to deriving any personal advantage from it. If I had absolute control over the appointment to which you refer, I should apply it to the satisfaction of one or other of the engagements into which I entered when I formed the government, and which (from the absolute want of means) remain unfulfilled. But I have informed the numerous parties who have applied to me on the subject of that appointment, that I feel it to be my duty, on account of the present condition of the board and the functions they have to perform, to select for it some experienced man of business connected with the naval profession, or some man distinguished in that profession.

Believe me, my dear Dean, affectionately yours,

ROBERT PEEL.

I applied again for another place of less importance : the answer was much the same as before :—

Whitehall, April 5, 1843.

MY DEAR DEAN OF YORK,—I must dispose of the appointment to which you refer upon the same principle on which I have uniformly disposed of every appointment of a similar nature.

I do not consider patronage of this kind (and, indeed, I may truly say it of all patronage) as the means of gratifying private wishes of any one. Those who have made locally great sacrifices and great exertions for the maintenance of the political cause which they espouse, have always been considered fairly entitled to be consulted in respect to the disposal of local patronage, and would justly complain if, in order to promote the interests of a relative of my own, I were to disregard their recommendations. It would subject me to great personal embarrassment, and be a complete departure from the rule to which I have always adhered.

All patronage of all descriptions, so far from being of the least advantage personally to a minister, involves him in nothing but embarrassment. Ever affectionately yours,

ROBERT PEEL.

I publish one more letter of the same kind, because all these letters exhibit the character of the writer, and contain matters of some public interest. The distributor of stamps died in the very place where my son was resident, and where he and I had exerted considerable interest in assisting the government members. I thought that now, perhaps, an exception might be made to the general rule, and I confidently recommended my eldest son for the vacancy. The following was the answer :—

Whitehall, May 1.

MY DEAR DEAN,—Whatever arrangements may be made with respect to the office of distributor of stamps, lately held by Mr. ——,

I do not feel myself justified in appropriating to myself any share of the local patronage of a county with which I have not the remotest connection by property, or any other local tie.

There are three members for the county of —— who support the government; and, in addition to the applications which I shall no doubt have from them, I have already received recommendations from the Duke of —— and Earl ——, each having certainly better claims than I have personally for local appointments in the county of ——.

I feel it quite impossible to make so complete a departure from the principles on which I have invariably acted, and which I feel to be nothing more than consistent with common justice, as to take — shire offices for my own private purposes.

Very faithfully yours,

ROBERT PEEL.

These letters show the noble principle on which Sir Robert's public life was founded. I am quite sure that he had a great regard for my sons. He invited them to his shooting-quarters, was pleased to find them amusement, and made them many handsome presents; but he steadily refused to enrich them out of the public purse merely because they were his nephews. Many prime ministers have not been so scrupulous.

And clearly *one* divine wishes Sir Robert Peel had not been so.

The changes of opinion which Sir Robert Peel underwent are often cited as indications of a want of conscientiousness. They really are, subject, of course, to the preceding remarks, proofs of his conscientiousness. We do not mean in the obvious sense of their being opposed to his visible interest, and having on two great occasions destroyed the most serviceable party organisation ever ruled by a statesman in a political age; but in a more refined sense, the timeliness of his transitions may, without overstraining, be thought a mark of their *bona fides*. He could not have changed with such felicitous exactness, if he had been guided by selfish calculation. The problems were too great and too wide. There have, of course, been a few men—Talleyrand and Theramenes are instances— who have seemed to hit, as if by a political sense, the fitting

moment to leave the side which was about to fall, and to join
the side which was about to rise. But these will commonly
be found to be men of a very different character from that of
Peel. Minds are divided into open and close. Some men
are so sensitive to extrinsic impressions, pass so easily from
one man to another, catch so well the tone of each man's
thought, use so well the opportunities of society for the purposes of affairs, that they are, as it were, by habit and practice,
metrical instruments of public opinion. Sir Robert was by
character, both natural and acquired, the very reverse. He was
a reserved, occupied man of business. In the arts of society
in the easy transition from person to person, from tone to
tone, he was but little skilled. If he had been left to pick up
his rules of conduct by mere social perception and observation,
his life would have been a life of miscalculations; instead
of admiring the timeliness of his conversions, we should
wonder at the perversity of his transitions. The case is not
new. In ancient times, at a remarkable moment, in the
persons of two selfish men of genius, the open mind was
contrasted with the close. By a marvellous combination of
successive manœuvres, Julius Cæsar rose from ruin to empire;
the spoiled child of society—sensitive to each breath of
opinion—ever living, at least among the externals of enjoyment—always retaining, by a genial kindliness of manner,
friends from each of the classes which he variously used. By
what the vulgar might be pardoned for thinking a divine
infatuation, Pompeius lost the best of political positions,
threw away every recurring chance, and died a wandering
exile. As a reserved, ungenial man, he never was able to
estimate the feeling of the time. ' I have only to stamp
with my foot when the occasion requires, to raise legions
from the soil of Italy!' were the words of one who could not,
in his utmost need, raise a force to strike one blow for Italy
itself. The fate of Pompeius would have been that of Peel,
if he too had played the game of selfish calculation. His

D

changes, as it has been explained, are to be otherwise accounted for.  He was always anxious to do right.  An occupied man of business, he was converted when other men of
business in the nation were converted.

It is not, however, to be denied that a calm and bland
nature like that of Peel is peculiarly prone to self-illusion.
Many fancy that it is passionate, imaginative men who most
deceive themselves; and of course they are more tempted—a
more vivid fancy and a more powerful impulse hurry them
away.  But they know their own weakness.  'Do you believe
in ghosts, Mr. Coleridge?' asked some lady.  'No, ma'am, I
have seen too many,' was the answer.  A quiet, calm nature,
when it is tempted by its own wishes, is hardly conscious that
it is tempted.  These wishes are so gentle, quiet, as it would
say, so 'reasonable,' that it does not conceive it possible to be
hurried away into error by them.  Nor *is* there any hurry.
They operate quietly, gently, and constantly.  Such a man will
very much believe what he wishes.  Many an imaginative out-
cast, whom no man would trust with sixpence, really forms his
opinions on points which interest him by a much more
intellectual process—at least has more purely intellectual
opinions beaten and tortured into him—than the eminent and
respected man of business, in whom every one confides, who is
considered a model of dry judgment, of clear and passionless
equanimity.  Doubtless Sir Robert Peel went on believing in
the corn-laws, when no one in the distrusted classes even
fancied that they were credible.

It has been bitterly observed of Sir Robert Peel, that he
was 'a Radical at heart;' and, perhaps with a similar thought
in his mind, Mr. Cobden said once, at a League meeting, 'I do
not altogether like to give up Peel.  You see he is a Lancashire man.'  And it cannot be questioned that, strongly opposed
as Sir Robert Peel was to the Reform Bill, he was really much
more suited to the reformed than to the unreformed House of
Commons.  The style of debating in the latter was described

by one who had much opportunity for observation, Sir James Mackintosh, as 'continuous, animated, after-dinner discussion.' The House was composed mainly of men trained in two great schools, on a peculiar mode of education, with no great real knowledge of the classics, but with many lines of Virgil and Horace lingering in fading memories, contrasting oddly with the sums and business with which they were necessarily brought side by side. These gentlemen wanted not to be instructed, but to be amused; and hence arose what, from the circumstance of their calling, may be called the class of conversationalist statesmen. Mr. Canning was the type of these. He was. a man of elegant gifts, of easy fluency, capable of embellishing anything, with a nice wit, gliding swiftly over the most delicate topics; passing from topic to topic like the *raconteur* of the dinner-table, touching easily on them all, letting them all go as easily; confusing you as to whether he knows nothing, or knows everything. The peculiar irritation which Mr. Canning excited through life was, at least in part, owing to the natural wrath with which you hear the changing talk of the practised talker running away about all the universe; never saying anything which indicates real knowledge, never saying anything which at the very moment can be shown to be a blunder; ever on the surface, and ever ingratiating itself with the superficial. When Mr. Canning was alive, sound men of all political persuasions—the Duke of Wellington, Lord Grey—ever disliked him. You may hear old Liberals to this day declaring he was the greatest charlatan who ever lived, angry to imagine that his very ghost exists; and when you read his speeches yourself, you are at once conscious of a certain dexterous insincerity which seems to lurk in the very felicities of expression, and to be made finer with the very refinements of the phraseology. Like the professional converser, he seems so apt at the *finesse* of expression, so prone to modulate his words, that you cannot imagine him putting his fine mind to tough thinking, really working, actually grappling with the rough substance of a great subject.  Of course, if this were the place for an estimate of Mr. Canning, there would be some limitation, and much excuse to be offered for all this.  He was early thrown into what we may call an aristocratic debating society, accustomed to be charmed, delighting in classic gladiatorship.  To expect a great speculator, or a principled statesman, from such a position, would be expecting German from a Parisian, or plainness from a diplomatist.  He grew on the soil on which he had been cast; and it is hard, perhaps impossible, to separate the faults which are due to it and to him.  He and it have both passed away.  The old delicate parliament is gone, and the gladiatorship which it loved.  The progress of things, and the Reform Bill which was the result of that progress, have taken, and are taking, the national representation away from the university classes, and conferring it on the practical classes.  Exposition, arithmetic, detail, reforms—these are the staple of our modern eloquence. The old boroughs which introduced the young scholars are passed away; and even if the young scholars were in parliament, the subjects do not need the classic tact of expression. Very plain speaking suits the 'passing tolls,' 'registration of joint-stock companies,' finance, the Post-office.  The petty regulation of the details of civilisation, which happily is the daily task of our government, does not need, does not suit, a *recherché* taste or an ornate eloquence.  As is the speech, so are the men.  Sir Robert Peel was inferior to Canning in the old parliament; he would have been infinitely superior to him in the new.  The aristocratic refinement, the nice embellishment, of the old time, were as alien to him as the detail and dryness of the new era were suitable.  He was admirably fitted to be where the Reform Bill placed him.  He was fitted to work and explain ; he was not able to charm or to amuse.

In its exact form this kind of eloquence and statesmanship is peculiar to modern times, and even to this age.  In ancient times the existence of slavery forbade the existence of a middle class eloquence. The Cleon who possessed the tone and the confidence of the people in trade was a man vulgar, coarse, speaking the sentiments of a class whose views were narrow and whose words were mean. So many occupations were confined to slaves, that there was scarcely an opening for the sensible, moderate, rational body whom we now see. It was, of course, always possible to express the sentiments and prejudices of people in trade. It is new to this era, it seems created for Sir Robert Peel to express those sentiments, in a style refined, but not too refined ; which will not jar people of high cultivation, which will seem suitable to men of common cares and important transactions.

In another respect Sir Robert Peel was a fortunate man. The principal measures required in his age were ' repeals.' From changing circumstances, the old legislation would no longer suit a changed community ; and there was a clamour, first for the repeal of one important act, and then of another. This was suitable to the genius of Peel. He could hardly have created anything. His intellect, admirable in administrative routine, endlessly fertile in suggestions of detail, was not of the class which creates, or which readily even believes an absolutely new idea. As has been so often said, he typified the practical intelligence of his time. He was prone, as has been explained, to receive the daily deposits of insensibly-changing opinion ; but he could bear nothing startling ; nothing bold, original, single, is to be found in his acts or his words. Nothing could be so suitable to such a mind as a conviction that an existing law was wrong. The successive gradations of opinion pointed to a clear and absolute result. When it was a question, as in the case of the Reform Bill, not of simple abolition, but of extensive and difficult reconstruction, he ' could not see his way.' He could be convinced that the anti-Catholic laws were wrong, that the currency laws were wrong, that the commercial laws were wrong ; especially he could be convinced that the *laissez-faire* system was right, and the real thing was to do nothing ; but he was incapable of the larger and higher political construction. A more imaginative genius is necessary to deal with the consequences of new creations, and the structure of an unseen future.

This remark requires one limitation. A great deal of what is called legislation is really administrative regulation. It does not settle what is to be done, but *how* it is to be done; it does not prescribe what our institutions shall be, but directs in what manner existing institutions shall work and operate. Of this portion of legislation Sir Robert Peel was an admirable master. Few men have fitted administrative regulations with so nice an adjustment to a prescribed end. The Currency Act of 1844 was an instance of this. If you consult the speeches by which that bill was introduced and explained to parliament, you certainly will not find any very rigid demonstrations of political economy, or dry compactness of abstract principle. Whether the abstract theory of the supporters of that Act be sound or unsound, no exposition of it ever came from the lips of Peel. He assumed the results of that theory; but no man saw more quickly the nature of the administrative machinery which was required. The separation of the departments of the Bank of England, the limitation of the country issues, though neither of them original ideas of Sir Robert's own mind, yet were not, like most of his other important political acts, forced on him from without. There was a general agreement among the received authorities in favour of a certain currency theory; the administrative statesman saw a good deal before other men what was the most judicious and effectual way of setting it at work and regulating its action.

We have only spoken of Sir Robert Peel as a public man, and if you wish to write what is characteristic about him, that is the way to do so. He was a man whom it requires an effort to think of as engaged in anything but political business. Disraeli tells us that some one said that Peel was never happy except in the House of Commons, or doing something which had some relation to something to be done there. In common life, we continually see men scarcely separable as it were from their pursuits: they are as good as others, but their visible nature seems almost all absorbed in a certain visible calling. When we speak of them we are led to speak of it, when we would speak of it we are led insensibly to speak of them. It is so with Sir Robert Peel. So long as constitutional statesmanship is what it is now, so long as its function consists in recording the views of a confused nation, so long as success in it is confined to minds plastic, changeful, administrative—we must hope for no better man. You have excluded the profound thinker; you must be content with what you can obtain—the business-gentleman.

## LORD BROUGHAM.[1]

[1857.]

It was a bold, perhaps a rash idea, to collect the writings of Henry Brougham. They were written at such distant dates; their subjects are so various; they are often so wedged into the circumstances of an age—that they scarcely look natural in a series of volumes. Some men, doubtless, by a strong grasp of intellect, have compacted together subjects as various; the finger-marks of a few are on all human knowledge; others, by a rare illuminative power, have lit up as many with a light that seems peculiar to themselves. *Franciscus Baconus sic cogitavit* may well illustrate an *opera omnia*. But Lord Brougham has neither power; his restless genius has no claim to the still, illuminating imagination; his many-handed, apprehensive intelligence is scarcely able to fuse and concentrate. Variety is his taste, and versatility his power. His career has not been quiet. For many years rushing among the details of an age, he has written as he ran. There are not many undertakings bolder than to collect the works of such a life and such a man.

The edition itself seems a good one. The volumes are convenient in size, well printed, and fairly arranged. The various writings it contains have been revised, but not over-revised, by their author. It is not, however, of the collection that we wish to speak. We would endeavour, so far as a few hasty pages may serve, to delineate the career and character of the writer. The attempt is among the most difficult. He is still among

[1] *Works of Henry Lord Brougham, F.R.S.*, Member of the National Institute of France and the Royal Academy of Naples. London: Griffin.

us; we have not the materials, possibly not the impartiality, of posterity. Nor have we the familiar knowledge of contemporaries; the time when Lord Brougham exerted his greatest faculties is beyond the political memory of younger men. There are no sufficient books on the events of a quarter of a century ago, we have only traditions; and this must be our excuse if we fall, or seem to fall, into error and confusion.

The years immediately succeeding the great peace were years of sullenness and difficulty. The idea of the war had passed away; the thrill and excitement of the great struggle were no longer felt. We had maintained, with the greatest potentate of modern times, a successful contest for existence. We had our existence, but we had no more; our victory had been great, but it had no fruits. By the aid of pertinacity and capital, we had vanquished genius and valour; but no visible increase of European influence followed. Napoleon said that Wellington had made peace as if he had been defeated. We had delivered the Continent; such was our natural idea: but the Continent went its own way. There was nothing in its state to please the everyday Englishman. There were kings and emperors; 'which was very well for foreigners, they had always been like that; but it was not many kings could pay ten per cent. income-tax.' Absolutism, as such, cannot be popular in a free country. The Holy Alliance, which made a religion of despotism, was scarcely to be reconciled with the British constitution. Altogether we had vanquished Napoleon, but we had no pleasure in what came after him. The cause which agitated our hearts was gone; there was no longer a noise of victories in the air; continental affairs were dead, despotic, dull; we scarcely liked to think that we had made them so; with weary dissatisfaction we turned to our own condition.

This was profoundly unsatisfactory. Trade was depressed; agriculture ruinous; the working class singularly disaffected. During the war, our manufacturing industry had grown most rapidly; there was a not unnatural expectation that, after a

general peace, the rate of increase would be accelerated. The
whole continent, it was considered, would be opened to us;
Milan and Berlin decrees no longer excluded us; Napoleon
did not now interpose between 'the nation of shopkeepers'
and its customers; now he was at St. Helena, surely those
customers would buy? It was half-forgotten that they could
not. The drain of capital for the war had been, at times,
heavily felt in England; there had been years of poverty and
discredit; still our industry had gone on, our workshops had
not stopped. We had never known what it was to be the
seat of war, as well as a power at war. We had never known
our burdens enormously increased, just when our industry was
utterly stopped; disarranged as trading credit sometimes was,
it had not been destroyed. No conscription had drained us of
our most efficient consumers. The Continent, south and north,
had, though not everywhere alike, suffered all these evils; its
populations were poor, harassed, depressed. They could not
buy our manufactures, for they had no money. The large preparations for a continental export lay on hand; our traders
were angry and displeased. Nor was content to be found in
the agricultural districts. During the war, the British farmer
had inevitably a monopoly of this market; at the approach of
peace, his natural antipathy to foreign corn influenced the
legislature. The Home Secretary of the time had taken into
consideration whether 76s. or 80s. was such a remunerating
price as the agriculturist should obtain, and a corn-law had
passed accordingly. But no law could give the farmer famine
prices, when there was scarcity here and plenty abroad. There
were riots at the passing of the 'Bread-tax,' as it was; in
1813, the price of corn was 120s.; the rural mind was sullen
in 1816, when it sunk to 57s. The protection given, though
unpopular with the poor, did not satisfy the farmer.

The lower orders in the manufacturing districts were, of
necessity, in great distress. The depression of trade produced
its inevitable results of closed mills and scanty employment.

Wages, when they could be obtained, were very low. The artisan population was then new to the vicissitudes of industry : how far they are, even now, instructed in the laws of trade, recent prosperity will hardly let us judge; but, at that time, they had no doubt that it was the fault of the State, and if not of particular statesmen, then of the essential institutions, that they were in want. They believed the Government ought to regulate their remuneration, and make it sufficient. During some straitened years of the war the name of 'Luddites' became known. They had principally shown their discontent by breaking certain machines, which they fancied deprived them of work. Afer the peace, the records of the time are full of 'Spencean Philanthropists,' 'Hampden Clubs,' and similar associations, all desiring a great reform—some of mere politics, others of the law of property and all social economy. Large meetings were everywhere held, something like those of the year 1839 : a general insurrection, doubtless a wild dream of a few hot-brained dreamers, was fancied to have been really planned. The name 'Radical' came to be associated with this discontent. The spirit which, in after years, clamoured distinctly for the five points of the Charter, made itself heard in mutterings and threatenings.

Nor were the capitalists, who had created the new wealth, socially more at ease. Many of them, as large employers of labour, had a taste for Toryism; the rule of the people to them meant the rule of their workpeople. Some of the wealthiest and most skilful became associated with the aristocracy, but it was in vain with the majority to attempt it. Between them and the possessors of hereditary wealth there was fixed a great gulf; the contrast of habits, speech, manners, was too wide. The two might coincide in particular opinions; they might agree to support the same institutions; they might set forth, in a Conservative creed, the same form of sound words: but, though the abstract conclusions were identical, the mode of holding them—to borrow a subtlety of Father Newman's—was exceedingly different. The refined, discriminating, timorous immobility of the aristocracy was distinct from the coarse, dogmatic, keep-downishness of the manufacturer. Yet more marked was the contrast, when the opposite tendencies of temperament had produced, as they soon could not but do, a diversity of opinion. The case was not quite new in England. Mr. Burke spoke of the tendency of the first East Indians to Jacobinism. They could not, he said, bear that their present importance should have no proportion to their recently-acquired riches. No extravagant fortunes have, in this century, been made by Englishmen in India; but Lancashire has been a California. Families have been created there, whose names we all know, which we think of when we mention wealth; some of which are now, by lapse of time, passing into the hereditary caste of recognised opulence. This, however, has been a work of time; and, before it occurred, there was no such intermediate class between the new wealth and the old. 'It takes,' it is said that Sir Robert Peel observed, 'three generations to make a gentleman.' In the meantime, there was an inevitable misunderstanding; the new cloth was too coarse for the old. Besides this, many actual institutions offended the eyes of the middle class. The state of the law was opposed both to their prejudices and interests: that you could only recover your debts by spending more than the debt, was hard; and the injury was aggravated, the money was spent in 'special pleading'—'in putting a plain thing so as to perplex and mislead a plain man.' 'Lord Eldon and the Court of Chancery,' as Sydney Smith expressed it, 'sat heavy on mankind.' The existence of slavery in our colonies, strongly supported by a strong aristocratic and parliamentary influence, offended the principles of middle-class Christianity, and the natural sentiments of simple men. The cruelty of the penal law—the punishing with death sheep-stealing and shop-lifting—jarred the humanity of that second order of English society, which, from their habits of reading and non-reading, may be called, *par excellence*, the scriptural classes. The routine harshness of a not very wise executive did not mitigate the feeling. The *modus operandi* of Government appeared coarse and oppressive.

We seemed to pay, too, a good deal for what we did not like. At the close of the war, the ten per cent. income tax was of course heavily oppressive. The public expenditure was beyond argument lavish; and it was spent in pensions, sinecures (for 'them idlers' in the speech of Lancashire), and a mass of sundries, that an economical man of business will scarcely admit to be necessary, and that even now, after countless prunings, produce periodically 'financial reform associations,' 'administrative leagues,' and other combinations which amply testify the enmity of thrifty efficiency to large figures and muddling management. There had remained from the eighteenth century a tradition of corruption, an impression that direct pecuniary malversation pervaded the public offices; an idea true in the days of Rigby or Bubb Dodington, but which, like many other impressions, continued to exist many years after the facts in which it originated had passed away. Government, in the hands of such a man as Lord Liverpool, was very different from government in the hands of Sir Robert Walpole: respectability was exacted: of actual money-taking there was hardly any. Still, especially among inferior officials, there was something to shock modern purity. The size of jobs was large: if the Treasury of that time could be revived, it would be depressed at the littleness of whatever is perpetrated in modern administration. There were petty abuses too in the country—in municipalities —in charitable trusts—in all outlying public moneys, which seemed to the offended man of business, who saw them with his own eyes, evident instances confirming his notion of the malpractices of Downing Street. 'There are only five little boys in the school of Richester; they may cost 200*l.*, and the income is 2000*l.*, and the trustees don't account for the balance; which is the way things are done in England: we keeps an aristocracy,' &c. The whole of this feeling was concentrated into a detestation of rotten boroughs. The very name was enough: that Lord Dover, with two patent sinecures in the Exchequer and a good total for assisting in nothing at the Audit office, should return two members for one house, while Birmingham, where they made buttons,—'as good buttons as there are in the world, sir,'—returned no members at all, was an evident indication that reform was necessary. Mr. Canning was an eloquent man; but 'even *he* could not say that a decaying stump was the *people*.' Gatton and Old Sarum became unpopular. The source of power seemed absurd, and the use of power was tainted. Side by side with the incipient Chartism of the northern operative, there was growing daily more distinct and clear the Manchester philosophy, which has since expressed itself in the Anti-Corn-Law League, and which for good and evil is now an element so potent in our national life. Both creeds were forms of discontent. And the counterpoise was wanting. The English constitution has provided that there shall always be one estate raised above the storms of passion and controversy, which all parties may respect and honour. The King is to be loved. But this theory requires, for a real efficiency, that the throne be filled by such a person as can be loved. In those times it was otherwise. The nominal possessor of the crown was a very old man, whom an incurable malady had long sequestered from earthly things. The actual possessor of the royal authority was a voluptuary of overgrown person, now too old for healthy pleasure, and half sickened himself at the corrupt pursuits in which, nevertheless, he indulged perpetually. His domestic vices had become disgracefully public. Whatever might be the truth about Queen Caroline, no one could say she had been well treated. There was no loyalty on which suffering workers, or an angry middle class, could repose: all through the realm there was a miscellaneous agitation, a vague and wandering discontent.

The official mind of the time was troubled. We have a record of its speculations in the life of Lord Sidmouth, who more

than any one perhaps embodied it. He had been Speaker, and was
much inclined to remedy the discontent of the middle classes
by 'naming them to the House.' A more conscientious man
perhaps has never filled a public position. If the forms of the
House of Commons had been intuitively binding, no one could
have obeyed them better: the 'mace' was a 'counsel of perfection' to him; all disorder hateful. In the Home Office it
was the same. The Luddites were people who would not
obey the Speaker. Constituted authority must be enforced.
The claims of a suffering multitude were not so much neglected
as unappreciated. A certain illiberality, as we should now
speak, pervades the whole kind of thought. The most striking
feature is an indisposition, which by long indulgence has
become an inability, to comprehend another person's view, to
put oneself in another's mental place, to think what he thinks,
to conceive what he inevitably is. Lord Sidmouth referred
to the file. He found that Mr. Pitt had put down disaffection
by severe measures. Accordingly, he suspended the Habeas
Corpus Act, passed six Acts, commended a Peterloo massacre,
not with conscious unfeelingness, but from an absorbed offi-
ciality, from a knowledge that this was what 'the department'
had done before, and an inference that this must be done again.
As for the reforming ideas of the middle classes, red tape
had never tied up such notions; perhaps it was the French
Revolution over again: you could not tolerate *them*.

Between such a dominant mind as this, and such a subject
mind as has been described, there was a daily friction. The situation afforded obvious advantages to enterprising men. Its peculiarity did not escape the shrewd eyes of John Lord Eldon. 'If,'
said the Conservative Chancellor, 'I were to begin life again,
d——n my eyes, but I would begin as an agitator.' Henry
Brougham did so begin. During the war he had distinguished
himself in the exposition of the grievances of the trading interest.
Our Government had chosen a mode of carrying it on specially
fitted to injure our commerce. 'Napoleon had said that no

vessel should touch a British port, and then enter a French one, or one under French control. The Orders in Council said that no vessel whatever should enter any such port without having first touched at some port of Great Britain.'[1] The natural results were the annihilation of our trade with the Continent and a quarrel with the United States. The merchants of the country were alarmed at both consequences. Perhaps until then men hardly knew how powerful our trading classes had become. Meetings were held in populous places; petitions in great numbers—an impressive and important thing in those times—were presented. Wherever foreign commerce existed, the discontent expressed itself in murmurs. The forms of the House of Commons were far more favourable than they now are to action from without; and this is not unnatural, since there had been as yet but few actions from without, and it had not been necessary to have a guard against them. 'The petitions, as has been said, were numerous; and on the presentation of each there was a speech from the member presenting it, trying to bring on a debate, and suggesting topics which might irritate the ministry and convince the country.' Mr. Brougham was always in his place. 'Hardly an hour passed without detecting some false statement or illogical argument; hardly a night passed without gaining some convert to the cause of truth.' The result was decisive. 'Although opposed by the whole weight of the Government both in public and out of doors; although at first vigorously resisted by the energy, the acuteness, the activity, and the expertness which made Mr. Perceval one of the first debaters of his day; although, after' his death, the struggle was maintained by the father of the system[2] with all his fire and with his full knowledge of the subject—nay, although' the Ministry risked their existence on the question, the victory remained with the petitioners. The Orders in Council were abolished, and the efficacy of

This and the following quotations are from the Speeches of Lord Brougham and the Introductions to them, published in 1838. The latter were written by himself.     [2] Mr. Stephen.

agitation proved. 'The session of 1816 offered an example yet more remarkable of the same tactics being attended with signal success. On the termination of the war, the Government were determined, instead of repealing the whole income-tax, which the law declared to be " for and during the continuance of the war, and no longer," to retain one-half of it.' 'As soon as this intention was announced, several meetings were held.' Some petitions were presented. Mr. Brougham declared that, if the motion 'were pressed on Thursday, he should avail himself of the forms of the House.' Of course the unpopularity of paying money was decisive; the income-tax fell. The same faculty of aggression, which had been so successful in these instances, was immediately so applied as to give voice to the sullenness of the country; to express forms of discontent as real, though not with an object as determinate.

Mr. Brougham did not understate his case : 'There is one branch of the subject which I shall pass over altogether—I mean the amount of the distresses which are now universally admitted to prevail over almost every part of the empire. Upon this topic all men are agreed ; the statements connected with it are as unquestionable as they are afflicting.' Nor did he shrink from detail. 'I shall suppose,' he observed to the House, 'a farm of 400 acres of fair, good land, yielding a rent of from 500*l.* to 600*l.* a-year.' 'It will require a four years' course— 200 acres being in corn, 100 in fallow, and 100 in hay and grass;' and he seems to prove that at least it *ought* not to answer, 'independently of the great rise in lime and all sorts of manure.' The commercial mania of the time takes its turn in the description. 'After the cramped state in which the enemy's measures, and our own retaliation (as we termed it) had kept our trade for some years, when the events of spring 1814 suddenly opened the Continent, a rage for exporting goods of every kind burst forth, only to be explained by reflecting on the previous restrictions we had been labouring under, and only to be equalled (though not in extent) by some of the mercantile delusions connected with South American speculations. Everything that could be shipped was sent off; all the capital that could be laid hold of was embarked. The frenzy, I can call it nothing less, after the experience of 1806 and 1810, descended to persons in the humblest circumstances and the farthest removed, by their pursuits, from commercial cares. It may give the committee some idea of this disease, if I state what I know to have happened in one or two places. Not only clerks and labourers, but menial servants, engaged the little sums which they had been laying up for a provision against old age and sickness; persons went round tempting them to adventure in the trade to Holland, and Germany, and the Baltic; they risked their mite in the hopes of boundless profits; it went with the millions of the more regular traders: the bubble soon burst, like its predecessors of the South Sea, the Mississippi, and Buenos Ayres; English goods were selling for much less in Holland and the north of Europe than in London and Manchester; in most places they were lying a dead weight without any sale at all; and either no returns whatever were received, or pounds came back for thousands that had gone forth. The great speculators broke; the middling ones lingered out a precarious existence, deprived of all means of continuing their dealings either at home or abroad; the poorer dupes of the delusion had lost their little hoards, and went upon the parish the next mishap that befel them; but the result of the whole has been much commercial distress —a caution now absolutely necessary in trying new adventures —a prodigious diminution in the demand for manufactures, and indirectly a serious defalcation in the effectual demand for the produce of land.'

Next year Mr. Brougham described as the worst season ever known. The year 1812, a year before esteemed one of much suffering, rose in comparison to one of actual prosperity. He began with the ' clothing, a branch of trade which, from accidental circumstances, is not as depressed as our other great

staples;' he passed to the iron trade, &c. &c. He dilated on
the distress, the discontent and suffering of the people. Of
course the Government were to blame. He moved that the
'unexampled' difficulties of trade and manufactures were
'materially increased by the policy pursued with respect
to our foreign commerce — that the continuance of these
difficulties is in a great degree owing to the severe pressure
of taxation under which the country labours, and which ought
by every practicable means to be lightened—that the system
of foreign policy pursued by his Majesty's ministers has not
been such as to obtain for the people of this country those
commercial advantages which the influence of Great Britain
in foreign countries fairly entitled them to expect.' As became a pupil of the Edinburgh University, Mr. Brougham was
not averse to political economy. He was ready to discuss the
theory of rent or the corn-laws. He made a speech, which he
relates as having had a greater success than any other which he
made in Parliament, in support of Mr. Calcraft's amendment,
to 'substitute 192,638*l*. 4*s*. 9*d*. for 385,276*l*. 9*s*. 6*d*., the estimate for the household troops.' Foreign policy was a favourite
topic. Almost unsupported, as he said some years after, he
attacked the Holy Alliance. Looking back through the softening atmosphere of reminiscence, he almost seems to have a
kindness for Lord Castlereagh. He remembers with pleasure
the utter ' courage with which he exposed himself unabashed to
the most critical audience in the world, while incapable of utter-
ing anything but the meanest matter, expressed in the most
wretched language;' nor has he 'forgotten the kind of pride
that mantled on the fronts of the Tory phalanx when, after being
overwhelmed with the fire of the Whig Opposition, or galled by
the fierce denunciations of the Mountain, or harassed by the
splendid displays of Mr. Canning, their chosen leader stood
forth, and presenting the graces of his eminently patrician
figure, flung open his coat, displayed an azure ribbon traversing
a snow-white chest, and declared 'his high satisfaction that he

could now meet the charges against him face to face, and repel with indignation all that his adversaries had been bold and rash enough to advance. But the 'Mr. Brougham' of that time showed no admiration; no denunciations were stronger than his; no sarcasm impinged more deeply; if the 'noble lord in the blue ribbon' wished anyone out of the House, the 'man from the Northern Circuit' was probably that one. Kings and emperors met with little mercy, and later years have shown how little was merited by the petty absolutism and unthinking narrowness of that time.

That Mr. Brougham indissolubly connected the education movement with his name everybody knows, but scarcely anyone remembers how unpopular that movement was. Mr. Windham had said, some years before, 'That the diffusion of knowledge was proper, might be supported by many good arguments; but he confessed he was a sceptic on that point. It was said, Look at the state of the savages as compared with ours. A savage among savages was *very well*, and the difference was only perceived when he came to be introduced into civilised society.' 'His friend Dr. Johnson was of opinion that it was not right to teach reading beyond a certain extent in society.' The same feeling continued. Mr. Peel, in his blandest tones, attacked the education committee. Lord Stowell, not without sagacity, observed, 'If you provide a larger amount of highly-cultivated talent than there is a demand for, the surplus is very likely to turn sour.' Such were the sentiments of some of the best scholars of that era; and so went all orthodox sentiment. That education was the same as republicanism, and republicanism as infidelity, half the curates believed. But, in spite of all this opposition, perhaps with more relish on account of it, Mr. Brougham was ever ready. He was a kind of prophet of knowledge. His voice was heard in the streets. He preached the gospel of the alphabet; he sang the praises of the primer all the day long. 'Practical observations,' 'discourses,' 'speeches,' exist, terrible to all men now. To the kind of edu-

cation then advocated there may be objections. We may object
to the kind of 'knowledge' then most sought after; but there
can be no doubt that those who then laboured in its behalf must
be praised for having inculcated, in the horrid heat of the day,
as a boring paradox what is now a boring commonplace.

Our space would fail us if we were to attempt to recount
Brougham's labours on the slavery question, on George IV.
and Queen Caroline, or his hundred encounters with the
routine statesmen. The series commenced at the Peace, but
it continued for many years. Is not its history written in the
chronicles of Parliament? You must turn the leaves—no
unpleasant reading—of those old debates, and observe how
often Mr. Brougham's name occurs, and on what cumbrous
subjects, before you can estimate the frequency of his attacks
and the harassing harshness of his labour. One especial subject was his more than any other man's—law reform. He had
Romilly and Mackintosh as fellow-labourers in the amelioration of the penal code; he had their support, and that of some
others, in his incessant narrations of the grievances of indi-
viduals, and denunciations of the unfeeling unthinkingness of
our Home administration; but no man grappled so boldly—we
had almost said so coarsely—with the crude complexities of our
civil jurisprudence: for a rougher nature, a more varied knowledge of action than we can expect of philanthropists were
needed for that task. The subject was most difficult to deal
with. The English commerce and civilisation had grown up in
the meshes of a half-feudal code, further complicated with the
curious narrowness and spirit of chicane which haunt everywhere the law-courts of early times. The technicality which
produced the evil made the remedy more difficult. There was
no general public opinion on the manner of reform; the public
felt the evil, but no one could judge of the efficacy of a remedy,
save persons studious in complicated learning, who would
hardly be expected to show how that learning could be rendered
useless—hardly, indeed, to imagine a world in which it did not

exist.  The old creed, that these ingenious abuses were the
last 'perfection of reason,' still lingered.  It must give Lord
Brougham some pride to reflect how many of the improvements
which he was the first to popularise, if not to suggest, have
been adopted—how many old abuses of detail, which he first
indicated to Parliament, exist no longer—how many more are
now admitted by everybody to be abuses, though the mode of
abolition is contested.  The speech on law reform, which he
published in the collected edition of his speeches, is nearly a
summary of all that has been done or suggested in common or
civil law reform for the last thirty years.  The effect which so
bold an attack on so many things by a single person produced
in that conservative time was prodigious.  'There never was
such a nuisance as the man is,' said an old lawyer whom we
knew; and he expressed the feeling of his profession.  If we
add, that beside all these minor reforms and secondary agita-
tions, Mr. Brougham was a bold advocate of Catholic emancipation and parliamentary reform—the largest heresies of that
epoch—we may begin to understand the sarcasm of Mr.
Canning : ' The honourable and learned gentleman having, in
the course of his parliamentary life, supported or proposed
*almost every species of innovation* which could be practised on
the constitution, it was not very easy for ministers to do anything without seeming to borrow from him.  Break away in
what direction they would, whether to the right or to the left,
it was all alike.  " Oh," said the honourable gentleman, " I was
there before you : you would not have thought of that if I had
not given you a hint."  In the reign of Queen Anne there was
a sage and grave critic of the name of Dennis, who in his old age
got it into his head that he had written all the good plays
which were acted at that time.  At last a tragedy came forth
with a most imposing display of hail and thunder.  At the first
peal, Dennis exclaimed : " That is my thunder ! "  So with the
honourable and learned gentleman ; there was no noise astir for
the good of mankind in any part of the world, but he instantly

claimed it for his thunder.' We may have wearied our readers
with these long references to old conflicts, but it was necessary.
We are familiar with the aberrations of the ex-Chancellor; we
forget how bold, how efficacious, how varied was the activity of
Henry Brougham.

There are several qualities in his genius which make such a
life peculiarly suited to him. The first of these is an aggressive,
impulsive disposition. Most people may admit that the world
goes ill; old abuses seem to exist, questionable details to
abound. Hardly anyone thinks that anything may not be
made better. But how to improve the world, to repair the
defects, is a difficulty. Immobility is a part of man. A sluggish
conservatism is the basis of our English nature. ' *Learn,* my
son,' said the satirist, ' to bear tranquilly the calamities of others.'
We easily learn it. Most men have a line of life, and it im-
poses certain duties which they fulfil; but they cannot be
induced to start out of that line. We dwell in ' a firm basis of
content.' ' Let the mad world go its own way, for it will go its
own way.' There is no doctrine of the English Church more
agreeable to our instinctive taste than that which forbids all
works of supererogation. ' You did a thing without being
obliged,' said an eminent statesman: 'then that must be
wrong.' We travel in the track. Lord Brougham is the
opposite of this. It is not difficult to him to attack abuses.
The more difficult thing for him would be to live in a world
without abuses. An intense excitability is in his nature. He
must ' go off.' He is eager to reform corruption, and rushes out to
refute error. A tolerant placidity is altogether denied to him.

And not only is this excitability eager, it is many-sided.
The men who have in general exerted themselves in labours for
others, have generally been rather of a brooding nature; certain
ideas, views and feelings have impressed themselves on them
in solitude; they come forth with them among the crowd, but
they have no part in its diversified life. They are almost
irritated by it. They have no conception except of their cause;

they are abstracted in one thought, pained with the dizziness of a heated idea. There is nothing of this in Brougham. He is excited by what he sees. The stimulus is from without. He saw the technicalities of the law-courts; observed a charitable trustee misusing the charity moneys; perceived that George IV. oppressed Queen Caroline; went to Old Sarum. He is not absorbed in a creed: he is pricked by facts. Accordingly, his activity is miscellaneous. The votary of a doctrine is concentrated, for the logical consequences of a doctrine are limited. But an open-minded man, who is aroused by what he sees, quick at discerning abuses, ready to reform anything which he thinks goes wrong—will never have done acting. The details of life are endless, and each of them may go wrong in a hundred ways.

Another faculty of Brougham (in metaphysics it is perhaps but a phase of the same) is the faculty of easy anger. The supine placidity of civilisation is not favourable to animosity. A placid Conservative is perhaps a little pleased that the world is going a *little* ill. Lord Brougham does not feel this. Like an Englishman on the Continent, he is ready to blow up anyone. He is a Jonah of detail; he is angry at the dust of life, and wroth with the misfeasances of *employés*. The most reverberating of bastinadoes is the official mind basted by Brougham. You did *this* wrong; why did you omit *that?* Document C ought to be on the third file; paper D is wrongly docketed in the ninth file. Red tape will scarcely succeed when it is questioned; you should take it as Don Quixote did his helmet, without examination, for a most excellent helmet. A vehement, industrious man proposing to untie papers and not proposing to spare errors is the terror of a respectable administrator. ' Such an impracticable man, sir, interfering with the *office*, attacking private character, messing in what cannot concern him.' These are the jibes which attend an irritable anxiety for the good of others. They have attended Lord Brougham through life. He has enough of misanthropy to be a philanthropist.

How much of this is temper, and how much public spirit, it

is not for anyone to attempt to say. That a natural pleasure in wrath is part of his character, no one who has studied the career of Brougham can doubt. But no fair person can doubt, either, that he has shown on many great occasions—and, what is more, on many petty occasions—a rare zeal for the public welfare. He may not be capable of the settled calm by which the world is best administered. There is a want of consistency in his goodness, of concentration in his action. The gusts of passion pass over him, and he is gone for a time you can scarcely say where. But, though he is the creature of impulse, his impulses are often generous and noble ones. No one would do what he has done, no one could have the intense motive power to do what he has done, without a large share of diffused unselfishness. The irritation of the most acute excitability would not suffice. It is almost an axiom in estimates of human nature, that in its larger operations all that nature must concur. Doubtless there is a thread of calculation in the midst of his impulses; no man rises to be lord-chancellor without, at least in lulls and intervals of impulse, a most discriminating and careful judgment of men and things and chances. But after every set-off and abatement, and without any softening of unamiable indications, there will yet remain—and a long series of years will continue to admire it—an eager principle of disinterested action.

Lord Brougham's intellectual powers were as fitted for the functions of a miscellaneous agitator as his moral character. The first of these, perhaps, is a singular faculty of conspicuous labour. In general, the work of agitation proceeds in this way: a conspicuous, fascinating popular orator is ever on the surface, ever ready with appropriate argument, making motions, attracting public attention; beneath and out of sight are innumerable workers and students, unfit for the public eye, getting up the facts, elaborating conclusions, supplying the conspicuous orator with the *data* on which he lives. There is a perpetual controversy, when the narrative of the agitation comes to be written, whether the merit of what is achieved belongs to the skilful advocate who makes a subtle use of what is provided for him, or the laborious inferiors and juniors who compose the brief and set in order the evidence. For all that comes before the public, Lord Brougham has a wonderful power : he can make motions, addresses, orations, when you wish and on what you wish. He is like a machine for moving amendments. He can keep at work any number of persons under him. Every agitation has a tendency to have an office ; some league, some society, some body of labourers must work regularly at its details. Mr. Brougham was able to rush hither and thither through a hundred such kinds of men, and gather up the whole stock of the most recent information, the extreme decimals of the statistics, and diffuse them immediately with eager comment to a listening world. This may not be, indeed is not, the strictest and most straining kind of labour; the anxious, wearing, verifying, self-imposed scrutiny of scattered and complicated details is a far more exhausting task; it is this which makes the eye dim and the face pale and the mind heavy. The excitement of a multifarious agitation will carry the energies through much ; the last touches, and it is these which exhaust, need not be put on any one subject. Yet, after all deductions, such a career requires a quantity far surpassing all that most men have of life and *verve* and mind.

Another advantage of Lord Brougham is his extreme readiness ; what he can do, he can do at a moment's notice. He has always had this power. Lord Holland, in his Memoirs referring to transactions which took place many years ago, gives an illustration of it. 'The management of our press,' he is speaking of the question of the general election of 1807, 'fell into the hands of Mr. Brougham. With that active and able individual I had become acquainted through Mr. Allen in 1805. At the formation of Lord Grenville's ministry, he had written, at my suggestion, a pamphlet called the "State of the Nation." He subsequently accompanied Lord Rosslyn to Lisbon. His early connection with the Abolitionists had familiarised him with the means of circulating political papers, and given him some weight with those best qualified to co-operate in such an undertaking. His extensive knowledge, his extraordinary readiness, his assiduity and habits of composition, enabled him to correct some articles, and to furnish a prodigious number himself. With partial and scanty assistance from Mr. Allen, myself, and one or two more, he in the course of a few days filled every bookseller's shop with pamphlets—most London newspapers, and all country ones without exception, with paragraphs—and supplied a large portion of the boroughs throughout the kingdom with handbills adapted to the local interests of the candidates, and all tending to enforce the conduct, elucidate the measures, or expose the adversaries of the Whigs.'

Another power which was early remarked of Brougham, and which is as necessary as any to an important leader in great movements, is a skilful manipulation of men. Sir James Mackintosh noted in his Journal, on January 30, 1818 : ' The address and insinuation of Brougham are so great, that nothing but the bad temper which he cannot always hide could hinder him from mastering everybody as he does Romilly. He *leads* others to his opinion ; he generally appears at first to concur with theirs, and never more than half opposes it at once. This management is helped by an air of easy frankness that would lay suspicion itself asleep. He will place himself at the head of an opposition among whom he is unpopular ; he will conquer the House of Commons, who hate, but now begin to fear him.' An observer of faces would fancy he noted in Lord Brougham this pliant astuteness marred by ill-temper. It has marked his career.

Another essential quality in multifarious agitation is an extreme versatility. No one can deny Lord Brougham this. An apparently close observer has described him: ' Take the routine of a day, for instance. In his early life he has been known to attend, in his place in court, on circuit, at an early hour in the morning. After having successfully pleaded the cause of his client, he drives off to the hustings, and delivers, at different places, eloquent and spirited speeches to the electors. He then sits down in the retirement of his closet to pen an address to the Glasgow students, perhaps, or an elaborate article in the " Edinburgh Review." The active labours of the day are closed with preparation for the court business of the following morning; and then, in place of retiring to rest, as ordinary men would after such exertions, he spends the night in abstruse study, or in social intercourse with some friend from whom he has been long separated. Yet he would be seen, as early as eight on the following morning, actively engaged in the court, in defence of some unfortunate object of government persecution, astonishing the auditory, and his fellow-lawyers no less, with the freshness and power of his eloquence. A fair contrast with this history of a day, in early life, would be that of one at a more advanced period; say, in the year 1832. A watchful observer might see the new Lord Chancellor seated in the court over which he presided, from an early hour in the morning until the afternoon, listening to the arguments of counsel, and mastering the points of cases with a grasp of mind that enabled him to give those speedy and un-embarrassed judgments that have so injured him with the profession. If he followed his course, he would see him, soon after the opening of the House of Lords, addressing their lordships on some intricate question of law, with an acuteness that drew down approbation even from his opponents; or, on some all-engrossing political topic, casting firebrands into the camp of the enemy, and awakening them from the complacent repose of conviction to the hot contests with more active and inquiring intellects. Then, in an hour or so, he might follow him to the Mechanics' Institution, and hear an able and stimulating discourse on education, admirably adapted to the peculiar capacity of his auditors; and towards ten, perhaps, at a Literary and Scientific Institution in Marylebone, the same Proteus-like intellect might be found expounding the intricacies of physical science with a never-tiring and elastic power. Yet, during all those multitudinous exertions, time would be found for the composition of a discourse on Natural Theology, that bears no marks of haste or excitement of mind, but presents as calm a face as though it had been the laborious production of a contemplative philosopher.' We may differ in our estimate of the *quality* of these various efforts; but no one can deny to him who was capable of them a great share in what Adam Smith mentioned as one of the most important facilities to the intellectual labourer—a quickness in 'changing his hand.'

Nor would any of these powers be sufficient, without that which is, in some sense, the principle of them all— an enterprising intellect. In the present day this is among the rarest of gifts. The speciality of pursuits is attended with a timidity of mind. Each subject is given up to men who cultivate it, and it only; who are familiar with its niceties and absorbed in its details. There is no one who dares to look at the whole. 'I have taken *all* knowledge to be my province,' said Lord Bacon. The notion, and still more the expression, of it seems ridiculous now. The survey of each plot in the world of knowledge is becoming more complete. We shall have a plan of each soon, on a seven-inch scale; but we are losing the picturesque pictures of the outside and surface of knowledge in the survey of its whole. We have the petty survey, as we say, but no chart, no globe of the entire world; no bold sketch of its obvious phenomena, as they strike the wayfarer and impress themselves on the imagination. The man of the speciality cannot describe the large outlines; he is too close upon the minutiæ; he does o t know the relations of other knowledge, and no one else dares to infringe on his province—on the 'study of his life'— for fear of committing errors in detail which he alone knows, and which he may expose. Lord Brougham has nothing of this cowardice. He is ready to give, in their boldest and most general form, the rough outlines of knowledge as théy strike the man of the world, occupied in its affairs and familiar with

its wishes.  He is not cooped up in a single topic, and he has
no dread of those who are.  He may fall into error, but he
exhibits a subject as it is seen by those who know other
subjects, by a man who knows the world ; he at least attempts
an embracing conception of his topic, he makes you feel its connection with reality and affairs.  He has exhibited this virtue
at all stages of his career, but it was most valuable in his
earlier time.  There is no requisite so important as intellectual courage in one who seeks to improve all things in all
ways.

His oratory also suits the character of the hundred-subject
agitator well.  It is rough-and-ready.  It abounds in sarcasm,
in vituperation, in aggression.  It does not shrink from detail.
It would batter any thing at any moment.  We may think
as we will on its merits as a work of art, but no one can deny
its exact adaptation to a versatile and rushing agitator—to a
Tribune of detail.

The deficiencies of Brougham's character—in some cases they
seem but the unfavourable aspects of its excellences—were also
fitted for his earlier career.  The first of these, to say it in a sentence, is the want of a thinking intellect.  A miscellaneous agitator must be ready to catch at anything, to attack everything,
to blame anyone.   This is not the life for a mind of anxious
deliberation.  The patient philosopher, who is cautious in his
positions, dubious of his data, slow in his conclusions, must fail
at once.  He would be investigating while he should attack, inquiring while he should speak.  He could not act upon a
chance ; the moment of action would be gone.  A sanguine and
speedy intellect, ready to acquire, by its very idea all but excludes the examining, scrupulous, hesitating intellect which
reflects.

Nor would a man of very sensitive judgment endure such a
career.  An agitator must err by excess ; a delicate nature errs
by defects.  There is a certain coarseness in the abusive breed.
A Cleon should not feel failure.  No man has ever praised very

highly Lord Brougham's judgment; but to have exceedingly
improved it would perhaps have impaired his earlier utility.
You might as fitly employ some delicate lady as a rough-rider,
as a man of a poising, refining judgment in the task of a
grievance-stater.

Harsh nerves, too, are no disadvantage. Perhaps they are
essential. Very nice nerves would shrink from a scattered and
jangled life. Three days out of six the sensitive frame would
be jarred, the agitator would be useless. It is possible, indeed,
to imagine that in a single noble cause—a cause that would
light up the imagination, that would move the inner soul, a
temperament the most delicate, a frame that is most poetic,
might well be absorbingly interested. A little of such qualities
may be essential. The apostle of a creed must have the nature
to comprehend that creed; his fancy must take it in, his
feelings realise it, his nature absorb it. To move the finer
nature, you need the deeper nature. Perhaps even in a
meaner cause, in a cause which should take a hold on the
moving mob, sway the masses, rule the popular fancy, rough as
the task of the mob-orator is, you require the delicate imagination. One finds some trace of it—still more of what is its
natural accompaniment, a sweet nature—buried in the huge
frame and coarse exterior of O'Connell. No unpoetic heart
could touch the Irish people. Lord Brougham is prose itself.
He was described, many years ago, as excelling all men in a
knowledge of the course of exchange. ' He is,' continued the
satirist, 'apprised of the exact state of our exports and imports,
and scarce a ship clears out its cargo at Liverpool or Hull but
he has the notice of the bill of lading.' To explain the grievances of men of business needs no poetic nature. It scarcely
needs the highest powers of invective. There is something
nearly ridiculous in being the ' Mirabeau of sums.'

There is a last quality, which is difficult to describe in the
language of books, but which Lord Brougham excels in, and
which has perhaps been of more value to him than all his

other qualities put together. In the speech of ordinary men it is called ' devil ; ' persons instructed in the German language call it ' the demonic element.' What it is one can hardly express in a single sentence. It is most easily explained by physiognomy. There is a glare in some men's eyes which seems to say, ' Beware, I am dangerous ; *noli me tangere.*' Lord Brougham's face has this. A mischievous excitability is the most obvious expression of it. If he were a horse, nobody would buy him ; with that eye, no one could answer for his temper. Such men are often not really resolute, but they are not pleasant to be near in a difficulty. They have an aggressive eagerness which is formidable. They would kick against the pricks sooner than not kick at all. A little of the demon is excellent for an agitator.

His peculiar adaptation to his peculiar career raised Mr. Brougham, in a few years, to a position such as few men have ever obtained in England—such as no other man perhaps has attained by popular agitation. When he became member for Yorkshire, in 1830, he was a power in the country. The cause which he was advocating had grown of itself. The power of the middle classes, especially of the commercial classes, had increased. Lord Eldon was retiring. Lord Sidmouth had retired. What we now call ' liberality' was coming into fashion. Men no longer regarded the half-feudal constitution as a ' form of thought.' Argument was at least thought fair. And this seems likely and natural. No one can wonder that the influence of men of business grew with the development of business, and that they adopted the plain, straightforward, cautious creed, which we now know to be congenial to them. It is much more difficult to explain how reform became a passion. The state of the public mind during the crisis of the Reform Bill is one which those who cannot remember it cannot understand. The popular enthusiasm, the intense excitement, the rush of converts, the union of rectors and squires with those against whom they had respectively so long preached and sworn, the acclamation for the ' whole bill and nothing but the bill,' are become utterly strange. As the first French Assembly in a single night abolished, with public outcry, the essential abuses of the old *régime,* so our fathers at once, and with enthusiasm, abolished the close boroughs and the old representation, the lingering abuses of half-feudal England. The present Frenchmen are said not to comprehend August 4 : we can hardly understand the year '32. An apathy has fallen upon us. But we can nevertheless, and without theorising, comprehend what an advantage such an enthusiasm was to the Liberals of that time. Most Whig ministries have been like Low-Church bishops. There is a feeling that the advocates of liberty ought scarcely to coerce ; they have ruled, but they seem to deny the succession by which they ruled ; they have been distrusted by a vague and half-conservative sentiment. In the tumult of 1832 all such feelings were carried away. Toryism was abolished with delight.

Mr. Brougham was among the first to share the advantage. There is a legend that in the first Whig ministry Lord Brougham was offered the post of Attorney-general, and that he only replied by disdainfully tearing up the letter containing the offer. Whether the anecdote be literally true or not, we cannot say. The first of the modern Whig ministries is in the post-historical period. We have not yet enough of contemporary evidence to be sure of its details : years must pass before the memoir-writers can accumulate. But in spirit the tale is doubtless accurate. Lord Grey did not wish to make Mr. Brougham Lord-Chancellor, and Mr. Brougham refused any inferior place as beneath his merits and his influence. The first Whig ministry were, indeed, in a position of some difficulty. The notion that a successful Opposition, as such, should take the reins of administration, has been much derided. ' Sir,' said a sceptic on this part of constitutional government, ' I would as soon choose for a new coachman the man who shied stones best at my old one !' And, without going the length of such critics, it

F

must be allowed that the theory may produce odd results, when the persons summoned by their victory to assume office have been for many years in opposition. The party cannot have acquired official habits; the traditions of business cannot be known to them; their long course of opposition will have forced into leadership men hardly fitted for placid government. There is said to have been much of this feeling when Lord Grey's ministry were installed; it seemed as if that 'old favourite of the public,' Mr. Buckstone, were called to license plays. Grave Englishmen doubted the gravity of the administration. To make Lord Brougham Chancellor was, therefore, particularly inconvenient. He was too mobile : you could not fancy him droning. He had attacked Lord Eldon during many years, of course ; but did he know law ? He was a most active person ; would he sit *still* upon the woolsack ? Of his inattention to his profession men circulated idle tales. 'Pity he hadn't known a little law, and then he would have known a little of everything,' was the remark of one who certainly only knows one thing. A more circumstantial person recounted that, when Brougham had been a pupil of Sir Nicholas Tindal, in the Temple, an uncle of his, having high hopes of his ability, asked the latter : 'I hope my nephew is giving himself up, soul and body, to his profession ?' 'I do not know anything,' replied the distinct special-pleader, 'as to his *soul*, but his body is very seldom in my chambers.' Putting aside with contempt this surface of tales, it could not be denied that Mr. Brougham's practice at the bar—large and lucrative as it was—immense as was the energy required to maintain it at the same time with his other labours—had yet not shown him to possess the finest discretion, the most delicate tact of the advocate. Mr. Scarlett stole verdicts away from him. 'He strikes hard, sir,' said an attorney ; 'but he strikes wrong.' His appointment as Chancellor scarcely strengthened the ministry of the time. Mr. Brougham was a hero ; Lord Brougham was 'a necessity.' It was like Mr. Disraeli being Chancellor of the Exchequer.

After the lapse of years, and with the actual facts before us, it is not difficult to see how far these anticipations have been falsified, and how far they have been justified by the result. All the notions as to Lord Brougham's ignorance of law may at once be discarded. A man of his general culture and vigorous faculties, with a great memory and much experience in forensic business, is no more likely to be ignorant of the essential bookwork of law than a tailor to be ignorant of scissors and seams. A man in business must be brought in contact with it; a man of mind cannot help grasping it. No one now questions that Lord Brougham was and is a lawyer of adequate attainments. But, at the same time, the judgments which supply the conclusive proof of this—the complete refutation of earlier cavillers—also would lead us to deny him the praise of an absolutely judicial intellect. Great judges may be divided into two classes—judges for the parties, and judges for the lawyers. The first class of these are men who always decide the particular case before them rightly, who have a nice insight into all that concerns it, are acute discerners of fact, accurate weighers of testimony, just discriminators of argument. Lord Lyndhurst is perhaps as great a judge in this kind as it is easy to fancy. If a wise man had a good cause, he would prefer its being tried before Lyndhurst to its being tried before anyone else. For the ' parties,' if they were to be considered in litigation, no more would be needed. By law-students, however, and for the profession, something more is desired. They like to find, in a judicial decision, not only a correct adjustment of the particular dispute in court, but also an ample exposition of principles applicable to other disputes. The judge who is peculiarly exact in detecting the precise peculiarities of the case before him, will be very apt to decide only what is essential to, absolutely needed by, that case. His delicate discrimination will see that nothing else is necessary; he will not bestow conclusions on after-generations; he will let posterity decide its own controversies. A judge of different kind has a professional interest in what comes before him: it is in his eyes not a pitiful dispute whether A or B is entitled to a miserable field, but a glorious opportunity of deciding some legal controversy on which he has brooded for years, and on which he has a ready-made conclusion.   Accordingly, his judgments are in the nature of essays.   They are, in one sense, applicable to the matter in hand—they decide it correctly; but they go so much into the antecedents of the controversy— give so much of principle—that the particular facts seem a little lost : the general doctrine fills the attention.   No one can read a judgment of the late Lord Cottenham without feeling that it fixed the law on the matter in hand upon a defined basis for future years.   Very likely he finds an authority for the case which has occurred in his practice ; he does not stay to inquire whether the litigants appreciated the learning ; perhaps they did not—possibly they would have preferred that a more exclusive prominence should be given to themselves.   Now Lord Brougham has neither of these qualities ; his intellect wants the piercing precision which distinguishes the judge—the unerring judge—of the case then present; and, though competently learned, he has never been absorbed in his profession as a judge of ' principle ' almost always must be.   A man cannot provide a dogma suiting all the cases of the past, and deciding all the cases for the future, without years of patient reflection.   His mind must be stored with doctrines.   No one can fancy this of Lord Brougham. He is not to be thought of as giving still attention to technical tenets, years of brooding consideration to an abstract jurisprudence.   Accordingly, though an adequate, and, in his time—for his speed cleared off arrears—a most useful judge, he cannot be said to attain the first rank in the judicial scale ; and such we believe is the estimation of the world.

Of the political duties of the Chancellor, and Lord Brougham's performance of them, it is not easy to speak.   Many of them are necessarily secret, and the history of those times cannot yet be written.   That he showed wonderful energy, zeal, and power, no one can doubt ; nor that the essential defects of his character soon showed him but little qualified for an administrator. In the year 1802, Francis Horner anticipated, that if ' an active career were opened to Brougham, he would show a want of prudence and moderation ; ' and it is curious to read, as a commentary on it, what the Duke of Wellington wrote to Sir R. Peel, on the 15th November, 1835. ' His Majesty mentioned that Lord Brougham[1] had threatened he would not put the great seal to a commission to prorogue the parliament; ' and afterwards correcting himself: ' It appears that Lord Brougham did not make the threat that he would not prorogue the parliament, but that Lord Melbourne said he was in such a state of excitement that he might take that course.' We must wait for Lord Brougham's memoirs before we know the exact history of that time ; but all the glimpses we get of it show the same picture of wildness and eccentricity.

The times—the most nearly revolutionary times which England has long seen—were indeed likely to try an excitable temperament to the utmost; but at the same time they afforded scope to a brilliant manager of men, which only such critical momentary conjunctures can do. Mr. Roebuck gives a curious instance of this :—

The necessity of a dissolution had long been foreseen, and decided on by the ministers, but the King had not yet been persuaded to consent to so bold a measure; and now the two chiefs of the administration were about to intrude themselves into the royal closet, not only to advise and ask for a dissolution, but to request the king on the sudden—on this very day, and within a few hours—to go down and put an end to his parliament in the midst of the session, and with all the ordinary business of the session yet unfinished. The bolder mind of the Chancellor took the lead, and Lord Grey anxiously solicited him to *manage* the King on the occasion. So soon as they were admitted, the Chancellor, with some care and circumlocution, propounded to the King the object of the interview they had sought. The startled monarch no sooner understood the drift of the Chancellor's somewhat

---

[1] The editors of Sir R. Peel's Memoirs have left this name in blank ; but if they had wished it not to be known, they should have suppressed the passage. Everybody knows who held the great seal at that time.

periphrastic statement, than he exclaimed in wonder and amazement against the very idea of such a proceeding. 'How is it possible, my lords, that I can after this fashion repay the kindness of parliament to the queen and myself? They have just granted me a most liberal civil-list, and to the queen a splendid annuity in case she survives me.' The Chancellor confessed that they had, as regarded his Majesty, been a liberal and wise parliament, but said that nevertheless their further existence was incompatible with the peace and safety of the kingdom. Both he and Lord Grey then strenuously insisted upon the absolute necessity of their request, and gave his Majesty to understand that this advice was by his ministers unanimously resolved on; and that they felt themselves unable to conduct the affairs of the country in the present condition of the parliament. This last statement made the King feel that a general resignation would be the consequence of a further refusal. Of this, in spite of his secret wishes, he was at the moment really afraid, and therefore he, by employing petty excuses, and suggesting small and temporary difficulties, soon began to show that he was about to yield. 'But, my lords, nothing is prepared; the great officers of state are not summoned.' 'Pardon me, sir,' said the Chancellor, bowing with profound apparent humility, 'we have taken the great liberty of giving them to understand that your Majesty commanded their attendance at the proper hour.' 'But, my lords, the crown and the robes, and other things needed, are not prepared.' 'Again I most humbly entreat your Majesty's pardon for my boldness,' said the Chancellor; 'they are all prepared and ready —the proper officers being desired to attend in proper form and time.' 'But, my lords,' said the King, reiterating the form in which he put his objection, 'you know the thing is wholly impossible; the guards, the troops, have had no orders, and cannot be ready in time.' This objection was in reality the most formidable one. The orders to the troops on such occasions emanate always directly from the King, and no person but the King can in truth command them for such service; and as the Prime Minister and daring Chancellor well knew the nature of royal susceptibility on such matters, they were in no slight degree doubtful and anxious as to the result. The Chancellor therefore, with some real hesitation, began again as before, 'Pardon me, sir, we know how bold the step is that, presuming on your great goodness, and your anxious desire for the safety of your kingdom, and happiness of your people, we have presumed to take. I have given orders, and the troops are ready.' The King started in serious anger, flamed red in the face, and burst forth with, 'What, my lords, have you dared

to act thus? Such a thing was never heard of. You, my Lord
Chancellor, ought to know that such an act is treason, high treason,
my lord.' 'Yes, sir,' said the Chancellor, 'I do know it; and nothing
but my thorough knowledge of your Majesty's goodness, of your
paternal anxiety for the good of your people, and my own solemn
belief that the safety of the state depends upon this day's proceedings,
could have emboldened me to the performance of so unusual, and, in
ordinary circumstances, so improper a proceeding. In all humility I
submit myself to your Majesty, and am ready in my own person to
bear all the blame, and receive all the punishment which your
Majesty may deem needful; but I again entreat your Majesty to
listen to us and to follow our counsel, and as you value the security
of your crown and the peace of your realms, to yield to our most
earnest solicitations.' After some further expostulations by both his
ministers, the King cooled down and consented. Having consented,
he became anxious that everything should be done in the proper
manner, and gave minute directions respecting the ceremonial. The
speech to be spoken by him at the prorogation was ready prepared
and in the Chancellor's pocket. To this he agreed, desired that everybody might punctually attend, and dismissed his ministers for the
moment with something between a menace and a joke upon the
audacity of their proceeding.

With the fall of Lord Melbourne's first administration terminated Lord Brougham's administrative career. As everyone
knows, on the defeat of Sir Robert Peel and the subsequent
return of the Whigs to power, he was not invited to resume
office. Since that time—for now more than twenty years—
he has had to lead the life, in general the most trying to political reputation, perhaps to real character, and more than any
other alien to the character of his mind and the tendencies of
his nature. We have had many recent instances how difficult it is to give what is variously termed an 'independent
support,' and a 'friendly opposition,' to a Government of which
you approve the general tendencies, but are inclined to criticise
the particular measures. The Peelites and Lord John Russell
have for several years been in general in this position, and
generally with a want of popular sympathy. As they agree
with the Government in principle, they cannot take, by way of

objection; what the country considers broad points; their suggestions of detail seem petty and trivial to others—the public hardly think of such things; but men who have long considered a subject, who have definite ideas and organised plans, can scarcely help feeling an eager interest in the smallest minutiæ of the mode of dealing with it. Sometimes they discern a real importance undiscerned by those less attentive; more commonly, perhaps, they fancy there is something peculiarly felicitous in contrivances settled by themselves and congenial to their habits or their notions. Lord Brougham was in a position to feel this peculiarly. The various ideas which he had struggled for in earlier life were successful one by one; the hundred reforms he suggested were carried; the hundred abuses he had denounced were abolished. The world which *was*, was changed to the world which *is*; but it was not changed by him. That he should have been favourably disposed to the existing liberal administrations was not likely; the separation was too recent, perhaps too abrupt. An eager and excitable disposition is little likely to excel in the measured sentences, the chosen moments, the polished calm of the *frondeur*. Accordingly, the life of Brougham for many years has not been favourable to his fame. On particular occasions, as on the abolition of Negro apprenticeship, he might attain something of his former power. But, in general, his position has been that of the agitator whose measure is being substantially carried, yet with differences of detail aggravating to his temper and annoying to his imagination. Mr. Cobden described Sir Robert Peel's mode of repealing the corn-laws with the microscopic sliding-scale for three years, as seventeen-and-sixpence on the demand of the Anti-corn-law League, and good security for the other half-crown. Yet excitable men at that very moment clamoured for the last half-crown; they could not bear the modification, the minute difference from that on which they had set their hearts. We must remember this in relation to what is now most familiar to us in the life of Lord Brougham.

To a man so active, to be out of action is a pain which
few can appreciate ; that other men should enter into your
labours is not pleasant ; that they should be Canningites does
not make it any better. We have witnessed many escapades
of Lord Brougham ; we perhaps hardly know his temptations
and his vexations.

Such is the bare outline of the career of Lord Brougham.
A life of early, broken, various agitation ; a short interval of
ordinary administration—occurring, however, at a time singularly extraordinary ; a long old age secluded from the actual
conduct of affairs, and driven to distinguish itself by miscellaneous objection and diversified sarcasm. Singular stories of
eccentricity and excitement, even of something more than
either of these, darken these latter years. On these we must
not dwell. There are many aspects of Brougham's varied character, a few of which we should notice by themselves.

The most connected with his political life is his career as a
law reformer. We have spoken of his early labours on this
subject ; we have said that few men who have devoted themselves to nothing else have exposed so many abuses, propounded
so many remedies ; that one of his early motions is a schedule of
half, and much more than half, that has been, or will be, done
upon a large portion of the subject. But here praise must end.
The completed, elaborated reforms by which Lord Brougham
will be known to posterity are few, are nothing in comparison with his power, his industry, and his opportunities.
There is nothing, perhaps, for which he is so ill qualified.
The bold vehement man who exposes an abuse has rarely the
skilful, painful, dissecting power which expunges it. Lord
Brougham once made a speech on conveyancing. ' I should
not,' said, on the next day, an eminent professor of that art,
' like him to draw a deed relating to my property.' A law
reformer, in order that his work may be perfect, requires the
conveyancing abilities. He must be able to bear in mind the
whole topic—to draw out what is necessary of it on paper—

to see what is necessary—to discriminate the rights of indi-
viduals—to distinguish, with even metaphysical nicety, the
advantage he would keep from the abuse he would destroy.
He must elaborate enacting clauses which will work in the
complicated future, repealing clauses which will not interfere
with the complicated machinery of the past.  His mind must
be the mind of a codifier.  A rushing man, like Lord Brougham,
cannot hope to have this.  A still and patient man, in quiet
chambers, apt in niceties, anxious by temperament, precise in
habit, putting the last extreme of perfection on whatever he
may attempt, is the man for the employment.  You must not
expect this quiet precision from an agitator.  There is the
same difference as that between the hard-striking pugilist and
the delicate amputating operator.

The same want of repose has impaired his excellence in a
pursuit to which, at first sight, it seems much less needful—
the art of oratory.  We are apt to forget that oratory is an
imaginative art.  From our habits of business, the name of
rhetoric has fallen into disrepute : our greatest artists strive
anxiously to conceal their perfection in it ; they wish their
address in statement to be such, that the effect seems to be
produced by that which is stated, and not by the manner in
which it is stated.  But not the less on that account is there a
real exercise of the imagination in conceiving of the events of
a long history, in putting them forward in skilful narration,
each fact seeming by nature to fall into its place, all the
details appearing exactly where they should—a group, to
borrow a metaphor from another art, collecting itself from
straggling and desultory materials.  Still more evidently is the
imagination requisite in expressing deep emotions, even common emotions, or in describing noble objects.  Now, it seems
to be a law of the imagination that it only works in a mind
of stillness.  The noise and crush of life jar it.  'No man,'
it has been said, 'can say, I *will* compose poetry :' he must

wait until—from a brooding, half-desultory inaction—poetry
may arise, like a gentle mist, delicately and of itself.

> I waited for the train at Coventry ;
> I hung with grooms and porters on the bridge
> To watch the three tall spires ; and there I shaped
> The city's legend into this.

Lord Brougham would not have waited so. He would have
rushed up into the town ; he would have suggested an improvement, talked the science of the bridge, explained its history to
the natives. The quiet race would think twenty people had
been there. And of course, in some ways this is admirable ;
such life and force are rare ; even the 'grooms and porters'
would not be insensible to such an aggressive intelligence—
so much *knocking* mind. But, in the meantime, no lightly-
touched picture of old story would have arisen on his imagination. The city's legend would have been thrust out : the 'fairy
frostwork' of the fancy would have been struck away : there
would have been talk on the schooling of the porter's eldest boy.
The rarity of great political oratory arises in a great measure from
this circumstance. Only those engaged in the jar of life have the
material for it ; only those withdrawn into a brooding imagination have the faculty for it. M. de Lamartine has drawn a striking picture of one who had the opportunity of action and the
dangerous faculty of leisure : 'Vergniaud s'enivrait dans cette
vie d'artiste, de musique, de déclamation et de plaisirs ; il se
pressait de jouir de sa jeunesse, comme s'il eût le pressenti-
ment qu'elle serait sitôt cueillie. Ses habitudes étaient médita-
tives et paresseuses. Il se levait au milieu du jour ; il écrivait
peu et sur des feuilles éparses ; il appuyait le papier sur ses
genoux comme un homme pressé qui se dispute le temps ; il
composait ses discours lentement dans ses rêveries et les re-
tenait à l'aide de notes dans sa mémoire ; il polissait son
éloquence à loisir, comme le soldat polit son arme au repos.'
This is not the picture of one who is to attain eminence in
stirring and combative times. Harsher men prevailed ; a

mournful fate swallowed up Vergniaud's delicate fancies. He died, because he was idle; but he was great, because he was idle. Idleness with such minds is only the name for the passive enjoyment of a justly-moving imagination.

We should only weary our readers with a repetition of what has been said a hundred times already, if we tried to explain that Lord Brougham has nothing of this. His merit is, that he was never idle in his life. He must not complain if he has the disadvantage of it also. That he was a most effective speaker in his great time, is of course undoubted. His power of sarcasm, his amazing readiness, his energetic vigour of language, made him, if not a very persuasive, at least a most formidable orator. His endless animation must tell even to excess upon his audience. But he has not acted wisely for his fame in publishing his speeches. They have the most unpardonable of all faults—the fault of dulness. It is scarcely possible to read them. Doubtless, at the time their influence was considerable; they may even have been pleasant, as you like to watch the play of a vicious horse; but now, removed from the hearing of the speaker's voice—out of the way of the motions of his face and the glare of his eye—even their evil-speaking loses its attractiveness. The sarcasm seems blunt—the denunciation heavy. They are crowded with a detail which may have been, though acute observers say it was not, attractive at the time, but which no one can endure now. Not only do you feel that you are bored, but you are not sure that you are instructed. An agitator's detail is scarcely to be trusted. His facts may be right, but you must turn historian in order to test them; you must lead a life of state-papers and old letters to know if they are true. It is perhaps possible for the imagination of man to give an interest to any considerable action of human life. A firmly-drawing hand may conduct us through the narration—an enhancing touch enliven the details; but, to achieve this with contested facts in a combative life, is among the rarest operations of a rare power. The imagination has few tasks so difficult. To Lord Brougham, least of all, has it been possible to attract men by the business detail and cumbrous aggressions of the last age. His tone is too harsh. He has shattered his contemporaries, but he will not charm posterity.

Lord Brougham has wished to be known, not only as an orator, but as a writer on oratory. He has written a ' Discourse ' on Ancient Oratory, recommending, and very deservedly, its study to those who would now excel in the art; and there is no denying that he has rivalled the great Greek orator, at least in one of his characteristic excellences. There is no more manly book in the world than Brougham's Speeches; he always ' calls a spade a spade '; the rough energy strikes; we have none of the tawdry metaphor, or half-real finery of the inferior orators, there is not a simile which a man of sense should not own. Nevertheless, we are inclined to question whether his studies on ancient oratory, especially on the great public oration of Demosthenes, have been entirely beneficial to him. These masterly productions were, as everyone knows, the eager expression of an intense mind on questions of the best interest; they have accordingly the character of vehemence. Speaking on subjects which he thought involved the very existence of his country, he could not be expected to speak very temperately; he did not, and could not admit, that there was fair ground for difference of opinion; that an equally patriotic person, after proper consideration, could by possibility arrive at an opposite conclusion. The circumstances of the parliamentary orator in this country are quite different. A man cannot discuss the dowry of the Princess Royal, the conditions of the Bank Charter, as if they were questions of existence— all questions arising now present masses of fact, antecedents in blue-books, tabulated statistics, on which it is impossible that there should not be a necessity for an elaborate inquiry—that there should not be discrepancy of judgment after that inquiry. The Demosthenic vehemence is out of place. The calm didactic exposition, almost approaching to that of the lecturer, is more efficacious than the intense appeal of an eager orator. That 'Counsellor Broom was all in a fume,' is a line in one of the best ludicrous poems of a time rather fertile in such things. On points of detail it is ridiculous to be in a passion ; on matters of business it is unpersuasive to be enthusiastic ; even on topics less technical, the Greek oratory is scarcely a model to be imitated precisely. A certain *nonchalant* ease pervades our modern world —we affect an indifference we scarcely feel ; our talk is light, almost to affectation ; our best writing is the same ; we suggest rather than elaborate, hint rather than declaim. The spirit of the ancient world was very different—the tendency of its conversation probably was to a rhetorical formality, an haranguing energy ; certainly it is the tendency of its written style. 'With every allowance,' says Colonel Mure, ' for the peculiar genius of the age in which the masterpieces of Attic prose were produced —a consideration which must always have a certain weight in literary judgments—still, the impartial modern critic cannot but discern in this pervading rhetorical tone a defect, perhaps the only serious defect, in the classical Greek style. . . . . It certainly is not natural for the historian or the popular essayist to address his readers in the same tone in which the defender of a client or the denouncer of a political opponent addresses a public assembly.' So great a change in the general world, in the audience to be spoken to, requires a change in the speaker. The light touch of Lord Palmerston is more effective than the most elaborated sentences of a formal rhetorician. Of old, when conversation and writing were half oratorical, oratory might be very oratorical ; now that conversation is very conversational, oratory must be a little conversational. In real life, Lord Brougham has too much of the orator's tact not to be half aware of this ; but his teaching forgets it.

That Lord Brougham should have adopted a theory enjoining vehemence in oratory, is an instance to be cited by those who hold that a man's creed is a justification for his inclinations.

He is by nature over-vehement; and what is worse, it is not vehemence of the best kind : there is something of a scream about
it. People rather laughed at his kneeling to beseech the peers.
No one is sure that there is real feeling in what he reads and
hears; it seems like a machine going. Lord Cockburn has an odd
anecdote. An old judge, who loved dawdling, disliked the ' dis-
composing qualities ' of Brougham. His revenge consisted in
sneering at Brougham's eloquence, by calling it or him *the
Harangue.* ' Well, gentlemen, what did *the Harangue* say next ?
Why it said this (misstating it); but here, gentlemen, *the
Harangue* was wrong and not intelligible.' We have some
feeling for the old judge. If you take a speech of Brougham,
and read it apart from his voice, you have half a notion that
it is a gong going, eloquence by machinery, an incessant talking
*thing.*

It is needless to point out how completely an excitable ungenial nature, such as we have so much spoken of, incapacitates
Lord Brougham for abstract philosophy. His works on that
subject are sufficiently numerous, but we are not aware that even
his most ardent admirers have considered them as works of really
the first class. It would not be difficult to extract from the
' Political Philosophy,' which is probably the best of them,
singular instances of inconsistency and of confusion. The error
was in his writing them : he who runs may *read*, but it does
not seem likely he will think. The brooding disposition, and
the still, investigating intellect, are necessary for consecutive
reasonings on delicate philosophy.

The same qualities, however, fit a man for the acquisition of
general information. A man who is always rushing into the
street will become familiar with the street. One who is for
ever changing from subject to subject will not become *painfully*
acquainted with any one, but he will know the outsides of them
all, and the road from each to the other. Accordingly, all the
descriptions of Lord Brougham, even in his earliest career,
speak of his immense information. Mr. Wilberforce, in perhaps

the earliest printed notice of him, recommended Mr. Pitt to employ him in a diplomatic capacity, on account of his familiarity with languages, and the other kinds of necessary knowledge. He began by writing on Porisms ; only the other day he read a paper on some absurdities imputed to the Integral Calculus, in French, at Paris. It would be in the highest degree tedious to enumerate all the subjects he knows something of. Of course, an extreme correctness cannot be expected. ' The most *mis*-informed man in Europe,' is a phrase of satire ; yet, even in its satire, it conveys a compliment to Brougham's information.

An especial interest in physical science may be remarked in Brougham, as in most men of impressible minds in his generation. He came into life when the great discoveries in our knowledge of the material world were either just made, or were on the eve of being made. The enormous advances, which have been actually made in material civilisation, were half anticipated. There was a vague hope in science. The boundaries of the universe, it was hoped, would move. Active, ardent minds were drawn with extreme hope to the study of new moving power ; a smattering of science was immeasurably less common then than now, but it exercised a stronger dominion, and influenced a higher class of genius. It was new, and men were sanguine. In the present day, younger men are perhaps repelled into the opposite extreme. We live among the marvels of science, but we know how little they change us. The essentials of life are what they were. We go by the train, but we are not improved at our journey's end. We have railways, and canals, and manufactures—excellent things, no doubt, but they do not touch the soul. Somehow, they seem to make life more superficial. With a half-wayward dislike, some in the present generation have turned from physical science and material things. ' We have tried these, and they fail,' is the feeling. ' What is the heart of man the better for galvanic engines and hydraulic presses ? Leave us to the old poetry and the old philosophy : there is at least a life and a mind.' It is the day after the feast. We do not care for its delicacies; we are rather angry at its profusion; we are cross to hear it praised. Men who came into active life half a century ago were the guests invited to the banquet; they did not know what was coming, but they heard it was something gorgeous and great; they expected it with hope and longing. The influence of this feeling was curiously seen in the Useful Knowledge Society, the first great product of the educational movement in which Lord Brougham was the most ardent leader. No one can deny that their labours were important, their intentions excellent, the collision of mind which they created most beneficial. Still, looking to their well-known publications, beyond question the knowledge they particularly wished to diffuse is, according to the German phrase, 'factish.' Hazlitt said 'they confounded a knowledge of useful things with useful knowledge.' An idea, half unconscious, pervades them, that a knowledge of the detail of material knowledge, even too of the dates and shell of outside history, is extremely important to the mass of men; that all will be well when we have a cosmical ploughboy and a mob that knows hydrostatics. We shall never have it; but even if we could, we should not be much the better. The heart and passions of men are moved by things more within their attainment; the essential nature is stirred by the essential life; by the real actual existence of love, and hope, and character, and by the real literature which takes in its spirit, and which is in some sort its undefecated essence. Thirty years ago the preachers of this now familiar doctrine were unknown, nor was their gospel for a moment the one perhaps most in season. It was good that there should be a more diffused knowledge of the material world; and it was good, therefore, that there should be partisans of matter, believers in particles, zealots for tissue, who were ready to incur any odium and any labour that a few more men might learn a few more things. How a man of incessant activity should pass easily to such a creed is evident. He would see the obvious ignorance. The less

G

obvious argument, which shows that this ignorance, in great measure inevitable, was of far less importance than would be thought at first sight, would never be found by one who moved so rapidly.

We have gone through now, in some hasty way, most of the lights in which Lord Brougham has been regarded by his contemporaries. There is still another character in which posterity will especially think of him. He is a great memoirist. His 'Statesmen of George III.' contains the best sketches of the political men of his generation, one with another, which the world has, or is likely to have. He is a fine painter of the exterior of human nature. Some portion of its essence requires a deeper character; another portion, more delicate sensations; but of the rough appearance of men, as they struck him in the law-court and in parliament—of the great debater struggling with his words—the stealthy advocate gliding into the confidence of the audience—the great judge unravelling all controversies, and deciding by a well-weighed word all complicated doubts—of such men as these, and of men engaged in such tasks as these, there is no greater painter perhaps than Brougham. His eager aggressive disposition brought him into collision with conspicuous men; his skill in the obvious parts of human nature has made him understand them. A man who has knocked his head against a wall—if such an illustration is to be hazarded—will learn the nature of the wall. Those who have passed fifty years in managing men of the world, will know their external nature, and if they have literary power enough, will describe it. In general, Lord Brougham's excellence as a describer of character is confined to men whom he had thus personally and keenly encountered. The sketches of the philosophers of the eighteenth century, of French statesmen, are poor and meagre. He requires evidently the rough necessities of action to make him observe. There is, however, a remarkable exception. He preserves a singularly vivid recollection of the instructors of his youth; he nowhere appears so amiable as in describing them.

He is over-partial, no doubt ; but an old man may be permitted to reverence, if he can reverence, his schoolmaster.

This is all that our limits will permit us to say of Lord Brougham. On so varied a life, at least on a life with such varied pursuits, one might write to any extent. The regular biographer will come in after years. It is enough for a mere essayist to sketch, or strive to sketch, in some rude outline, the nature of the man.

## MR. GLADSTONE.[1]

[1860.]

WE believe that Quarterly essayists have a peculiar mission in relation to the characters of public men. We believe it is their duty to be personal. This idea may seem ridiculous to some of our readers; but let us consider the circumstances carefully. We allow that personality abounds already, that the names of public men are for ever on our lips, that we never take up a newspaper without seeing them. But this incessant personality is wholly fragmentary; it is composed of chance criticism on special traits, of fugitive remarks on temporary measures, of casual praise and casual blame. We can expect little else from what is written in haste, or is spoken without limitation. Public men must bear this criticism as they can. Those whose names are perpetually in men's mouths must not be pained if singular things are sometimes said of them. Still *some* deliberate truth should be spoken of our statesmen, and if Quarterly essayists do not speak it, who will? We fear it will remain unspoken.

Mr. Gladstone is a problem, and it is very remarkable that he should be a problem. We have had more than ordinary means for judging of him. He has been in public life for seven and twenty years; he has filled some of the most conspicuous offices in the State; he has been a distinguished member of the Tory party; he *is* a distinguished member of the Liberal party; he has brought forward many measures; he

[1] *Speech of the Chancellor of the Exchequer on the Finance of the Year and the Treaty of Commerce with France.* Delivered in the House of Commons on Friday, February 10, 1860. Corrected by the Author.

has passed many years in independent Opposition, which is unquestionably the place most favourable to the display of personal peculiarities in Parliament; he is the greatest orator in the House of Commons; he never allows a single important topic to pass by without telling us what he thinks of it;—and yet, with all these data, we are all of us in doubt about him. What he will do, and what he will think, still more, why he will do it, and why he will think it, are *quæstiones vexatæ* at every political conjuncture. At the very last ministerial crisis, when the Government of Lord Derby was on the verge of extinction, when every voice on Lord John's resolution was of critical importance, no one knew till nearly the last hour how Mr. Gladstone would vote, and in the end he voted against his present colleagues. The House of Commons gossips are generally wrong about him. Nor is the uncertainty confined to parliamentary divisions; it extends to his whole career. Who can calculate his future course? Who can tell whether he will be the greatest orator of a great administration; whether he will rule the House of Commons; whether he will be, as his gifts at first sight mark him out to be, our greatest statesman? or whether, below the gangway, he will utter unintelligible discourses; will aid in destroying many ministries and share in none; will pour forth during many hopeless years a bitter, a splendid, and a vituperative eloquence?

We do not profess that we can solve all the difficulties that are suggested even by the superficial consideration of a character so exceptional. We do not aspire to be prophets. Mr. Gladstone's destiny perplexes us—perhaps as much as it perplexes our readers. But we think that we can explain much of his past career; that many of his peculiarities are not so unaccountable as they seem; that a careful study will show us the origin of most of them; that we may hope to indicate some of the material circumstances and conditions on which his future course depends, though we should not be so bold as to venture to foretell it.

During the discussion on the Budget, an old Whig who did not
approve of it, but who had to vote for it, muttered of its author,
' Ah, Oxford on the surface, *but* Liverpool below.' And there
is truth in the observation, though not in the splenetic sense
in which it was intended. Mr. Gladstone does combine, in a
very curious way, many of the characteristics which we generally
associate with the place of his education and many of those
which we usually connect with the place of his birth. No one
can question the first part of the observation. No man has
through life been more markedly an Oxford man than Mr.
Gladstone. His 'Church and State,' published after he had
been several years in public life, was instinct with the very
spirit of the Oxford of that time. His 'Homer,' published the
other day, bears nearly equal traces of the school in which he
was educated. Even in his ordinary style there is a tinge half
theological, half classical, which recalls the studies of his youth.
Many Oxford men much object to the opinions of their distinguished representative; but none of them would deny, that
he remarkably embodies the peculiar results of the peculiar
teaching of the place.

And yet he has something which his collegiate training
never would have given him, which it is rather remarkable it
has not taken away from him. There is much to be said in
favour of the University of Oxford. No one can deny to it
very great and very peculiar merits. But certainly it is not an
exciting place, and its education operates as a narcotic rather
than as a stimulant. Most of its students devote their lives to
a single profession, and we may observe among them a kind of
sacred torpidity. In many rural parsonages there are men of
very great cultivation, who are sedulous in their routine duties,
who attend minutely to the ecclesiastical state of the souls in
their village, but who are perfectly devoid of general intellectual interests. They have no anxiety to solve great problems;
to busy themselves with the speculations of their age; to

impress their peculiar theology—for peculiar it is both in its expression and its substance—on the educated mind of their time. Oxford, it has been said, 'disheartens a man early.' At any rate, since Newmanism lost Father Newman, few indeed of her acknowledged sons attain decided eminence in our deeper controversies. Jowett she would repudiate, and Mansel is but applying the weapons of scepticism to the service of credulity. The most characteristic of Oxford men labour quietly, delicately, and let us hope usefully, in a confined sphere ; they hope for nothing more, and wish for nothing more. Even in secular literature we may observe an analogous tone. The 'Saturday Review' is remarkable as an attempt on the part of 'university men' to speak on the political topics and social difficulties of the time. And what do they teach us? It is something like this : 'So-and-so has written a tolerable book, and we would call attention to the industry which produces tolerable books. So-and-so has devoted himself to a great subject, and we would observe that the interest now taken in great subjects is very commendable. Such-and-such a lady has delicate feelings, which are desirable in a lady, though we know that they are contrary to the facts of the world. All common persons are doing as well as they can, but it does not come to much after all. All statesmen are doing as ill as they can, and let us be thankful that *that* does not come to much either.' We may search and search in vain through this repository of the results of 'university teaching' for a single truth which it has established, for a single high cause which it has advanced, for a single deep thought which is to sink into the minds of its readers. We have, indeed, a nearly perfect embodiment of the corrective scepticism of a sleepy intellect. 'A B says he has done something, but he has not done it; C D has made a parade of demonstrating this or that proposition, but he does not prove his case; there is one mistake in page 5, and another in page 113; a great history has been written of this or that century, but the best authorities as to that period have not been consulted, which, however, is not very remarkable, as there is nothing in them.' We could easily find, if it were needful, many traces of the same indifferent habit, the same apathetic culture, in the more avowed productions of Oxford men. The shrewd eye of Mr. Emerson, stimulated doubtless by the contrast to America, quickly caught the trait. 'After all,' says the languid Oxford gentleman of his story, 'there is nothing true and nothing new, and no matter!'

To this, as to every other species of indifferentism, Mr. Gladstone is the antithesis. Oxford has not disheartened *him.* Some of his colleagues would say they wished it had. He is interested in everything he has to do with, and often interested too much. He proposes to put a stamp on contract notes with an eager earnestness as if the destiny of Europe, here and hereafter, depended upon its enactment. He cannot let anything alone. 'Sir,' said an old distributor of stamps in Westmoreland, 'my head, sir, is worn out. I must resign. The Chancellor, sir, is imposing of things that I can't understand.' The world is not well able to understand them either. The public departments break down under the pressure of the industry of their superior. Mr. Gladstone is ready to work as long as his brain will hold together—to make speeches as long as he has utterance (words he is sure to have); but the subordinate officials will not work equally hard. They have none of the excitement of origination; they will not share the credit of success. They do, however, share the discredit of failure. In the high pressure season of this year's Budget, Acts of Parliament have been passed in which essential provisions were not to be found, in which what was intended to be enacted was omitted or exceeded, in which the marginal notes were widely astray of the text. In his literary works Mr. Gladstone is the same. His book on Homer is perhaps the most zealous work which this generation has produced. He has the enthusiasm of a German professor for the scholastic detail, for the exact meaning of word No. 1, for the precise number of times which word No. 2 is used by the poet ; he has the enthusiasm of a lover for Helen, the enthusiasm of an orator for the speeches. Of his theological books we need not speak ; every reader will recall the curious succession of need· less *quæstiunculæ* by which their interest is marred.

Some of this energy Mr. Gladstone probably owes to the place of his birth. Lancashire is sometimes called ' America-and-water : ' we suspect it is America and very little water. The excessive energy natural to half-educated men who have but a single pursuit cannot, indeed, in any part of England, produce the monstrous results which it occasionally produces in the United States ; it is kept in check by public opinion, by the close vicinity of an educated world. But in its own pursuit, in commerce, we question whether New York itself is more intensely eager than Liverpool—at any rate, it is difficult to conceive how it can be. Like several other remarkable men whose families belong to the place, Mr. Gladstone has carried into other pursuits the eagerness, the industry—we are loth to say the rashness, but the boldness—which Liverpool men apply to the business of Liverpool. Underneath the scholastic polish of his Oxford education, he has the speculative hardihood, the eager industry of a Lancashire merchant.

Such is one of the principal peculiarities which Mr. Gladstone's character presents even to a superficial observer. But something more than superficial observation is necessary really to understand a character so complicated and so odd. We will touch upon some of the traits which are among the most important ; and if our minute analysis has, or seems to have, some of the painfulness of a vivisection, we would observe that a defect of this kind is in some degree inseparable from the task we have undertaken. We cannot explain the special peculiarities of a singular man of genius without a somewhat elaborate and a half-metaphysical discussion.

It is needless to say that Mr. Gladstone is a great orator. Oratory is one of the pursuits as to which there is no error.

The criterion is ready.   Did the audience feel? were they excited? did they cheer?   These questions, and others such as
these, can be answered without a mistake.   A man who can
move the House of Commons—still, after many changes, the
most severe audience in the world—must be a great orator.
The most sincere admirers and the most eager depreciators of
Mr. Gladstone are agreed on this point, and it is almost the
only point on which they are agreed.

It will be well, however, to pause upon this characteristic
of Mr. Gladstone's genius, and to examine the nature of it
rather anxiously, because it seems to afford the true key to
some of his most perplexing peculiarities.   Mr. Gladstone has,
beyond any other man in this generation, what we may call
the oratorical *impulse*.   We are in the habit of speaking of
rhetoric as an art, and also of oratory as a faculty, and in
both cases we speak quite truly.   No man can speak without a special intellectual gift, and no man can speak well
without a special intellectual training.   But neither this gift
of the intellect nor this education will suffice of themselves.
A man must not only know what to say, he must have a
vehement longing to get up and say it.   Many persons, rather
sceptical persons especially, do not feel this in the least.   They
see before them an audience—a miscellaneous collection of
odd-looking men—but they feel no wish to convince them of
anything.   'Are not they very well as they are?   They believe what they have been brought up to believe.'   'Confirm
every man in *his own* manner of conceiving,' said one great
sage.   'A savage among savages is very well,' remarked another.   You may easily take away one creed and then not be
able to implant another.   'You may succeed in unfitting men
for their own purposes without fitting them for your purposes'
—thus thinks the *cui bono* sceptic.   Another kind of sceptic
is distrustful, and speaks thus: 'I know *I can't* convince
these people; if I could, perhaps I would, but I can't.   Only
look at them! they have all kinds of crotchets in their heads.

There is a wooden-faced man in spectacles. How can you convince a wooden-faced man in spectacles ? And see that other man with a narrow forehead and compressed lips—is it any use talking to him ? It is of no use ; do not hope that mere arguments will impair the prepossessions of nature and the steady convictions of years.' Mr. Gladstone would not feel these sceptical arguments. He would get up to speak. He has the *didactic* impulse. He has the ' courage of his ideas.' He will convince the audience. He knows an argument which will be effective, he has one for one and another for another ; he has an enthusiasm which he feels will rouse the apathetic, a demonstration which he thinks must convert the incredulous, an illustration which he hopes will drive his meaning even into the heads of the stolid. At any rate, he will try. He has *a nature*, as Coleridge might have said, towards his audience. He is sure, if they only knew what he knows, they would feel as he feels, and believe as he believes. And by this he conquers. This living faith, this enthusiasm, this confidence, call it as we will, is an extreme power in human affairs. One *croyant*, said the Frenchman, is a greater power than fifty *incrédules*. In the composition of an orator, the hope, the credulous hope, that he will convince his audience, is the *primum mobile*, it is the primitive incentive which is the spring of his influence and the source of his power. Mr. Gladstone has this incentive in perhaps an excessive and dangerous measure. Whatever may be right or wrong in pure finance, in abstract political economy, it is certain that no one save Mr. Gladstone would have come down with the Budget of 1860 to the Commons of 1860. No other man would have believed that such a proposal would have a chance. Yet after the warning—the disheartening warning of a reluctant cabinet—Mr. Gladstone came down from a depressing sick-bed, with semi-bronchitis hovering about him, entirely prevailed for the moment, and three parts conquered after all. We will not say that *the world* is given to men of this temperament and this energy ; on the contrary, there is

often a turn in the tide, the ovation of the spring may be the
prelude to unpopularity in the autumn; but we see that
*audiences* are given them; we see that unimpressible men are
deeply moved by them— that the driest topics of legislation and
finance are for the instant affected by them—that the prolonged effects of that momentary influence may be felt for many
years, sometimes for centuries.  The orator has a dominion
over the critical instant, and the consequences of the decisions
taken during that instant may last long after the orator and
the audience have both passed away.

Nor is the didactic impulse the only one which is essential
to a great political orator; nor is it the only one which Mr.
Gladstone has.  We say it with respect, but he has the *contentious* impulse.  He illustrates the distinction between the
pacific and the peaceful.  On all great questions, on the controversies of states and empires, Mr. Gladstone is the most
pacific of mankind.  He hates the very rumour of war; he
trusts in moral influences; he detests the bare idea of military
preparations.  He will not believe that preparations are necessary till the enemy is palpable.  In the early part of 1853 he
did not believe that the Russian war was impending; after the
conversations of the Emperor Nicholas with Sir Hamilton Sey-
mour, he proposed to Parliament a scheme for converting some
portions of the National Debt, which could only be successful
if peace continued, and which, after the outbreak of the war,
failed ignominiously.  In 1860, *mutatis mutandis*, he has done
the same.  He staked his financial reputation upon a fine calculation; he gave us a Budget in which the two ends scarcely
met.  The Chinese war came, and they no longer meet.  We believe that Mr. Gladstone so much hates the bare idea of the
possibility of war, that after many warnings, after at least one
failure which must have been painful, and which should have
been instructive, he has refused to take even the contingency
of hostilities into his calculations.  Some one said he was not
only a Christian, but a morbid Christian.  He cannot imagine

that anything so coarse as war will occur; when it does occur, he has a tendency to disapprove of it as soon as he can. During the Russian war he soon joined, in fact if not in name, the peace-at-all-price party; he exerted his finest reasonings and his most persuasive eloquence against a war which was commenced with his consent. At the present moment no Englishman, not Mr. Bright himself, *feels* so little the impulse to arm. He will not believe in a war till he sees men fighting. He is the most pacific of our statesmen in theory and in policy. When you hear Mr. Gladstone, he is about the most combative. He can bear a good deal about the politics of Europe; but let a man question the fees on vatting, or the change in the game-certificate, or the stamp on bills of lading—what melodious thunders of loquacious wrath! The world, he hints, is likely to end at such observations, and it is dreadful that they should be made by the honourable member who made them— ' by the honourable member who four years ago said so-and-so, and five years before that moved,' &c. &c. The number of well-intentioned and tedious persons whom Mr. Gladstone annually scolds into a latent dislike of him must be considerable.

But though we may smile at the minutiæ in which this contentious impulse sometimes shows itself, we must remember that the impulse itself is essential to a great political orator, everywhere in some degree, but in England especially. To be an influential speaker in the House of Commons, a man must be a great debater. He must excel not only in elaborate set speeches, but likewise in quick occasional repartee. No one but a rather contentious person will ever so excel. Mr. Fox, the most genial of men, was asked why he disputed so vehemently about some trifle or other. He said, ' I *must* do so; I can't live without discussion.' And this is the temperament of a great debater. It must be a positive pain to him to be silent under questionable assertions, to hear others saying that which he cannot agree with. An indifferent sceptic, such as we

formerly spoke of, endures this very easily. ' He thinks, no
doubt, that what the speaker is saying is quite wrong ; but people
do not understand what he is saying ; very likely they won't
understand the answer : besides, we've a majority ; what is the
use of arguing when you have a majority ?   Let us outvote him
on the spot, and go to bed.'   And so, report says, have whips
argued to Mr. Gladstone, but he is ever ready.   He takes up
the parable of disputation at a quarter-past twelve, and goes on
till he has exhausted argument, illustration, ingenuity, and
research.   To hardly any man have both the impulses of the
political orator been given in so great a measure : the didactic
orator is usually felicitous in exposition only ; the great debater
is, like Fox, only great when stung to reply by the *œstrus* of
contention.   But Mr. Gladstone is by nature, by vehement
overruling nature, great in both arts ; he longs to pour forth
his own belief ; he cannot rest till he has contradicted everyone
else.

In addition to this oratorical temperament, Mr. Gladstone
has in a high degree the most important intellectual talent of
an orator ; he has what we may call an adaptive mind.   He has
described this himself better than most people would describe
it :—

Poets of modern times have composed great works in ages
that stopped their ears against them.  ' Paradise Lost' does not
represent the time of Charles the Second, nor the ' Excursion' the
first decades of the present century.   The case of the orator is entirely
different.   His work, from its very inception, is inextricably mixed
up with practice.   It is cast in the mould offered to him by the mind
of his hearers.   It is an influence principally received from his
audience (so to speak) in vapour, which he pours back upon them in
a flood.   The sympathy and concurrence of his time, is, with his own
mind, joint parent of his work.   He cannot follow nor frame ideals ;
his choice is, to be what his age will have him, what it requires in
order to be moved by him, or else not to be at all.   And as when we
find the speeches in Homer, we know that there must have been men
who could speak them, so, from the existence of units who could speak
them, we know that there must have been crowds who could feel them.

We may judge of the House of Commons in the same way from the great 'Budget' speech. No one, indeed, half guides, half follows the moods of his audience more quickly, more easily, than Mr. Gladstone. There is a little playfulness in his manner, which contrasts with the dryness of his favourite topics, and the intense gravity of his earnest character. He has the same sort of control over the minds of those he is addressing that a good driver has over the animals he guides: he feels the minds of his hearers as the driver the mouths of his horses.

The species of intellect that is required for this task is pre-eminently the advocate's intellect. The instrument of oratory, at least of this kind of oratory, is the *argumentum ad hominem.* It is 'inextricably mixed up with practice.' It argues from the data furnished to him ' by the mind of his hearers.' He receives his premises from them ' like a vapour,' and pours out his ' conclusions upon them like a flood.' Such an orator may believe his conclusions, but he can rarely believe them for the reasons which he assigns for them. He may be an enthusiast in his creed, he may be a zealot in his faith, but not the less will he be an advocate in his practice; not the less will he catch at disputable premises because his audience accepts them; not the less will he draw inferences from them which suit his momentary purpose; not the less will he accept the most startling varieties of assertion, for he will imbibe from one audience a different ' vapour ' of premises from that which he will receive from another; not the less will he have the chameleon-like character which we associate with a consummate advocate; not the less will he be one thing to-day, with the colour of one audience upon him; not the less will he be another to-morrow, when he has to address, persuade, and influence some different set of persons.

We scarcely think, with Mr. Gladstone, that this style of oratory is the very highest, though it is very natural that he should think so, for it exactly expresses the oratory in which

he is the greatest living master.   Mr. Gladstone's conception
of oratory, in theory and in practice, is the oratory of Pitt, not
the oratory of Chatham or of Burke : it is the oratory of adaptation.   We do not deny that this is the kind of oratory which
is most generally useful, the only kind which is commonly per-
missible, the only one which in general would not be a *bore*;
but, we must remember that there is an eloquence of great
principles which the hearers scarcely heed, and do not accept
—such as, in its highest parts, is the eloquence of Burke—we
must remember that there is an eloquence of great passions, of
high-wrought intense feeling, which is nearly independent of
the peculiarities of its audience, because it appeals to our ele-
mental human nature—which is the same, or much the same,
in almost every audience, which is everywhere and always
susceptible to the union of vivid genius and eager passion.
Such as this last was, if we may trust tradition, the eloquence
of Chatham, the source of his rare, magical, and occasional
power.   Mr. Gladstone has neither of these.   Few speakers
equally great have left so few passages which can be quoted—
so few which embody great principles in such a manner as to
be referred to by coming generations.   He has scarcely given
us a sentence that lives in the memory ; nor is his declama-
tion, facile and effective as it always is, the very highest de-
clamation : it is a nearly perfect expression of intellectualised
sentiment, but it wants the volcanic power of primitive passion.

The prominence of advocacy in Mr. Gladstone's mind is in
appearance, though not in reality, diminished by the purity and
intensity of his zeal.   There is an elastic heroism about him.
When he begins to speak, we may know that we are going to
hear what we shall not agree with.   We may believe that the
measures he proposes are mischievous ; we may smile at the
emphasis with which some of their minutiæ are insisted upon ;
but we inevitably feel that we have left the ordinary earth.
We know that high sentiments will be appealed to by one

who feels high sentiments; that strong arguments will be strongly stated by one who believes that argument should decide controversy. We know that we are beyond the realm of the patronage Secretary; we have left behind us the doctrine that corruption is the ruling power in popular assemblies, that patronage is the purchase-money of power. We are not alleging that in the real world in which we live there is not some truth —more or less of truth—in these lower maxims; but they do not rule in Mr. Gladstone's world. He was not born to be a Secretary of the Treasury. If he tried his hand at it, he would perplex the borough attorneys out of their lives. And he *could* not keep the office a month; he would evince a real disgust at detestable requests, and guide with odd impulsiveness the delicate and latent machinery. His natural element is a higher one. He has—and it is one of the springs of great power—a real faith in the higher parts of human nature; he believes, with all his heart and soul and strength, that there *is* such a thing as truth; he has the soul of a martyr with the intellect of an advocate.

Another of Mr. Gladstone's characteristics is an extraordinary love of labour. We have alluded several times to his taste, we might almost say his whimsical taste, for minutiæ. He is ready with whatever detail may be necessary on any subject, no matter of what kind. He covers his greatest schemes with a crowd of irrelevant appendages, till it is difficult to see their outline. The Budget of 1860 was large enough and complicated enough, one would have thought, in its essential irremovable features; but its author did not think so. He had supplementary provisions respecting game-certificates, respecting the transmission of newspapers by the post, respecting 'several other minuter changes with which he was almost ashamed to trouble the committee.' The labour necessary to all these accessories must have been enormous. Many of the alterations may have—must have—been lying ready in his memory, or in some old note-book, for many years. But the industry to fur-

H

bish them up, to get them into a practicable, or even into a proposable shape, would frighten not only most persons, but most laborious persons. And Mr. Gladstone's energy seems to be strictly intellectual. Nothing in his outward appearance indicates the iron physique that often carries inferior men through heavy tasks. Whatever he does that is peculiar, he does by the peculiarity of his mind. He is carried through his work, or seems to be so, by pure will, zeal, and effort.

The last characteristic of Mr. Gladstone which is very remarkable, or which we shall mention, is his scholastic intellect. We have not much of this in conspicuous men in the present day, but in former times there was a good deal of it. Lord Bacon had something like it in his eye when he spoke of minds which were not 'discursive' or skilful in discovering analogies, but were *discriminative* or skilful in detecting differences. The best scene for training this sort of intellect is the law-court. Lord Bacon must have seen much of it in the work of Gray's Inn when he was young, and traces of the discipline which he then underwent may perhaps be found even in books which were written by him many years afterwards. When, as in positive law, the first principles are fixed, there is no room for the highest originality; the only admissible controversy is whether a particular case comes or does not come within a particular principle. On this point there is room for endless distinctions and eternal hair-splitting. When the principles settled by authority are not entirely consistent, the function of this kind of distinguishing reason is even greater; it has to suggest nice refinements, which may reconcile the apparent differences between the principles themselves, as well as to settle the exact relation of the case, or the facts, to the doctrine of the authorities. Accordingly the scholastic theologians of mediæval times were the most expert masters of the discriminative ratiocination which the world has ever seen. They had to reconcile the recognised authorities of the Catholic Church— authorities vast in size, and scattered over centuries in time—

with one another, with good sense, with the facts of special cases, with the general exigencies of the age. By their labour was formed that acute logic, that subtle, if unreal philosophy which fell at the Reformation, when the authorities of the Catholic Church were no longer conclusive, and the art of arranging them was no longer important. We have learned to smile at the scholastic distinctions of former times ; the inductive philosophy, which is now our most conspicuous pursuit, does not need them ; the popular character of our ordinary discussion does not admit of them. In a free country we must use the sort of argument which plain men understand—and plain men certainly do not appreciate or apprehend scholastic refinements. So at least we should say beforehand. Yet Mr. Gladstone is the statesman whose expositions have, for good or for evil, more power than those of any other ; his voice is a greater power in the country of plain men than any other man's ; nevertheless, his intellect is of a thoroughly scholastic kind. He can distinguish between any two propositions ; he never allowed, he could not allow, that any two were identical. If anyone on either side of the House is bold enough to infer anything from anything, Mr. Gladstone is ready to deny that the inference is correct—to suggest a distinction which he says is singularly important—to illustrate an apt subtlety which, in appearance at least, impairs the validity of the deduction. No schoolman could be readier at such work. We may find the same tendency of mind even more strikingly illustrated in his writings. At the time of the Gorham case, for example, he wrote a pamphlet on the Royal Supremacy. For the purposes of that case, it was of the last importance to determine the exact position of the Crown with respect to ecclesiastical affairs, and especially to the offence of heresy. The law at first seems distinct enough on the matter. The 1st of Elizabeth provides 'that such jurisdictions, privileges, superiorities, and pre-eminences, spiritual and ecclesiastical, as by any spiritual or ecclesiastical power or authority hath here-

tofore been or may lawfully be exercised or used for the visita-
tion of the ecclesiastical state and persons, and for reformation,
order, and correction of the same, and of all manner of errors,
heresies, schisms, abuses, offences, contempts, and enormities,
shall for ever, by authority of this present parliament, be united
and annexed to the imperial crown of this realm.' These words
would have seemed distinct and clear to most persons. They
would have seemed to give to the Crown all the power it could
wish to exercise—all that any spiritual authority had ever
' theretofore exercised '—all that any temporal authority could
ever use. We should think it was clear that Queen Elizabeth
would have applied a rather summary method of instruction
to anyone who attempted to limit the jurisdiction conferred by
this enactment. If Mr. Gladstone had lived in the times about
which he was writing, he might have had to make a choice
between being silent and being punished; but in the times of
Queen Victoria he is not subjected to an alternative so painful.
He writes securely:—

We have now before us the terms of the great statute which,
from the time it was passed, has been the actual basis of the royal
authority in matters ecclesiastical; and I do not load these pages by
reference to declarations of the Crown, and other public documents
less in authority than this, in order that we may fix our view the
more closely upon the expressions of what may fairly be termed a
fundamental law in relation to the subject-matter before us.

The first observation I make is this : there is no evidence in the
words which have been quoted that the Sovereign is, according to the
intention of the statute, the source or fountain-head of ecclesiastical
jurisdiction. They have no trace of such a meaning, in so far as it
exceeds (and it does exceed) the proposition, that this jurisdiction has
been by law united or annexed to the Crown.

I do not now ask what have been the glosses of lawyers—what are
the reproaches of polemical writers—or even what attributes may be
ascribed to prerogative, independent of statute, and therefore applicable
to the Church before as well as after the Reformation. I must for
the purposes of this argument assume what I shall never cease to
believe until the contrary conclusion is demonstrated by fact, namely,

that, in the case of the Church, justice is to be administered from the English bench upon the same principles as in all other cases—that our judges, or our judicial committees, are not to be our legislators—and that the statutes of the realm, as they are above the sacred majesty of the Queen, so are likewise above their ministerial interpreters. It was by statute that the changes in the position of the Church at that great epoch were measured—by statute that the position itself is defined; and the statute, I say, contains no trace of such a meaning as that the Crown either originally was the source and spring of ecclesiastical jurisdiction, or was to become such in virtue of the annexion to it of the powers recited; but simply bears the meaning, that it was to be master over its administration.

So that which seems a despotism is gradually pruned down into a vicegerency. 'All the superiorities and pre-eminences spiritual and ecclesiastical,' which had ever been lawfully exercised, are restricted to the single function of regulation; and by a judicious elaboration the Crown becomes scarcely the head of the Church, but only the *visitor* and corrector of it, as of several other corporations. We are not now concerned with the royal supremacy—we have no wish to hint or intimate an opinion on a vast legal discussion; but we *are* concerned with Mr. Gladstone. And we venture to say that a subtler gloss, more scholastically expressed, never fell from lawyer in the present age, or from schoolmen in times of old.

The great faculties we have mentioned give Mr. Gladstone, it is needless to say, an extraordinary influence in English politics. England is a country governed mainly by labour and by speech. Mr. Gladstone will work and can speak, and the result is what we see. With a flowing eloquence and a lofty heroism; with an acute intellect and endless knowledge; with courage to conceive large schemes, and a voice which will persuade men to adopt those schemes—it is not singular that Mr. Gladstone is of himself a power in parliamentary life. He can do there what no one else living can do.

But the effect of these peculiar faculties is by no means unmixedly favourable. In almost every one of them some faulty

tendency is latent, which may produce bad effects—in Mr. Gladstone's case has often done so, perhaps does so still.   His greatest characteristic, as we have indicated, is the singular vivacity
of his oratorical impulse.   But great as is the immediate
power which a vehement oratorical propensity, when accompanied by the requisite faculties, secures to the possessor, the
advantage of possessing it, or rather of being subject to it, is
by no means without an alloy.   We have all heard that Paley
said he knew nothing against some one *but* that he was a
popular preacher.   And Paley knew what he was saying.   The
oratorical impulse is a *disorganising* impulse.   The higher
faculties of the mind require a certain calm, and the excitement
of oratory is unfavourable to that calm.   We know that this is
so with the hearers of oratory; we know that they are carried
away from their fixed principles, from their habitual tendencies,
by a casual and unexpected stimulus.   We speak commonly of
the power of the orator.   But the orator is subject himself to
much the same calamity.   The force which carries away his
hearers must first carry away himself.   He will not persuade
any of his hearers unless he has first succeeded, for the
moment at least, in persuading his own mind.   Every exciting
speech is conceived, planned, and spoken with excitement.
The orator feels in his own nerves, even in a greater degree,
that electric thrill which he is to communicate to his hearers.
The telling ideas take hold of him with a sort of *seizure*.   They
fasten close upon his brain.   He has a sort of passionate
impulse to tell them.   He hungers, as a Greek would have said,
till they are uttered.   His mind is full of them.   He has the
vision of the audience in his mind.   Until he has persuaded
these men of these things, life is tame, and its other stimulants
are uninteresting.   So much excitement is evidently unfavourable to calm reflection and deliberation.   Mr. Pitt is said
to have thought more of the manner in which his measures
would strike the House than of the manner in which, when
carried, they would work.   Of course he did—every great

orator will do so, unless he has a supernatural self-control. An ordinary man sits down—say to make a Budget: he arranges the accounts; adds up the figures; contrasts the effects of different taxes; works out steadily hour after hour their probable incidence, first of one, then of another. Nothing disturbs him. With the orator it is different. During that whole process he is disturbed by the vision of his hearers. How they will feel, how they will think, how they will like his proposals—cannot but occur to him. He hears his ideas rebounding in the cheers of his hearers; he is disheartened, at fancying that they will fall tamely on an inanimate and listless multitude. He is subject to two temptations; he is turned aside from the conceptions natural to the subject by an imagination of his audience; his own eager temperament naturally inclines him to the views which will excite that audience most effectually. The tranquil deposit of ordinary ideas is interrupted by the sudden eruption of volcanic forces. We know that the popular instinct suspects the judgment of great orators; we know that it does not give them credit for patient equanimity; and the popular instinct is right.

Nor is cool reflection the only higher state of mind which the oratorical impulse interferes with; we believe that it is singularly unfavourable also to the exercise of the higher kind of imagination. Several great poets have written good dramatic harangues; but no great practical orator has ever written a great poem. The creative imagination requires a singular calm: it is 'the still unravished bride of quietness,' as the poets say 'the foster-child of silence and slow time.' No great work has ever been produced except after a long interval of still and musing meditation. The oratorical impulse interferes with this. It breaks the exclusive brooding of the mind upon the topic; it brings in a new set of ideas, the faces of the audience and the passions of listening men; it *jerks* the mind, if the expression may be allowed, just when the delicate poetry of the mind is crystallising into symmetry. The process is stayed, and the result is marred.

Mr. Gladstone has suffered from both these bad effects of the oratorical temperament. His writings, even on imaginative subjects, even on the poetry of Homer, are singularly devoid of the highest imagination. They abound in acute remarks; they excel in industry of detail; they contain many animated and some eloquent passages. But there is no central conception running through them; there is no binding idea in them; there is nothing to fuse them together; they are elaborate aggregates of varied elements; they are not shaped and consolidated wholes. Nor, it is remarkable, has his style the delicate graces which mark the productions of the gentle and meditative mind; there is something hard in its texture, something dislocated in its connections. In his writings, where he is removed from the guiding check of the listening audience, he starts off, just where you least expect it. He hurries from the main subject to make a passing and petty remark. As he has not the central idea of his work vividly before him, he overlays it with tedious, accessory, and sometimes irrelevant detail.

His intellect has suffered also. He is undeniably defective in the tenacity of first principle. Probably there is nothing which he would less like to have said of him, and yet it is certainly true. We speak, of course, of intellectual consistency, not of moral probity. And he has not an *adhesive* mind; such adhesiveness as he has is rather to projects than principles. We will give—it is all we have space to give—a single remarkable instance of his peculiar mutability. He has adhered in the year 1860 to his project of reducing the amount levied in England by indirect taxation. He announced in 1853 that he would do so, and, what was singular enough, he was able to do it when the time came. But this superficial consistency must not disguise from us the entire inconsistency in abstract principle between the Budget of 1853 and the Budget of 1860. The most important element in English finance at present is the income-tax. In 1853 that tax was, Mr. Gladstone explained to us, an occasional, an exceptional, a sacred reserve. It had done much that was wonderful for our fathers in the French war ; Sir R. Peel had used it with magical efficiency in our own time ; but it was to be kept for first-rate objects. In 1860 the income-tax has become the tax *of all work.* Whatever is to be done, whatever other tax is to be relinquished, it is but a penny more or a penny less of this ever-ready and omnipotent impost. We do not blame Mr. Gladstone for changing his opinion. We believe that an income-tax of moderate amount should be a permanent element in our financial system. We think that additions to it from time to time are the best ways of meeting any sudden demand for exceptional expenditure. But we cannot be unaware of the transition which he has made. His opinion as to our most remarkable tax has varied, not only in detail but in essence. It was to be a rare and residuary agency ; it is now a permanent and principal force. The inconsistency goes further. He used to think that he would be guilty of a ' high political offence ' if he altered the present mode of assessing the income-tax, if he equalised the pressure on industrial and permanent incomes. But he is now ready to *consider* any plan with that object—in other words, he is ready to do it if he can. A great change in his funda-mental estimate of our greatest tax has made an evident and indisputable change in his mode of viewing proposed reforms and alterations in it.

Mr. Gladstone's inclination—his unconscious inclination for the art of advocacy—increases his tendency to suffer from the characteristic temptations of his oratorical temperament. It is scarcely necessary to say that professional advocacy is un-favourable to the philosophical investigation of truth ; a more battered commonplace cannot be found anywhere. To catch at whatever turns up in favour of your own case ; to be obviously blind to everything which tells in favour of the case of your adversary ; to imply doubts as to principles which it is not expedient to deny; to suggest with delicate indirectness the conclusive arguments in favour of principles which it is not wise directly to affirm—these, and such as these, are the arts of the advocate. A political orator has them almost of necessity, and Mr. Gladstone is not exempt from them. Indeed, without any fault of his own, he has them, if not to an unusual extent, at least with a very unusual conspicuousness. His vehement temperament, his 'intense and glowing mind,' drive him into strong statements, into absolute and unlimited assertions. He lays down a principle of tremendous breadth to establish a detail of exceeding minuteness. He is not a 'hedging' advocate. He does not understand the art which Hume and Peel—different as were their respective spheres—practised with almost equal effect in those spheres. Mr. Gladstone dashes forth to meet his opponents. He will believe easily—he will state strongly whatever may confute them. An incessant use of ingenious and unqualified principles is one of Mr. Gladstone's most prominent qualities; it is unfavourable to exact consistency of explicit assertion, and to latent consistency of personal belief. His scholastic intellect makes matters worse. He will show that any two principles are or may be consistent; that if there is an apparent discrepancy, they may still, after the manner of Oxford, 'be held together.' One of the most remarkable of Father Newman's Oxford Sermons explains how science teaches that the earth goes round the sun, and how Scripture teaches that the sun goes round the earth; and it ends by advising the discreet believer to accept *both*. Both, it is suggested, may be accommodations to our limited intellect—aspects of some higher and less discordant unity. We have often smiled at the recollection of the old Oxford training in watching Mr. Gladstone's ingenious 'reconcilements.' It must be pleasant to have an argumentative acuteness which is quite sure to extricate you, at least in appearance, from any intellectual scrape. But it is a dangerous weapon to use, and particularly dangerous to a very conscientious man. He will not use it unless he believes in its results; but he will try and believe in its results, in order that he may use it. We need not spend further words in proving that a kind of advocacy at once acute, refined, and vehement, is unfavourable both to consistency of statement and to tenacious sluggishness of belief.

In this manner, the disorganising effects of his greatest peculiarities have played a principal part in shaping Mr. Gladstone's character nd course. They have helped to make him annoy the old Whigs, confound the country gentlemen, and puzzle the nation generally. They have contributed to bring on him the long array of depreciating adjectives, 'extravagant,' 'inconsistent,' 'incoherent,' and 'incalculable.'

Mr. Gladstone's intellectual history has aggravated the unfavourable influence of his characteristic tendencies. Such a mind as his required, beyond any man's, the early inculcation of a steadying creed. It required that the youth, if not the child, should be father to the man: it required that a set of fixed and firm principles should be implanted in his mind in its first intellectual years—that those principles should be precise enough for its guidance, tangible enough to be commonly intelligible, true enough to stand the wear and tear of ordinary life. The tranquil task of developing coherent principle might have calmed the vehemence of Mr. Gladstone's intellectual impulses—might have steadied the impulsive discursiveness of his nature. A settled and plain creed, which was in union with the belief of ordinary men, might have kept Mr. Gladstone in the common path of plain men—might have made him intelligible and safe. But he has had no such good fortune. He began the world with a vast religious theory; he embodied it in a book on 'Church and State;' he defended it, as was said, mistily—at any rate, he defended it in a manner which requires much careful pains to appreciate, and much preliminary information to understand; he puzzled the ordinary mass of English Churchmen; he has been half out of sympathy with

them ever since.   The creed which he had chosen, or which his
Oxford training stamped upon him, was one not likely to be
popular with common Englishmen.   It had a scholastic appearance and a mystical essence which they dislike almost equally.
But this was not its worst defect.   It was a theory which broke
down when it was tried.   It was a theory with definite practical
consequences, which no one in these days will accept—which
no one in these days will propose.   It was a theory to be
shattered by the slightest touch of real life, for it had a definite
teaching which was inconsistent with the facts of that life—
which all persons who were engaged in it were, on some ground
or other, unanimous in rejecting.   In Mr. Gladstone's case it
has been shattered.   He maintained, that a visible church
existed upon earth; that every state was bound to be directed
by that church; that all members of that state should, if
possible, be members of that church; that at any rate none of
the members should be utterly out of sympathy with her; that
the state ought to aid her in her characteristic work, and
refrain from aiding her antagonists in that work; that within her own sphere the church, though thus aided, is substantially independent; that she has an absolute right to elect her
own bishops, to determine her own creed, to make her own de-
finitions of orthodoxy and heresy.   This is the high Oxford creed;
and, in all essential points, it was Mr. Gladstone's first creed.

But a curious series of instructive events proved that
England at least would not adopt it,—that the actual Church
of England is not the church of which it speaks,—that the
actual English State is by no means the state of which it
speaks.   The additional endowment of the Maynooth College
which Sir Robert Peel proposed was an express relinquishment
of the principle that the Church of England had an exclusive
right to assistance from the State; it proved that the Conservative party—the special repository of constitutional traditions—
was ready to aid a different and antagonistic communion.   The
removal of the Jewish disabilities struck a still deeper blow: it

proved that persons who could not be said to participate in even the rudiments of Anglican doctrine might be prime ministers and rulers in England. The theory of the exclusive union of a visible church with a visible state vanished into the air. The real world would not endure it. We fear it must be said that the theory of the substantial independence of the English church has vanished too. The case of Dr. Hampden proved conclusively that the intervention of the English church in the election of her bishops was an ineffectual ceremony; that it could not be galvanised into effective life; that it was one of those lingering relics of the past which the steady English people are so loth to disturb. Undisputed practice shows that the prime minister, who is clearly secular prince, is the dispenser of ecclesiastical dignities. And the judgment of her Majesty's Council in the Gorham case went further yet. It touched on the finest and tenderest point of all. It decided that, on the critical question, heresy or no heresy, the final appeal was not to an ecclesiastical court, but to a lay court—to a court, not of saintly theologians, but of tough old lawyers, to men of the world most worldly. The Oxford dream of an independent church, the Oxford dream of an exclusive church, are both in practice forgotten; their very terms are strange in our ears; they have no reference to real life. Mr. Gladstone has had to admit this. He has voted for the endowment of Maynooth; he has voted for the admission of Jews to the House of Commons; he has acquiesced in the Hampden case; he sees daily the highest patronage of the church distributed by Lord Palmerston, the very man who, on any high-church theory, ought not to dispense it, to the very men who, on any high-church theory, ought not to receive it. He wrote a pamphlet on the Gorham case, but he does not practically propose to alter the constitution of the judicial committee of the privy council; he has never proposed to bring in a bill for that purpose; he acquiesces in the supreme decision of the most secular court which can exist over the most peculiarly ecclesiastical questions

that can be thought of.   These successive changes do credit to
Mr. Gladstone's good sense ; they show that he has a susceptible
nature, that he will not live out of sympathy with his age.
But what must be the effect of such changes upon any mind,
especially on a delicate and high-toned mind.   They tend, and
must tend, to confuse the first principles of belief; to disturb
the best landmarks of consistency ; to leave the mind open to
attacks of oratorical impulse ; to foster the catching habit of
advocacy ; to weaken the guiding element in a disposition
which was already defective in that element.   The 'movement
of 1833,' as Father Newman calls it, has wrecked many fine
intellects, has broken many promising careers.   It could not do
either for Mr. Gladstone, for his circumstances were favourable,
and his mental energy was far too strong ; but it has done him
harm, nevertheless ; it has left upon his intellect a weakening
strain and a distorting mark.

Mr. Gladstone was a likely man to be enraptured with the
first creed with which he was thrown, and to push it too far.
He wants the warning instincts.   Some one said of him formerly, 'He may be a good Christian, but he is an atrocious
pagan ;' and the saying is true.   He has not a trace of the
protective morality of the old world, of the *modus in rebus*,
the μέσον, the shrinking from an extreme, which are the prominent characteristics of the ethics of the old world, which are
still the guiding creed of the large part of the world that is,
—scarcely altered after two thousand years.   And this much we
may concede to the secular moralists—unless a man have from
nature a selective tact which shuns the unlimited, unless he
have a detective instinct which unconsciously but sensitively
shrinks from the extravagant, he will never enjoy a placid life,
he will not pass through a simple and consistent career.   The
placid moderation which is necessary to coherent success cannot be acquired, it must be born.

Perhaps we may seem already to have more than accounted
for the prominence of Mr. Gladstone's characteristic defects.

We may seem to have alleged sufficient reasons for his being changeable and impulsive, a vehement advocate and an audacious financier. But we had other causes to assign which have aggravated these faults. We shall not, indeed, after what we have said, venture to dwell on them at length. We will bear in mind the precept, ' If you wish to exhaust your readers, exhaust your subject.' But we will very slightly allude to one of them.

A writer like Mr. Gladstone, fond of deriving illustration from the old theology, might speak of public life in England as an *economy*. It is a world of its own, far more than most Englishmen are aware of. It presents the characters of public men in a disguised form; and by requiring the seeming adoption of much which is not real, it tends to modify and to distort much which is real. An English statesman in the present day lives by following public opinion; he may profess to guide it a little; he may hope to modify it in detail; he may help to exaggerate and to develop it; but he hardly hopes for more. Many seem not willing to venture on so much. And what does this mean except that such a statesman has to follow the varying currents of a varying world; to adapt his public expressions, if not his private belief, to the tendencies of the hour; to be in no slight measure the slave—the petted and applauded slave, but still the slave—of the world which he seems to rule. Nor is this all. A minister is not simply the servant of the public, he is likewise the advocate of his colleagues. No one supposes that a cabinet can ever agree; when did fifteen able men—fifteen able men, more or less rivals—ever agree on anything? We are aware that differences of opinion, more or less radical, exist in every cabinet; that the decisions of every cabinet are in nearly every case modified by concession; that a minority of the cabinet frequently dissents from them. Yet all this latent discrepancy of opinion is never hinted at, much less is it ever avowed. A cabinet minister comes down to the House habitually to vote and occasionally to speak in favour of measures which he much dislikes, from which he has in vain

attempted to dissuade his colleagues. The life of a great
minister is the life of a great advocate. No life can be imagined which is worse for a mind like Mr. Gladstone's. He was
naturally changeable, susceptible, prone to unlimited statements—to vehement arguments. He has followed a career in
which it is necessary to follow a changing guide and to obey
more or less, but always to some extent, a fluctuating opinion ;
to argue vehemently for tenets which you dislike ; to defend
boldly a given law to-day, to propose boldly that the same law
should be repealed to-morrow. Accumulated experience shows
that the public life of our parliamentary statesmen is singularly unsteadying, is painfully destructive of coherent principle ;
and we may easily conceive how dangerous it must be to a
mind like Mr. Gladstone's—to a mind, by its intrinsic nature,
impressible, impetuous, and unfixed.

What, then, is to be the future course of the remarkable
statesman whose excellences and whose faults we have ventured to analyse at such length ? No wise man would venture
to predict. A wise man does not predict much in this complicated world, least of all will he predict the exact course of
a perplexing man in perplexing circumstances. But we will
hazard three general remarks.

First, Mr. Gladstone is essentially a man who cannot impose
his creed *on* his time, but must learn his creed *of* his time.
Every parliamentary statesman must, as we have said, do so in
some measure ; but Mr. Gladstone must do so above all men.
The vehement orator, the impulsive advocate, the ingenious but
somewhat unsettled thinker, is the last man from whom we
should expect an original policy, a steady succession of mature
and consistent designs. Mr. Gladstone may well be the ex-
positor of his time, the advocate of its conclusions, the admired
orator in whom it will take pride ; but he cannot be more.
Parliamentary life rarely admits the autocratic supremacy of
an original intellect ; the present moment is singularly
unfavourable to it ; Mr. Gladstone is the last man to obtain it.

Secondly, Mr. Gladstone will fail if he follow the seductive example of Sir Robert Peel. It is customary to talk of the unfavourable circumstances in which the latter was placed, but in one respect those circumstances were favourable. He had very unusual means of learning the ideas of his time. They were forced upon him by a loud and organised agitation. The repeal of the corn-laws, the repeal of the Catholic disabilities, —the two acts by which he will be remembered—were not chosen by him, but exacted from him. The world around him clamoured for them. But no future statesman can hope to have such an advantage. The age in which Peel lived was an age of destruction; the measures by which he will be remembered were abolitions. We have now reached the term of the destructive period. We cannot abolish all our laws; we have few remaining with which educated men find fault. The questions which remain are questions of construction—how the lower classes are to be admitted to a share of political power without absorbing the whole power; how the natural union of Church and State is to be adapted to an age of divided religious opinion, and to the necessary conditions of a parliamentary government. These, and such as these, are the future topics of our home policy. And on these the voice of the nation will never be very distinct. Destruction is easy, construction is very difficult. A statesman who will hereafter learn what our real public opinion is, will not have to regard loud agitators, but to disregard them; will not have to yield to a loud voice, but to listen for a still small voice; will have to seek for the opinion which is treasured in secret rather than for that which is noised abroad. If Mr. Gladstone will accept the conditions of his age; if he will guide himself by the mature, settled, and cultured reflection of his time, and not by its loud and noisy organs; if he will look for that which is thought, rather than for that which is said—he may leave a great name, be useful to his country, may steady and balance his own mind. But if not, not. The coherent efficiency of his career will depend on the guide which

he takes, the index which he obeys, the δαίμων which he con-
sults.

There are two topics which are especially critical. Mr.
Gladstone must not object to war because it is war, or to expenditure because it is expenditure. Upon these two points
Mr. Gladstone has shown a tendency—not, we hope, an uncon-
trollable tendency, but still a tendency—to differ from the best
opinion of the age. He has been unfortunately placed. His
humane and Christian feelings are opposed to war; he has a
financial ideal which has been distorted, if not destroyed, by
a growing expenditure. But war is often necessary; finance is
not an end; money is but a means. A statesman who would
lead his age must learn its duties. It may be that the defence
of England, the military defence, is one of our duties. If so,
we must not sit down to count the cost. If so, it is not the age
for arithmetic. If so, it is for our statesmen—it is especially
for Mr. Gladstone, who is the most splendidly gifted amongst
them—to sacrifice cherished hopes; to forego treasured schemes;
to put out of their thoughts the pleasant duties of a pacific
time; to face the barbarism of war; to vanquish the instinctive
shrinkings of a delicate mind.

Lastly, Mr. Gladstone must beware how he again commits
himself to a long period of bewildering opposition. Office is a
steadying situation. A minister has means of learning from his
colleagues, from his subordinates, from unnumbered persons
who are only too ready to give him information, what the truth
is, and what public opinion is. Opposition, on the other hand,
is an exciting and a misleading situation. The bias of every
one who is so placed is to oppose the ministry. Yet on a
hundred questions the ministry are likely to be right. They
have special information, long consultations, skilled public
servants to guide them. On most points there is no misleading
motive. Every minister decides, to the best of his ability, upon
most of the questions which come before him. A bias to oppose
him, therefore, is always dangerous. It is peculiarly dangerous

to those in whom the contentious impulse is strong, whose life is in debate. If Mr. Gladstone's mind is to be kept in a useful track, it must be by the guiding influence of office, by an exemption from the misguiding influence of opposition.

No one desires more than we do that Mr. Gladstone's future course should be enriched, not only with oratorical fame, but with useful power. Such gifts as his are amongst the rarest that are given to men ; they are amongst the most valuable ; they are singularly suited to our parliamentary life. England cannot afford to lose such a man. If in the foregoing pages we have seemed often to find fault, it has not been for the sake of finding fault. It is *necessary* that England should comprehend Mr. Gladstone. If the country have not a true conception of a great statesman, his popularity will be capricious, his power irregular, and his usefulness insecure.

## WILLIAM PITT.[1]

### [1861.]

LORD STANHOPE'S Life of Mr. Pitt has both the excellences and the defects which we should expect from him, and neither of them are what we expect in a great historical writer of the present age. Even simple readers are becoming aware that historical investigation, which used to be a sombre and respectable calling, is now an audacious pursuit. Paradoxes are very bold and very numerous. Many of the recognised 'good people' in history have become bad, and all the very bad people have become rather good. We have palliations of Tiberius, eulogies on Henry VIII., devotional exercises to Cromwell, and fulsome adulation of Julius Cæsar and of the first Napoleon. The philosophy of history is more alarming still. One school sees in it but a gradual development of atheistic belief, another threatens to resolve it all into 'the three simple agencies, starch, fibrin, and albumen.' But in these exploits of audacious ingenuity and specious learning Lord Stanhope has taken no part. He is not anxious to be original. He travels, if possible, in the worn track of previous historians; he tells a plain tale in an easy plain way; he shrinks from wonderful novelties; with the cautious scepticism of true common sense, he is always glad to find that the conclusions at which he arrives coincide with those of former inquirers. His style is characteristic of his matter. He narrates with a gentle sense and

---

[1] *Life of the Right Honourable William Pitt.* By Earl Stanhope, author of the *History of England from the Peace of Utrecht.*

languid accuracy, very different from the stimulating rhetoric and exciting brilliancy of his more renowned contemporaries.

In the present case Lord Stanhope has been very fortunate both in his subject and in his materials. Mr. Pitt has never had even a decent biographer, though the peculiarities of his career are singularly inviting to literary ambition. His life had much of the solid usefulness of modern times, and not a little also of the romance of old times. He was skilled in economical reform, but retained some of the majesty of old-world eloquence. He was as keen in small figures as a rising politician now ; yet he was a despotic premier at an age when, in these times, a politician could barely aspire to be an Under-Secretary. It is not wonderful that Lord Stanhope should have been attracted to a subject which is so interesting in itself, and which lies so precisely in the direction of his previous studies. From his high standing and his personal connections, he has been able to add much to our minuter knowledge. He has obtained from various quarters many valuable letters which have not been published before. There is a whole series from George III. to Mr. Pitt, and a scarcely less curious series from Mr. Pitt to his mother. We need not add that Lord Stanhope has digested his important materials with great care ; that he has made of them almost as much as could be made ; that he has a warm admiration and a delicate respect for the great statesman of whom he is writing. His nearest approach to an ungentle feeling is a quiet dislike to the great Whig families.

Mr. Pitt is an example of one of the modes in which the popular imagination is, even in historical times, frequently and easily misled. Mankind judge of a great statesman principally by the most marked and memorable passage in his career. By chance we lately had the honour to travel with a gentleman who said, that Sir Robert Peel was the 'leader of the Whigs ;' and though historical evidence will always prevent common opinion from becoming so absurd as this, it is unde-

niable that, in the popular fancy of younger men, Sir Robert
Peel is the Liberal minister who repealed the Corn-laws and
carried Catholic Emancipation. The world is forgetting that
he was once the favourite leader of the old Tory party—the
steady opponent of Mr. Canning, and the steady adherent of
Lord Sidmouth and Lord Eldon. We remember his great reforms, of which we daily feel the benefit; we forget that, during
a complete political generation, he was the most plausible sup-
porter of ancient prejudices, and the most decent advocate of
inveterate abuses. Mr. Pitt's fate has been very similar, but
far less fortunate. The event in his life most deeply implanted in the popular memory is his resistance to the French
Revolution; it is this which has made him the object of
affection to extreme Tories, and of suspicion and distrust to
reasonable Liberals. Yet no rash inference was ever more unfounded and more false. It can be proved that, in all the other
parts of Mr. Pitt's life, the natural tendency of his favourite
plan was uniformly Liberal; that, at the time of the French
Revolution itself, he only did what the immense majority of the
English people, even of the cultivated English people, deli-
berately desired; that he did it anxiously, with many mis-
givings, and in opposition to his natural inclinations; that it
is very dubious whether, in the temper of the French nation
and the temper of the English nation, a war between them
could by possibility have been avoided at that juncture; that,
in his administration and under his auspices, the spirit of
legislative improvement which characterises modern times may
almost be said to begin; that he was the first English minister
who discussed political questions with the cultivated thoughtfulness and considerate discretion which seem to characterise
us now; that, in political instruction, he was immeasurably
superior to Fox, and that, in the practical application of just
principles to ordinary events, he was equally superior to Burke.

There are two kinds of statesmen to whom, at different
times, representative government gives an opportunity and a

career—dictators and administrators. There are certain men who are called in conjunctures of great danger to save the State. When national peril was imminent, all nations have felt it needful to select the best man who could be found—for better, for worse ; to put unlimited trust in him ; to allow him to do whatever he wished, and to leave undone whatever he did not approve of. The qualities which are necessary for a dictator are two—a commanding character and an original intellect. All other qualities are secondary. Regular industry, a conciliatory disposition, a power of logical exposition, and argumentative discussion, which are necessary to a parliamentary statesman in ordinary times, are not essential to the selected dictator of a particular juncture. If he have force of character to overawe men into trusting him, and originality of intellect sufficient to enable him to cope with the pressing, terrible, and critical events with which he is selected to cope, it is enough. Every subordinate shortcoming, every incidental defect, will be pardoned. 'Save us !' is the cry of the moment ; and, in the confident hope of safety, any deficiency will be overlooked, and any frailty pardoned.

The genius requisite for a great administrator is not so imposing, but it is, perhaps, equally rare, and needs a more peculiar combination of qualities. Ordinary administrators are very common : every-day life requires and produces every-day persons. But a really great administrator thinks not only of the day but of the morrow ; does not only what he must but what he wants ; is eager to extirpate every abuse, and on the watch for every improvement ; is on a level with the highest political thought of his time, and persuades his age to be ruled according to it—to permit him to embody it in policy and in laws. Administration in this large sense includes legislation, for it is concerned with the far-seeing regulation of future conduct, as well as with the limited management of the present. Great dictators are doubtless rare in political history ; but they are not more so than great administrators, such as we have just defined them. It is not easy to manage any age; it is not easy to be on a level with the highest thought of any age; but to manage that age according to that highest thought is among the most arduous tasks of the world. The intellectual character of a dictator is noble but simple; that of a great administrator and legislator is also complex.

The exact description of Mr. Pitt is, that he had in the most complete perfection the faculties of a great administrator, and that he added to it the commanding temperament, though not the creative intellect, of a great dictator. He was tried by long and prosperous years, which exercised to the utmost his peculiar faculties, which enabled him to effect brilliant triumphs of policy and of legislation: he was tried likewise by a terrible crisis, with which he had not the originality entirely to cope, which he did not understand as we understand it now, but in which he showed a hardihood of resolution and a consistency of action which captivated the English people, and which impressed the whole world.

A very slight survey of Mr. Pitt's career is all we have room for here; indeed, it is not easy within the compass of an article to make any survey, however slight; but we hope at least to show that peculiar training, peculiar opportunity, and peculiar ability, combined to make him what he was.

It may seem silly to observe that Mr. Pitt was the son of his father, and yet there is no doubt that it was a critical circumstance in the formation of his character. When he was born, as Lord Macaulay has described, his father's name was the most celebrated in the whole civilised world; every post brought the news of some victory or some great stroke of policy, and his imagination dwelt upon the realities before him. 'I am glad I am not the eldest son,' he said. 'I should like to speak in the House of Commons, like papa.' And there are other sayings indicating an early ambition and an early consciousness of power. There is nothing extraordinary in this. Most boys are conceited; most boys have a wonderful belief in their own power. 'At sixteen,' says Mr. Disraeli, 'everyone believes he is the most peculiar man who ever lived.' And there is certainly no difficulty in imagining Mr. Disraeli thinking so. The difficulty is, not to entertain this proud belief, but to keep it; not to have these lofty visions, but to hold them. Manhood comes, and with it come the plain facts of the world. There is no illusion in them; they have a distinct teaching. 'The world,' they say definitely, 'does not believe in you. You fancy you have a call to a great career, but no one else even imagines that you fancy it. You do not dare to say it out loud.' Before the fear of ridicule and the touch of reality, the illusions of youth pass away, and with them goes all intellectual courage. We have no longer the hardihood, we have scarcely the wish to form our own creed, to think our own thoughts, to act upon our own belief; we try to be sensible, and we end in being ordinary; we fear to be eccentric, and we end in being commonplace. It is from this fate that the son of a commanding prime minister is at any rate preserved; the world thinks about him; the world alludes to him. He can speak 'in the grand style,' and he will not be laughed at, or not much. When we wonder at the indomitable resolution and the inflexible self-reliance which Mr. Pitt through life displayed, we may lessen our wonder by remembering that he never endured the bitter ignominy of youth; that his self-confidence was never disheartened by being 'an unknown man;' that he early received from fortune the inestimable permission *to be himself.*

The education of Mr. Pitt was as favourable to the development of his peculiar powers as his position. The public education of England has very great merits, and is well fitted for the cultivation of the average Englishman; but one at least of the qualities which fit it for training ordinary men unfit it for training an extraordinary man. Its greatest value to the mass of those who are brought up in it, is its influence in diminishing their self-confidence. They are early brought into a little but rough world, which effects on a small scale what the real world

will afterwards effect still more thoroughly on a large one.  It
teaches boys, who are no better than other boys, that they are
no better than other boys; that the advantages of one are
compensated by the advantages of others; that the world is a
miscellaneous and motley medley, in which it is not easy to
conquer, and over which it is impossible to rule.  But it is
not desirable that a young man in Pitt's position should learn
this lesson.  If you are to train a man to be prime minister at
five and twenty, you must not dishearten his self-confidence,
though it be overweening; you must not tame his energy,
though it seem presumptuous.  Ordinary men should and must
be taught to fear the face of the world; they are to be guided
by its laws and regulated by its manners; the one exceptional
man, who is in his first youth to rule the world, must be trained
not to fear it, but to despise it.

The legitimate food of a self-relying nature is early solitude,
and the most stimulating solitude is solitude in the midst of
society.  Mr. Pitt's education was of this kind entirely.  He
was educated at home during his whole boyhood.  He was sent
to Cambridge at a most unusually early age.  He lived there
almost wholly with Mr. Pretyman, his tutor.  'While Mr. Pitt
was undergraduate,' writes that gentleman, 'he never omitted
attending chapel morning and evening in the public hall,
except when prevented by indisposition.  Nor did he pass a
single evening out of the college walls; indeed, most of his
time was spent with me.  During his whole residence at the
University,' Mr. Pretyman continues, 'I never knew him spend
an idle day, nor did he ever fail to attend me at the appointed
hour.'  He did not make any friends, scarcely any social
acquaintances till he had taken his degree.  He passed very
much of his time, his tutor tells us, in very severe study, and
very much of it, as we may easily believe, in the most absorbing
of early pleasures—the monotonous excitement of ambitious
anticipation.  On an inferior man, this sort of youth could have
had but one effect—it must have made him a prig.  But it

had not that effect on Pitt. It contributed to make him a shy, haughty, and inaccessible man. Such he emerged from Cambridge, and such he continued through life to be; but he was preserved from the characteristic degradation of well-intentioned and erudite youth by two great counteracting influences, —a strong sense of humour and a genuine interest in great subjects. His sense of fun was, indeed, disguised from the vulgar by a rigid mask of grave dignity; but in private it was his strongest characteristic. 'Don't tell me,' he is said to have remarked, 'of a man's being able to talk sense; everyone can talk sense: can he talk nonsense?' And Mr. Wilberforce, the most cheerful of human beings, who had seen the most amusing society of his generation, always declared that Pitt's wit was the best which he had ever known. And it was likely to be; humour gains much by constant suppression, and at no time of life was Pitt ever wanting in dexterous words. No man who really cares for great things, and who sees the laughable side of little things, ever becomes a 'prig.'

While at Cambridge likewise Pitt paid, as his tutor tells us, great attention to what are now, in popular estimation, the characteristic studies of the place. His attainments in mathematics were probably not much like the elaborate and exact knowledge which the higher wranglers now yearly carry away from the University, but they were considerable for his time, and they comprehended the most instructive part of the subject, the first principles; a vague hope, too, is expressed that he may read Newton's 'Principia' 'after some summer circuit,' which, as we may easily suppose, was not realised.

Though the tutor's information is not very exact, we may accept his general testimony that Pitt was a good mathematician, according to the academic standing of that day. There is, indeed, strong corroborative evidence of the fact in Mr. Pitt's financial speeches. It is not easy to draw out the evidence in writing, and it would be very tiresome to read the evidence if it were drawn out; but a skilful observer of the contrast between educated and uneducated language will find in Pitt many traces of mathematical studies. Raw argument and common-sense correctness come by nature, but only a preliminary education can give the final edge to accuracy in statement, and the last nicety to polished and penetrating discussion. In later life, the facile use of financial rhetoric was as familiar to Mr. Pitt as to Mr. Gladstone.

His classical studies were pursued upon a plan suggested by his father, which was certainly well adapted for, the particular case, though it would not be good for mankind in general. A sufficient experience proves that no one can be taught any language thoroughly and accurately except by composition in it; and Mr. Pitt had apparently never practised any sort of composition in Greek or Latin, whether verse or prose. But, for the purpose of disciplining a student in *his own* language, the reverse practice of translating from the classical languages is the best single expedient which has ever been made use of. And to this Mr. Pitt was trained by his father from early boyhood. He was taught to read off the classics into the best English he could find, never inserting a word with which he was not satisfied, but waiting till he found one with which he *was* satisfied. By constant practice he became so ready that he never stopped at all; the right word always presented itself immediately. When he was asked in later life, how he had acquired the mellifluous abundance of appropriate language with which he amazed and charmed the House of Commons, it was to this suggestion of his father that he at once imputed it.

To the probably unconscious influence of the same instructor we may ascribe his early interest in parliamentary conflict. We have before quoted the naïve expression of his boyish desire to be in the House of Commons. There is a still more curious story of him in very early youth. It is said, ' He was introduced, on the steps of the throne in the House of Lords, to Mr. Fox, who was his senior by ten years, and already in the fulness of his fame. Fox used afterwards to relate that, as the discussion proceeded, Pitt repeatedly turned to him and said, " But surely, Mr. Fox, that might be met thus ; " or, " Yes, but he lays himself open to retort." What the particular criticisms were, Fox had forgotten ; but he said that he was much struck at the time by the precocity of a lad who through the whole sitting was thinking only how all the speeches on both sides could be answered.'

Nor were his political studies confined to the studious cultivation of oratorical language, or to a thorough acquisition of the art of argumentative fence : he attended also to the *substance* of political science. He was the first great English statesman who read, understood, and valued the ' Wealth of Nations.' Fox had ' no great opinion of *those* reasonings ; ' and the doctrines of free trade, though present, like all great political ideas, to the overflowing mind of Burke, were, like all his ideas, at the daily mercy of his eager passions and his intense and vivid imagination. Mr. Pitt, as it would seem, while still at college, acquired and arranged them with the collected consistency which was the characteristic of his mind. So thorough a training, in the superficial accomplishments, the peculiar associations, and the abstract studies of political life, has not perhaps fallen to the lot of any other English statesman.

Nor was the political opportunity of Mr. Pitt at all inferior to his political training. The history of the first twenty years of the reign of George III. is a history of his struggles with the aristocratic proprietors of parliamentary boroughs. Neither the extension of the power of the Crown, nor the maintenance of the political ascendency of the Whig families, was very popular with the nation at large; the popular element in the constitution was for the most part neutral in the conflict; it reserved the greater part of its influence for objects more interesting to itself; but between the two parties, between the Crown and the great borough proprietors, the strife was eager, intense, and unremitting.

As the present writer has elsewhere explained, the situation in which a constitutional king was placed under the old system of an unreformed Parliament was more than an energetic man could endure. According to the theory of that government, the patronage of the Crown was to be used to purchase votes in Parliament, and to maintain a parliamentary majority by constant bargains with borough proprietors.

But who is to use the patronage? The theory assumes that it is to be used by the minister of the day. According to it, the head of the party which is predominant in Parliament is to employ the patronage of the Crown for the purpose of confirming that predominance. But suppose that the Crown chooses to object to this; suppose that the King for the time being should say, ' This patronage is mine; the places in question are places in my service; the pensions in question are pensions from me. I will myself have at least some share in the influence that is acquired by the conferring of those pensions and the distribution of those places.' George III. actually did say this. He was a king in one respect among a thousand; he was willing to do the work of a Secretary of the Treasury; his letters for very many years are filled with the petty details of patronage; he directed who should have what, and stipulated who should not have anything. This interference of the King must evidently in theory, and did certainly in fact, destroy the efficiency of the alleged expedient. Very much of the patronage of the Crown went, not to the adherents of the prime minister, because they were his adherents, but to the King's friends, because they were his friends. Many writers have been very severe on George III. for taking the course which he did take, and have frequently repeated the well-known maxims, which show that what he did was a deviation from the constitution. Very likely it was; but what is the use of a constitution which takes no account of the ordinary motives of human nature? It was inevitable that an ambitious king, who had industry enough to act as he did, would so act. Let us consider his position. He was invested with authority which was apparently great. He was surrounded by noblemen and gentlemen who passed their life in paying him homage, and in professing perhaps excessive doctrines of loyal obedience to him. When the Duke of Devonshire, or the Duke of Bedford, or the Duke of Newcastle, approached the royal closet, they implied by words and manner that he had immeasurably more power than they had. In fact, it was expected that he should have immeasurably less. It was expected that, though these noblemen daily acknowledged that he was their superior, he should constantly act as if he were their inferior. The prime minister was in reality appointed by them, and it was expected that the King should do what the prime minister told him; that he should assent to measures on which he was not consulted; that he should make peace when Mr. Grenville said peace was right; that he should make war whenever Mr. Grenville said war was right; that he should allow the offices of his household and the dignities of his court to be used as a means for the support of cabinets whose members he disliked, and whose policy he disapproved of. It is evident that no man who was not imbecile would be content with such a position. It is not difficult to bear to be without power, it is not very difficult to bear to have only the mockery of power; but it is unbearable to have real power, and to be told that you must content yourself with the mockery of it; it is unendurable to have in your hands an effectual instrument of substantial influence, and also to act day by day as a pageant, without any influence whatever. Human nature has never endured this, and we may be quite sure that it never will endure it. It is a fundamental error in the ‘esoteric theory’ of the Tory party, that it assumed the King and the prime minister to be always of the same mind, while they often were of different minds.[1]

By a series of stratagems George III. at last obtained, in the person of Lord North, a minister who combined a sufficient amount of parliamentary support with an unlimited devotion to the royal pleasure. He was a minister of great ability, great parliamentary tact, unbounded good humour, and no firmness. He yielded everything to the intense, eager, petty incisiveness of his sovereign. The King was the true minister for all purposes of policy and business. Lord North was only the talking minister of the present French Assemblies, who is bound to explain and to defend measures which he did not suggest, and about which he was not consulted.

It is difficult to say how long Lord North's government might not have continued, if it had not been for the military calamities of the American war. That war had been very popular at its commencement, and continued popular as long

[1] *History of the Unreformed Parliament, and its lessons.* An essay, published in 1868, p. 28.

as it was likely to be successful: it became unpopular as soon
as it was likely to fail. The merchants began to murmur at
the stoppage of trade. The country gentlemen began to murmur at the oppressive burden of war-taxes. The nation began
to reconsider its opinion as to the justice of the quarrel, as
soon as it appeared that our military efforts would probably be
disastrous. Lord North shared in these feelings ; he did not
believe the war would succeed; no longer hoped it would
succeed ; no longer thought that there was any motive for continuing to carry it on, but for several years he did continue to
carry it on. The will of George III. was a very efficient force
on everyone just about him, and his personal ascendency over
many men intellectually far his superiors is a curious example
of the immense influence of a distinct judgment and inflexible
decision, with fair abilities and indefatigable industry, and
placed in a close contact with great men and great affairs.

At length, in March, 1782, the calamitous issue of the
American war became too evident, and Lord North resigned.
Lord Holland gives us a curious history of the mode in which he
announced to the House that he was no longer prime minister.

I have heard my uncle Fitzpatrick give a very diverting account
of the scene that passed in the House of Commons on the day of
Lord North's resignation, which happened to be a remarkably cold
day with a fall of snow. A motion of Lord Surrey's, for the dismissal
of ministers, stood for that day, and the Whigs were anxious that it
should come on before the resignation of Lord North was officially
announced, that his removal from office might be more manifestly
and formally the act of the House of Commons. He and Lord
Surrey rose at the same instant. After much clamour, disorder, and
some insignificant speeches on order, Mr. Fox, with great quickness
and address, moved, as the most regular method of extricating the
House from its embarrassment, ' That Lord Surrey be now heard.' But
Lord North, with yet more admirable presence of mind, mixed with
pleasantry, rose immediately and said, 'I rise to speak to that
motion ;' and, as his reason for opposing it, stated his resignation and
the dissolution of the Ministry. The House, satisfied, became
impatient, and after some ineffectual efforts of speakers on both sides
to procure a hearing, an adjournment took place. Snow was falling,

and the night tremendous. All the members' carriages were dismissed, and Mrs. Bennet's room at the door was crowded. But Lord North's carriage was waiting. He put into it one or two of his friends, whom he had invited to go home with him, and turning to the crowd, chiefly composed of his bitter enemies, in the midst of their triumph, exclaimed, in this hour of defeat and supposed mortification, with admirable good humour and pleasantry, ' I have my carriage. You see, gentlemen, the advantage of being in the secret. Good-night.'

Such acquiescent *bonhomie* is admirable, no doubt; but easy good-nature is no virtue for a man of action, least of all for a practical politician in critical times. It was Lord North's ' happy temper' which first made him the mean slave of George III., which afterwards induced him to ally himself with the most virulent assailants of that monarch, and, at a preceding period, of himself.

When Lord North resigned, it was natural that the leaders of the Opposition should come at once into predominant power; but a ministerial crisis in the early part of George III.'s reign was never permitted to proceed in what is now fixed as the constitutional etiquette. The King always interfered with it. On this occasion, the only political party who could take office was that which, under the judicious guidance of Lord Rocking-ham, and supported by the unequalled oratory of Fox and Burke, had consistently opposed the American War. But the leaders of this party were personally disliked by George III. Lord Rockingham he had once before called ' one of the most insignificant noblemen in my service.' Mr. Fox, from a curious combination of causes, he hated. Accordingly, though it was necessary for him to treat with Lord Rockingham and his friends, he did not treat with them directly. He employed as an intermediate agent Lord Shelburne, the father of the present Marquis of Lansdowne, a politician whom it is not difficult to describe, but whom it is difficult really to understand. Police-men tell us that there is such a character as a ' reputed thief,' who has never been convicted of any particular act of thievery.

Lord Shelburne was precisely that character in political life ;
everyone always said he was dishonest, but no particular act of
dishonesty has ever been brought home to him. It is not for
us now to discuss the dubious peculiarities of so singular a
character. But it will be admitted, that it was a most unfortunate one for conducting the delicate personal negotiations
inevitable on the formation of a cabinet, and that it specially
unfitted the person believed to possess it to be a good go-between
between a King who hated the Opposition and an Opposition
who distrusted the King. The inevitable result followed : every
member of the incoming party was displeased with the King ;
everyone disbelieved the assertions of Lord Shelburne ; everyone distrusted the solidity of a ministry constructed in a
manner so anomalous. A ministry, however, was constructed,
of which Lord Shelburne and Lord Rockingham were both
members ; and both, Mr. Fox said, intended to be prime
ministers.

Lord Rockingham must evidently have been a man of very
fine and delicate judgment. He could not speak in the House
of Lords, and his letters are rather awkwardly expressed ; but
those who compare the history of the Whig party for some
years before his death with the history of that party for some
years after it, and those who compare the career of Burke for
the same two periods, will perceive that both over the turbulence of the great party and the turbulence of the great orator
the same almost invisible discretion exercised a guiding and
restraining control. After Lord Rockingham's death, both
the Whig party and Mr. Burke committed great errors and fell
into lamentable excesses, which were entirely unlike anything
which happened while he was yet alive. If he had been permitted to exercise a composing influence, it is possible that the
ministry we have described might have lasted ; but, unfortunately, within three months after its formation he fell ill and
died. Mr. Fox, who had just been quarrelling with Lord Shelburne, refused to serve under him and sent in his resignation ;

and his example was followed by Burke, and by most of the followers of Lord Rockingham.

Lord Shelburne, however, still intended to be prime minister. The King was in his favour. The Whigs had no great aristocratic leader. The Duke of Portland, who was put forward as such, had no powers of speech and but feeble powers of thought. There was no difference of political opinion which need have separated any Whig from Shelburne. He was therefore justified in hoping that if he persevered, he might rally round him in no long time the greater portion of the Whig party, notwithstanding the secession of its present leaders. He doubtless hoped also, by taking advantage of the various influences of the Crown, to attach to himself very many of the followers of Lord North, who were the old adherents of the Crown. But these were anticipations only. For the moment he was more completely separated from the parliamentary ability of his age than any minister has since been. He came into office in opposition to Lord North and one great party; he remained in office in opposition to Fox and Burke, the leaders of the other great party. The trained leaders of the old Ministry and the trained leaders of the old Opposition were both opposed to him. If he decided to remain prime minister, it was necessary for him to take some bold step. He did so. He made Mr. Pitt Chancellor of the Exchequer and the leader of the House of Commons, though he was but twenty-three.

Such singular good fortune has never happened to any English statesman since parliamentary government in this country has been consolidated into its present form, and it is very unlikely that anything like it can ever happen again. Perhaps no man of twenty-three could get through the quantity of work that is now required to fill the two offices of Finance Minister and leader of the House of Commons. In Pitt's time the Chancellor of the Exchequer (he himself tells us) needed no private secretary; he had no business requiring any. The leader of the House of Commons did not even require one-tenth part of the ready available miscellaneous information which he must now have at his command, and most of which cannot be learned from any books. To fill the offices which Mr. Pitt filled at twenty-three, it would in this age be necessary that a man should have a trained faculty of transacting business rapidly, which no man of twenty-three can have; and that he should have also a varied knowledge of half a hundred subjects, which no college can teach, and which no book of reference will ever contain. Mr. Pitt, however, met with no difficulty. Though the finances of the country had been disordered by the American War, and though the ministry was daily assailed by the dexterous good-humour of Lord North and the vehement invectives of Fox and Burke, 'the boy,' as they called him, was successful in his Budget, and successful in his management of the House of Commons. It soon, however, became evident that Lord Shelburne's ministry could not stand long. There were three parties in the House, and a coalition of any two was sufficient to outnumber any one. According to a calculation preserved in a letter from Gibbon, everything depended on the decision of Mr. Fox. If he returned to the Government, it would be strong; if he allied himself with Lord North, it must fail. He did ally himself with Lord North, and Lord Shelburne resigned.

The coalition between Fox and Lord North is not defended even by Lord John Russell, who defends almost every act in the political life of his great hero. Indeed, it was not likely that he would defend it; for to it we owe the almost unbroken subjection of the Whigs, and the almost unbroken reign of the Tories, for five and twenty years.

No political alliance in English history has been more unpopular than this coalition. For once the King and the people were on the same side, and that side the right side. During by far the greater part of his reign the wishes of George III. were either opposed to the wishes of his people, or the wishes of the two, though identical, were pernicious.

During the first part of his reign his attempts to increase the royal influence were generally unpopular; during the latter part, he and his people were both favourable to the American War and to the French War, with what result history shows. But at the period of which we are speaking, both the prominent prejudices of the King and the deepest feelings of the people were offended by the same event. The Coalition deeply annoyed the King. It was hateful to him that his favourite, Lord North, who had been his confidential minister for years, who was enriched with the marks of his bounty and good-will, who was the leader of many politicians, always biassed in favour of the Crown, and always anxious to support its influence, if they could, should after all ally himself with Mr. Fox, who had opposed the Crown for years; who had called its latent influence 'an infernal spirit;' who was the leader of the party opposed to the American War, and therefore, in the King's view, of the party which had advocated treason and abetted the disruption of the empire; who, worse than all, was the companion and encourager of the Prince of Wales in every species of dissipation; who introduced him to haunts and countenanced him in habits which made the very heart of an economical and decorous monarch horrified and angry; who at that very moment was endeavouring to make 'capital,' as we should now say, out of the political prospects and present influence of his profligate associate. George III. used to call the 'coalition ministry' his 'son's ministry;' and he could not embody his detestation of it in terms more expressive, to those who knew their meaning. On the other hand, the people were not unnaturally offended also. The Coalition brought into very clear prominence the most characteristic weakness of our unreformed constitution. Though it professed to be, and really was, a popular constitution, the people could not be induced to believe that they had much concern in it. The members chosen by popular election were a minority; those nominated by aristocratic and indirect influence were a majority.

Accordingly most men believed, or were prone to believe, that
the struggles in Parliament were faction-fights for place and
power; that the interest of the nation had little to do with
them, or nothing; that they were contests for political power,
and for the rich pecuniary rewards which influential office
then conferred. The Coalition seemed to prove that this was
so even to demonstration. If there ever had been a *bonâ fide*,
and not a simulated, struggle in Parliament, it was the struggle
between Fox and Lord North. They had opposed one another
for years; Fox had heaped on Lord North every term of invective, opprobrium, and contempt; Lord North had said everything which a good-natured and passive man *could* say in
reply. They had taken different sides both on the obvious
question which had been the dividing and critical one of the
last few years, and on the latent question which was the real
one underlying the greater part of the controversies of the age
and giving to them most of their importance. Lord North was
the great parliamentary advocate of the American War; Fox
was its most celebrated and effective opponent. Lord North
was the most decent agent, and the most successful co-operator,
whom George III. had yet found in his incessant policy of
maintaining and augmenting the power of the Crown. Fox
was known to be opposed to that policy with all his mind, soul,
and strength; he was known to have heaped upon that policy
every bitter term of contempt, opprobrium, and execration
which the English language contains; he was known to have
incurred the bitter hatred of George III. by so doing. With
these facts before them, what could the nation infer when they
saw these two statesmen combine for the evident purpose of
obtaining immediate office? They could only say what they
did. They said at once that the Coalition must be dishonest if
the previous opposition had been real, and that the coalescing
statesmen were utterly untrustworthy if that opposition had
been simulated.

The government of the Coalition was not, however, destined

to be durable. George III. was a dangerous man to drive to extremity. Though without great creative ability, he had dexterous powers of political management, cultivated by long habit and experience; he had an eager obstinacy allied to the obstinacy of insanity; it was not safe to try him too far. The Coalition Government, however, tried him as far as it was possible. They framed an India Bill, giving the patronage of India to commissioners, to be from time to time nominated by Parliament, to be irremovable by the Crown, the first of whom were to be nominated by themselves. The King was enraged at a scheme so injurious to his secret influence. He considered that it was a scheme for enabling Mr. Fox to buy votes in Parliament. Lord Fitzwilliam, his intimate political friend, was to be at the head of the new Board; and it was expected, perhaps intended, that the Board should be an independent instrument of parliamentary power at the service of the aristocratic Whigs, and in daily opposition to the influence of the Crown—to that personal influence which George III. had all his life been hoarding and acquiring. The people were almost as much enraged at the scheme as the King himself. They thought that the politicians who had just formed a corrupt coalition to obtain office were now providing a corrupt expedient for retaining that office. ' Being dishonest themselves,' it was said, ' they are providing themselves with the means of purchasing the votes of others who are dishonest likewise.' The exact value of these accusations we have not space to estimate now; something might certainly be said in extenuation, if it were needful, but at the time the popular feeling was powerfully excited by them; they were expressed by Pitt with marvellous force and marvellous variety, and re-echoed through the nation.

The parliamentary influence of the Coalition Government, which was supported by the greater part of the borough proprietors, both Whig and Tory, was, however, sufficient to carry their India Bill through the House of Commons by majorities which would now be considered very large. It reached the House of Lords, and would have passed that House too, if George III. had not taken one of the most curious steps in our constitutional history. He wrote on a card: ' His Majesty allowed Earl Temple to say that whoever voted for the India Bill was not only not his friend, but would be considered by him as an enemy; and if these words were not strong enough, Earl Temple might use whatever words he might deem stronger and more to the purpose.'

Such was the influence of the Crown, such was especially the personal influence which George III. had acquired by steady industry and incessant attention to the personalities of politics, that the fate of the India Bill in the Lords very soon became dubious. ' The bishops wavered;' the staunchest followers of Lord North especially, being high Tories, became uncertain; and in the end the Bill was rejected by a majority of ninety-five over seventy-six.

Nor did the King's active influence stop here. The Coalition Ministry did not resign; although their principal measure had been rejected in the Lords, they kept their places; they induced the House of Commons to resolve that it was a breach of the privilege of Parliament to attempt to influence votes in either House by announcing ' any opinion or pretended opinion of his Majesty.' The ministry was passive in its place; but George III. was never deterred by minor difficulties. He sent his commands at midnight to Mr. Fox and Lord North to deliver up the seals of office, and to send them by their under-secretaries, as he must decline to see them in person. By this parliamentary *coup d'état* he broke up an administration which, though unpopular in the country, was supported by the ' great owners' of parliamentary influence and an overwhelming majority in the House of Commons.

But who was to come in? That the King could turn out the old ministry was very clear, for he had done so; but that he could form a ministry that could last in such circumstances

seemed unlikely; that he could form any ministry at all was
not evident. Political expectation was very eager. As soon as
the House met on the day after the midnight dismissal, a new
writ was moved for the borough of Appleby, 'in the room of
the Right Honourable William Pitt, who, since his election,
has accepted the office of First Lord of the Treasury and Chancellor of the Exchequer.' The announcement was received
with laughter, for it seemed unlikely that an ambitious boy
(such was the speech of the time) should be able to carry on
the government, and to lead the House of Commons in the
face of an adverse majority, in direct opposition to the most
experienced statesmen, the most practised debaters, and the
most skilful manœuvrers of his age.

Mr. Pitt was only twenty-five, and he had no one to rely
on. Mr. Dundas was a useful subordinate and an efficient
man of business, but he was not a great statesman or a great
orator, and he *was* a Scotch adventurer. In the Lords, Mr. Pitt
was confident of the support of Lord Temple, who had effected
the defeat of the India Bill by the use of the King's name; but
Lord Temple wanted to be paid. He had great borough connections, which gave him permanent claims on every government; he had just turned out the old government, which gave
him a peculiar claim upon the favour of the new. He asked
for a dukedom, and was refused. The King thought he had
asked too much, and perhaps believed that it would be most
dangerous at that critical moment to give the highest of hono-
rary rewards to the principal agent in an alarming act of royal
influence. At any rate, the application was declined, and Lord
Temple resigned. Mr. Pitt was thus left almost alone. His
cabinet consisted but of seven persons, and he himself was
the only member of the House of Commons among those seven.

Everybody expected that Parliament would be immediately
dissolved. As Mr. Pitt was evidently in a minority in the House
of Commons which then existed, it was confidently believed that
he would at once see whether he would not have a majority in

a new House of Commons. He was too wary, however, to do so. In that age, public opinion formed itself slowly and declared itself slowly. The nation, as far as it had an opinion, was in favour of the new administration ; but in many parts of the country there was no opinion. Delay was in favour of the side which had the advantage in telling argument ; and so strong were the objections of reasonable and moderate men to the coalition between Fox and Lord North—so entirely was their India Bill interpreted by the help of that connection, and regarded in its relation to it—that every day's discussion made converts. The members for close boroughs, and for counties in which individual interest predominated, were, it is true, a majority in the House of Commons, and they adhered for the most part to the Coalition. But the strength so obtained was always weak at a trying crisis. The same influences acted on the borough proprietors which acted upon others, and they never liked to be opposed to the national will when it was distinctly declared. Nor had the extreme partisans of either party ever liked the coalition of the two parties. The warmest Whigs were alienated from Fox, and the strongest Tories were alienated from Lord North. The majority of Fox began to waver, and the minority of Pitt began to augment. Every division showed a tendency in the same direction. Pitt maintained the struggle with dauntless courage, and unbounded dialectical dexterity, against all the orators in the House of Commons. The event began to be doubtful. In the unreformed Parliament no more was necessary. A large section of every party was attached to it by the hope of patronage ; it had been bought by promises of that patronage. As the present writer has elsewhere explained, the strength so obtained was unstable.

It especially failed at the moment at which it was especially wanted. A majority in Parliament which is united by a sincere opinion, and is combined to carry out that opinion, is in some sense secure. As long as that opinion is unchanged, it will remain ; it can only be destroyed by weakening the conviction which binds it together. A majority which is obtained by the employment of patronage is very different; it is combined mainly by *an expectation.* Sir Robert Walpole, the great master in the art of dispensing patronage, defined gratitude as an anticipation of future favours; he meant that the majority which maintained his administration was collected, not by recollection, but by hope; they thought not so much of favours which were past as of favours which were to come. At a critical moment this bond of union was ordinarily weak.[1]

As soon as it seemed likely that Mr. Pitt would be victorious, the selfish part of the followers of the Coalition—a very large part—began to go over to Mr. Pitt. The last motion of Mr. Fox was carried by a majority of *one.*

Mr. Pitt then saw that his time had come; he dissolved Parliament, and his triumph was complete. The popular feeling was overwhelming. It prevailed even in the strongholds of the Whig aristocracy. 'Thus in Norfolk,' says Lord Stanhope, 'the late member had been Mr. Coke, lord of the vast domains of Holkham, a gentleman who, according to his own opinion, as stated in his address to the county, had played " a distinguished part " in opposing the American war. But notwithstanding his alleged claims of distinction, and his much more certain claims of property, Mr. Coke found it necessary to decline the contest.' But of all the contests of this period, the most important in that point of view was for the county of York. That great county, not yet at election times severed into Ridings, had been under the sway of the Whig houses. Bolton Abbey, Castle Howard, and Wentworth Park had claimed the right to dictate at the hustings. It was not till 1780 that the spirit of the county rose. 'Hitherto'—so in that year spoke Sir George Savile—'I have been elected in Lord Rockingham's dining-room. Now I am returned by my constituents.' And in 1784 the spirit of the county rose higher still. In 1784 the independent freeholders of Yorkshire boldly confronted the great houses, and insisted on returning, in conjunction with

[1] *History of the Unreformed Parliament, and its Lessons,* p. 29.

the heir of Duncombe Park, a banker's son, of few years and of scarcely tried abilities, though destined to a high place in his country's annals—Mr. Wilberforce. With the help of the country gentlemen, they raised the vast sum of 18,662*l.* for the expense of the election ; and so great was their show of numbers and of resolution, that the candidates upon the other side did not venture to stand a contest. Wilberforce was also returned at the head of the poll by his former constituents at Hull. 'I can never congratulate you enough on such glorious success,' wrote the Prime Minister to his young friend. One hundred and sixty followers of Mr. Fox lost their seats, and were called ' Fox's martyrs.' The majority for Pitt in the new Parliament was complete, overwhelming, and enthusiastic.

The constitutional aspect of the events of 1784 has been much discussed, and well merits discussion. It is certain that George III. did much that was, according to the good notions now fixedly established, thoroughly unconstitutional ; it is certain that scarcely anyone will, upon any constitutional doctrines, new or old, defend the ' card ' displayed by Lord Temple. But, if we had room to argue the subject, we think it might be shown that it would have been inexpedient to apply, in the year 1784, the strict constitutional maxims on which we should act in the year 1861 ; that the beneficial relations, and that the inevitable relations of the Parliament and the Crown, were different then from what they are now ; that, under such an aristocratic legislature as the unreformed Parliament principally was, it was needful that the Crown should sometimes intervene, when the opinion of Parliament was opposed to the opinion of the people; that, in times when public opinion was formed but slowly, it was advisable that the Crown should do so, not by an instant dissolution of the House of Commons, as we should now exact, but by a deferred dissolution, which would enable the thinking part of the community to reflect, and give the whole country, far and near, time to form a real judgment.

But, at present, we have to deal with the events of 1784,

not in their relation to the constitution of England, but in their relation to the life of Mr. Pitt. They were the completion of his opportunity. But a short time previously the political isolation of Lord Shelburne had made him Chancellor of the Exchequer at a boyish age ; the isolation of George III. now made him prime minister while still very young. The first good fortune would have been a marvel in the life of any other man, but was nothing to the marvel of the second. By a strange course of great incidents, he was in the most command-ing position which an English subject has ever occupied since parliamentary government was thoroughly established in the country. The victory was so complete, that the mercenaries of the enemy had deserted to his standard. The Crown was ne-cessarily on his side, for he alone stood between George III. and the hated Coalition, which he had discarded and insulted ; the people were on his side, from a hatred of the official cor-ruption of which they considered his opponents to be the representatives and the embodiments, from a firm belief in his true integrity, from a proud admiration of his single-handed courage and audacious self-reliance. He had the power to do what he would.

Nor was this all. The opportunity was not only a great opportunity, but was an opportunity in the hands of *a young man.* Half of our greatest statesmen would have been wholly unprepared for it. When Lord Palmerston was in office in the spring of 1857 with a large majority, a shrewd observer, now no longer among us, said, ' Well, it is a large majority ; but what is he to do with it ? ' He did not know himself ; by paltry errors and frivolous haughtiness he frittered it away immediately. An old man of the world has no great objects, no telling enthusiasm, no large proposals, no noble reforms ; his advice is that of the old banker, ' Live, sir, from day to day, and don't trouble yourself! ' Years of acquiescing in proposals as to which he has not been consulted, of voting for measures which he did not frame, and in the wisdom of which he often

did not believe, of arguing for proposals from half of which he
dissents—usually de-intellectualise a parliamentary statesman
before he comes to half his power. From all this Pitt was
exempt. He came to great power with a fresh mind. And
not only so; he came into power with the cultivated thought
of a new generation. Too many of us scarcely remember how
young a man he was. He was born in 1759, and might have
well been in the vigour of life in 1830. Lord Sidmouth, his
contemporary, did not die till after 1840; he was younger
than his cousin, Mr. Thomas Grenville, who long represented
in London society the traditions of the past, and who died in
1846. He governed men of the generation before him. Alone
among English statesmen, while yet a youth he was governing
middle-aged men. He had the power of applying the eager
thought of five and twenty, of making it rule over the petty
knowledge and trained acquiescence of five and fifty. Alone
as yet, and alone perhaps for ever in our parliamentary history, while his own mind was still original, while his own
spirit was still unbroken, he was able to impose an absolute
yoke on acquiescent spirits whom the world had broken for
him.

We have expended so much space on a delineation of the
peculiar opportunities which Mr. Pitt enjoyed, that we must be
very concise in showing how he used them. Three subjects
then needed the attention of a great statesman, though none of
them were so pressing as to force themselves on the attention
of a little statesman. These were, our economical and financial
legislation, the imperfection of our parliamentary representation, and the unhappy condition of Ireland. Pitt dealt with
all three.

Our economical legislation was partly in an uncared-for
state, and partly in an ill-cared-for state. Our customs laws
were a chaos of confusion. Innumerable Acts of Parliament
had been passed on temporary occasions and for temporary
purposes; blunders had been discovered in them; other Acts

were passed to amend those blunders; those other Acts contained other blunders; new corrective legislation was required,
and here too there were errors, omissions, and imperfections.
And in so far as our economical legislation was based upon a
theory, that theory was a very mistaken one; it was the theory
of Protection. The first duty of the English Legislature, it
was believed, was to develop English industry and to injure
foreign industry. Our manufactures, it was thought, could be
made better by Acts of Parliament; the manufactures of our
rivals, it was believed, could be made worse. The industry of
the nation worked in a complicated network of fetters and
bonds.

Mr. Pitt applied himself vigorously to this chaos. He
brought in a series of resolutions consolidating our customs
laws, of which the inevitable complexity may be estimated by
their number. They amounted to 133, and the number of
Acts of Parliament which they restrained or completed was
much greater. He attempted, and successfully, to apply the
principles of Free Trade, the principles which he was the first
of English statesmen to learn from Adam Smith, to the actual
commerce of the country, and to the part of our commerce
which afforded the greatest temptations to a philosophic statesman, and presented the greatest accumulation of irritable and
stupid prejudice. France and England were near one another,
but had no trade with one another; no such trade at least as
two countries so different in soil, in climate, and in natural
aptitude, ought to have. So far from either nation much wish
ing to trade with the other, neither wished to depend on the
other for anything. The national dignity was supposed to
be compromised by buying from an ancient rival. Mr. Pitt,
however, framed a treaty which, if its consequences had not
been swept away with so much else, both good and evil, in
the European storm of the French Revolution, would have
been quoted as the true commencement of free-trade legislation; would have been referred to as we now refer to the ten-

tative reforms of Huskisson, and to the earlier budgets of Sir
Robert Peel.  So little was the subject then understood, even
by those most likely to understand it, that both Fox and Burke
opposed the treaty with virulence and vehemence ; declaring
that France was our natural enemy, and that it was unworthy
of anyone who pretended to be a statesman to create a
' peddling traffic,' and maintain ' huckstering ' relations with
her.

The financial reputation of Pitt has greatly suffered from
the absurd praise which was once lavished on the worst part
of it.  The dread of national ruin from the augmentation of
the national debt was a sort of nightmare in that age ; the
evil was apparent, and the counteracting force was not seen.
No one perceived that English industry was yearly growing
with an accelerating rapidity ; no one foresaw that in a few
years it would be aided by a hundred wonderful inventions—
by the innumerable results of applied science ; no one comprehended that the national estate was augmenting far faster
than the national burden.  The popular mind was apprehensive, and wished to see some remedy applied to what
seemed to be an evident and dangerous evil.  Mr. Pitt sympathised with the general apprehension and created the well-
known ' Sinking Fund.'  He proposed to apply annually a certain fixed sum to the payment of the debt, which was in itself
excellent, but he omitted to provide real money to be so paid.
The only source out of which debt can be defrayed, as everyone now understands, is a surplus revenue ; out of an empty
exchequer no claims can ever be liquidated by possibility : an
excess of income over outlay is a prerequisite of a true repayment.  Mr. Pitt, however, not only did not see this, but persuaded a whole generation that it was not so.  He proposed to
borrow the money to pay off the debt, and fancied that he
thus diminished it.  He had framed a puzzle in compound
interest, which deceived himself, and everyone who was en-
trusted with the national finances, for very many years.

The exposure of this financial juggle, for though not intended to be so, such in fact it was, has reacted very unfavourably upon Mr Pitt's deserved fame. It was so long said ' that he was a great financier *because* he invented the Sinking Fund,' that it came at last to be believed that he could not be a great financier inasmuch as he had invented it. So much merit had been claimed for something bad, that no search was made for anything good. But an accurate study of these times will prove that Pitt was really one of the greatest financiers in our history, that he repaired the great disorders of the American war, that he restored a surplus revenue, that he understood the true principles of taxation, that he even knew that the best way to increase a revenue from the consumption of the masses is to lower the rate of duty and develop their consuming power.

The subject of parliamentary reform is the one with which, in Mr. Pitt's early days, the public most connected his name, and is also that with which we are now least apt to connect it. We have so long and so often heard him treated as the great Conservative minister, that we can hardly realise to ourselves that he was an unsparing and ardent reformer. Yet such is the indisputable fact. He proposed the abolition of the worst of the rotten boroughs fifty years before Lord Grey accomplished it. The period was a favourable one for reform. The failure of the American War had left behind it a bitter irritation and an anxious self-reproach. Why had we, with our great wealth, our great valour, our long experience, failed in what seemed a trivial enterprise ? Why had we been put to shame in the face of Europe ? Why had we been forced to humble ourselves in the face of Europe ? Why had we been compelled to make an ignominious peace ? Why had we, as one of the greatest of civilised states, failed to conquer a raw and unknown colony ? The popular answer was, that our arms had been unsuccessful because our Government was corrupt. The practical working of our unreformed constitution has been tersely described as the barter of patronage for power; the parliamentary majorities of that age were kept by an incessant commerce between the proprietors of seats who sold and the Secretary of the Treasury who bought. In the present day refined arguments are often brought forward to justify or to palliate the system of government. But whatever may be the abstract worth of those arguments, their practical worth is not great. They will never convince the mass of men; they will never satisfy the unsophisticated instinct of ordinary men; they will not remove their natural distrust of what they believe to be unpatriotic selfishness; they will not lessen their conscientious repugnance to that which they call corruption. After the disasters of the American War, this feeling was very strong and very diffused. An unpopular tree was judged of by unpopular fruits; our calamities were evident, and our corruption was conspicuous. A most distinct association of the two was formed in the popular mind. Of this Mr. Pitt took advantage. If the strong counteracting influence of the French Revolution had not changed the national opinion, he would unquestionably have amended our parliamentary representation. Even after the French Revolution he never changed his own opinion; he considered that the time was not favourable for what we now call organic changes; and he judged wisely, for the mass of the nation was wildly and frantically Conservative; but he did not abandon his early principles: he never became a 'Pittite.'

The state of Ireland was a more pressing difficulty than our financial confusion, our economical errors, or our parliamentary corruption. It had an independent legislature, which might at any time take a dangerously different view of national interests, of the expediency of a peace, or the expediency of a war, from the English Parliament. That legislature was a Protestant legislature in the midst of a Catholic people; it was the legislature of a small and hated minority in the midst of an excitable, tumultuous, oppressed people. The mass of the

Irish Catholics believed that the mass of the property, which
belonged in fact to the Protestants, was in strict right theirs;
they believed that they were the true owners of the soil, and
that the Protestants were intruders; they believed that they
had a right to govern the country, and that the Protestants
were usurpers; they believed that the Church which the State
supported was a heretic Church; that the Church which the
State did not support was the true Church—the only true
Church in Christendom. In every parish the distinction between Protestant and Catholic was periodically ruled by the
most critical of tests—the pecuniary test. The collection of
the tithe in detail over the country, from the Catholic population for the Protestant Church, was the source of chronic confusion and incessant bloodshed. Mr. Pitt proposed to remedy
all these evils in turn, and effectually. He proposed to remedy
the most immediate and pressing cause of trouble throughout
the country by changing—as has since been done—the period-
ical extortion of the Irish tithe from the hostile farmer into
an equivalent payment by a rent-charge, which could be easily
collected, and could give rise to no disgraceful scenes. He proposed to put the Catholic majority and the Protestant minority
upon a perfect equality so far as civil rights were concerned.
He was desirous that Catholics should be eligible to all offices,
and be electors for all offices. He was ready likewise to
destroy the prevalent religious agitation at its very root, by
paying the ministers of the Church of the poor as well as the
ministers of the Church of the rich. He proposed at once to
remedy the national danger of having two Parliaments, and to
remove the incredible corruption of the old Irish Parliament,
by uniting the three kingdoms in a single representative system, of which the Parliament should sit in England. He
framed, in a word, a scheme which would have cured the internal divisions of Ireland, which would have united her effectually to the empire without impairing her real liberty.

Of these great reforms he was only permitted to carry a

few into execution. His power, as we have described it, was great when his reign commenced, and very great it continued to be for very many years; but the time became unfavourable for all forward-looking statesmanship—for everything which could be called innovation. The French Revolution and the French War destroyed for many years our national taste for political improvement. But, notwithstanding these calamities, Pitt achieved some part of all his cherished schemes save one.

No opportunity would have enabled Pitt to effect these great reforms, no peculiar situation would have suggested them to him, if he had not had certain more than ordinary tendencies and abilities—the tendencies and abilities of a great administrator. Contrary to what might at first sight be supposed, using the word 'administrator' in its most enlarged sense —in the sense in which we used it at the commencement of this article—the first qualification of the highest administrator is, that he should think of something which he need not think of—of something which is not the pressing difficulty of the hour. For inferior men no rule could be so dangerous. Ambitious mediocrity is dangerous mediocrity: ordinary men find what they must do amply enough for them to do; the exacting difficulty of the hour, which will not be stayed, which must be met, absorbs their whole time and all their energies. But the ideal administrator has time, has mind—for that is the difficulty—for something more: he can do what he must, and he will do what he wishes. This is Mr. Pitt's peculiarity among the great English statesmen of the eighteenth century. As a rule, the spirit of Sir Robert Walpole ruled over all these statesmen. They respected his favourite maxim, *quieta non movere*; to deal shrewdly and adroitly with what must be dealt with; to leave alone whatever might be left alone; to accumulate every possible resource against the inevitable difficulties of the present moment, and never to think or dream or treat of what was not inevitable;—these were then, as always, the justifiable aims of commonplace men. They did *their* possible; they did all that they could with their strength and their faculties in their day and generation. The philosophy of the time, with its definite problems and its un-aspiring tendencies, encouraged them; it made them unalive to the higher possibilities they were forgetting, to the higher duties they were half-consciously, half-unconsciously passing over. It was with reference to this oblivious neglect of the future, this short-sighted absorption in the present, that Dr. Arnold called this century the 'misused trial-time of modern Europe.' It is the distinctive characteristic of Pitt that, having a great opportunity, having power such as no par-liamentary statesman has ever had, having in his mind a fresh stock of youthful thought such as no similar statesman has ever possessed—he applied *that* power steadily and per-severingly to embody that thought. To persons who think but slightly, this may seem only a very slight merit. The first remark of many a commonplace man would be, 'If I had great power, I would carry out my own ideas.' A modern Socrates, if there were such a person, would answer, 'But, my good friend, what are your ideas?' When explained to an exact and scrutinising questioner, still more when confronted with the awful facts—the inevitable necessities of the real world—these 'ideas' would melt away; after a little while the commonplace person, who was at first so proud of them, would cease to believe that he ever entertained them; he would say, 'Men of *business* do not indulge in those speculations.' The characteristic merit of Pitt is, that in the midst of harass-ing details, in the midst of obvious cares, in the face of most keen, most able, and most stimulated opposition, he applied his whole power to the accomplishment of great but practicable schemes.

The marvel, or at any rate the merit, is greater. Pitt was by no means an excited visionary. He had by no means one of those minds upon which great ideas fasten as a fanaticism. There was among his contemporaries a great man, who was in

the highest gifts of abstract genius, in the best acquisitions
of political culture, far superior to him.  But in the mind of
Burke great ideas were a supernatural burden, a superincum-
bent inspiration.  He saw a great truth, and he saw nothing
else.  At all times, with the intense irritability of genius, in
later years with the extreme one-sidedness of insanity, he was
content, in season and out of season, with the great visions
which had been revealed to him, with the great lessons which
he had to teach, and which he could but very rarely induce
anyone to hear.  But Pitt's mind was an absolute contrast to
this.  He had an extreme discretion, tested at the most trying
conjunctures.  In 1784, when he had no power, when there
was a hostile majority in the House of Commons, when he had
no sure majority in the House of Lords, when the support
of the King, which he undeniably had, was an undeniable
difficulty;—for he did not intend to be a second Lord North;
he did not intend to be a servitor of the Palace; he would not
have stooped to carry out measures which he disapproved of;
he would not have been willing to enunciate measures as to
which he had not been consulted;—at this very moment with
most of the constitutional powers against him, with the very
greatest greatly against him, with no useful part of it truly for
him—he never made a false step; he guided the most feeble
administration of modern times so ably and so dexterously that
in a few months it became the strongest.  A mind with so delicate a tact as this is entitled to some merit for adhering to
distant principles.  It is those who understand the present that
feel the temptation of the present; it is those who comprehend
the hour that feel the truly arduous, though upon paper it may
seem the petty, difficulty of thinking beyond the hour.  It is
no merit in those who cannot have the present to attempt to
act for posterity.  There is nothing else left to them; they
have no other occupation open to them.  But it is a great merit
in those who can have what is plain, apparent, and immediate,
to think of the unseen, unasking, impalpable future.

It is this singular discretion which is Mr. Pitt's peculiar merit, because he belongs to the class of statesmen who are most apt to be defective in that discretion. He was an oratorical statesman; and an oratorical statesman means, *ex vi termini*, an excitable statesman. His art consists in the power of giving successfully in a more than ordinary manner the true feelings and sentiments of ordinary men; not their superficial notions, nor their coarser sentiments, for with these any inferior man may deal, but their most intimate nature, that which in their highest moments is most truly themselves. How is the exercise of this art to be reconciled with terrestrial discretion? Is the preacher to come down from his pedestal? is he who can deal worthily with great thoughts to be asked also to deal fittingly with small details? is it possible that the same mind which can touch the hearts of all men can also be alive to the petty interests of itself? is the microscopic power to be added to the telescopic power? is the capacity for careful management to be added to the power of creating unbounded enthusiasm? Yet this is the perpetual difficulty of parliamentary statesmen. A dry man can do the necessary business; an excitable man can give to the popular House of Parliament the necessary excitement. Mr. Pitt was able, with surpassing ability and surpassing ease, to do both; scarcely anyone else has been so.

This great parliamentary position he owed to a combination of parliamentary abilities, of which only one or two can be, within our necessary limits, distinctly specified, but one or two of which are very prominent.

First, his singular oratorical power. He was, Lord Macaulay tells us, 'at once the one man who could explain a budget without notes, and who could speak that most unmeaningly evasive of human compositions, a Queen's speech, offhand.' He had the eloquence of business both in its expressive and its inexpressive forms, and he had likewise the eloquence of character; that is, he had the singular power, which not half a dozen men in a generation possess, of imparting to a large audience the exact copy of the feelings, the exact impress of the determination, with which they are themselves possessed. On a matter of figures, ' Pitt said so,' was enough ; on a question of legislative improvement, an apathetic Parliament caught some interest from his example ; in the deepest moments of national despair, an anxious nation could show some remains of their characteristic courage, from his bold audacity, and unwearied, inflexible, and augmenting determination.

No man could have achieved this without a sanguine temperament, and accordingly good observers pronounced Mr. Pitt the most sanguine man they had ever known. In no stage of national despondency, in no epoch of national despair, was his capacity of hope, one of the important capacities for great men in anxious affairs, ever shaken. At the crisis of his early life, Lord Temple's resignation, which seemed the last possible addition to the coalition of difficulties under which he was labouring, is said to have deprived him of sleep ; but nothing else ever did so after his power attained its maturity, and while his body retained its strength.

Over the House of Commons, too, his anxious love of detail had an influence which will not surprise those who know how sensitive that critical assembly is to every sort of genuineness, and how keenly watchful it is for every kind of falsity. The labour bestowed on his reform of the Customs Acts, on his Indian measures, on his financial proposals from year to year, is matter of history ; no one can look with an instructed eye at these measures without instantly being conscious of it. In addition to his other great powers, Mr. Pitt added the rare one of an intense capacity for work, in an age when that capacity was rarer than it is now, and in a Parliament where the element of dandies and idlers was far more dominant than it has since become.

Nor would this enumeration of Pitt's great parliamentary qualities be complete ; it would want, perhaps, the most strik-

ing and obvious characteristic, if we omitted to mention Pitt's
well-managed shyness and his surpassing pride.

In all descriptions of Pitt's appearance in the House of
Commons, a certain aloofness fills an odd space. He is a 'thing
apart,' different somehow from other members. Fox was the
exact opposite. He was a good fellow ; he rolled into the House,
fat, good-humoured, and popular. Pitt was spare, dignified,
and reserved. When he entered the House, he walked to the
place of the Premier, without looking to the right or to the left,
and he sat at the same place. He was ready to discuss important business with all proper persons, upon all necessary occasions; but he was not ready to discuss business unnecessarily
with anyone, nor did he discuss anything but business with any
save a very few intimate friends, with whom his reserve at once
vanished, and his wit and humour at once expanded, and his
genuine interest in all really great subjects was at once displayed.
In a popular assembly this sort of reserve rightly manipulated
is a power. It is analogous to the manner which the accomplished author of 'Eöthen' recommends in dealing with Orien-
tals: 'it excites terror and inspires respect.' A recent book of
memoirs illustrates it. During Addington's administration, a
certain rather obscure 'Mr. G.' was made a privy-councillor,
and the question was raised in Pitt's presence as to the mode
in which he could have obtained that honour. Some one said,
'I suppose he was always talking to the Premier, and bothering
him.' Mr. Pitt quietly observed, 'In *my* time I would much
rather have made him a privy-councillor *than have spoken to
him.*' It is easy to conceive the mental exhaustion which this
well-managed reserve spared him, the number of trivial conversations which it economised, the number of imperfect ambitions
which it quelled before they were uttered. An ordinary man
could not of course make use of it. But Pitt at the earliest
period imparted to the House of Commons the two most important convictions for a member in his position : he convinced
them that he would not be the King's creature, and that he

desired no pecuniary profit for himself. As he despised royal favour and despised real money, the House of Commons thought he might well despise them.

We have left ourselves no room to speak of Mr. Pitt's policy at the time of the French Revolution. It would require an essay of considerable length to do it substantial justice. But we may observe, that the crisis which that revolution presented to an English statesman was one rather for a great dictator than for a great administrator. The English people were at first in general pleased with the commencement of the French Revolution. ' *Anglo-manie*,' it seemed, had been prevalent on the Continent; the English constitution it was hoped would be transplanted; the fundamental principles of the English Revolution it was, at any rate, hoped, would be imitated. The essay of Burke by its arguments, the progress of events by an evident experience, proved that such would not be the history. What was to come was uncertain. There was no precedent on the English file; the English people did not know what they ought to think; they were ready to submit to anyone who would think for them. The only point upon which their opinion was decided was, that the French Revolution was very dangerous; that it had produced awful results in France; that it was no model for imitation for sober men in a sober country. They were ready to concede anything to a statesman who allowed this, who acted on this, who embodied this in appropriate action.

Mr. Pitt saw little further than the rest of the nation; what the French Revolution was he did not understand; what forces it would develop he did not foresee; what sort of opposition it would require he did not apprehend. He was, indeed, on one point much in advance of his contemporaries. The instinct of uncultivated persons is always towards an intemperate interference with anything of which they do not approve. A most worthy police-magistrate in our own time said, that ' he intended to put down *suicide*.' The English people, in the very same spirit of uncultured benevolence, wished to 'put down the French Revolution.' They were irritated at its excesses; they were alarmed at its example; they conceived that such impiety should be punished for the past and prohibited for the future. Mr. Pitt's natural instinct, however, was certainly in an entirely opposite direction. He was by inclination and by temperament opposed to all war; he was very humane, and all war is inhuman; he was a great financier, and all war is opposed to well-regulated finance. He postponed a French war as long as he could; he consented to it with reluctance, and continued it from necessity.

Of the great powers which the sudden excitement of democratic revolution would stimulate in a nation seemingly exhausted, Mr. Pitt knew no more than those who were around him. Burke said that, as a military power, France was 'blotted from the map of Europe;' and though Pitt, with characteristic discretion, did not advance any sentiment which would be so extreme, or any phrase which would adhere so fixedly to everyone's memory, it is undeniable that he did not anticipate the martial power which the new France, as by magic, displayed; that he fancied she would be an effete country; that he fancied he was making war with certain scanty vestiges of the *ancien régime*, instead of contending against the renewed, excited, and intensified energies of a united people. He did not know that, for temporary purposes, a revolutionary government was the most powerful of all governments; for it does not care for the future, and has the entire legacy of the past. He forgot that it was possible, that from a brief period of tumultuous disorder, there might issue a military despotism more compact, more disciplined, and more overpowering than any which had preceded it, or any which has followed it.

But, as we have said, the conclusion of a prolonged article is no place for discussing the precise nature of Mr. Pitt's anti-revolutionary policy. Undoubtedly, he did not comprehend the Revolution in France ; as Lord Macaulay has explained, with his habitual power, he over-rated the danger of a revolution in this country ; he entirely over-estimated the power of the democratic assailants, and he entirely under-estimated the force of the conservative, maintaining, restraining, and, if need were, reactionary, influence. He saw his enemy ;— he did not see his allies. But it is not given to many men to conquer such difficulties ; it is not given to the greatest of administrators to apprehend entirely new phenomena. A highly imaginative statesman, a man of great moments and great visions, a greater Lord Chatham, might have done so, but the educated sense and equable dexterity of Mr. Pitt failed. All that he could do he did. He burnt the memory of his own name into the Continental mind. After sixty years, the French people still half believe that it was the gold of Pitt which caused many of their misfortunes ; after half a century it is still certain that it was Pitt's indomitable spirit and Pitt's hopeful temper which was the soul of every continental coalition, and the animating life of every anti-revolutionary movement. He showed most distinctly how potent is the influence of a commanding character just when he most exhibited the characteristic limitation of even the best administrative intellect.

## BOLINGBROKE AS A STATESMAN.

### [1863.]

WHO now reads Bolingbroke? was asked sixty years ago. Who knows anything about him? we may ask now. Professed students of our history or of our literature may have special knowledge; but out of the general mass of educated men, how many could give an intelligible account of his career? How many could describe even vaguely his character as a statesman? Our grandfathers and their fathers quarrelled for two generations as to the peace of Utrecht, but only an odd person here and there could now give an account of its provisions. The most cultivated lady would not mind asking, 'The peace of Utrecht! yes—what was that?' Whether Mr. St. John was right to make that peace; whether Queen Anne was right to create him a peer for making it; whether the Whigs were right in impeaching him for making it—the mass of men have forgotten. So is history *un*made. Even now, the dust of forgetfulness is falling over the Congress of Vienna and the peace of Paris; we are forgetting the last great pacification as we have wholly forgotten the pacification before that; in another fifty years 'Vienna' will be as 'Utrecht,' and Wellington be no more than Marlborough.

In the meantime, however, Mr. Macknight has done well to collect for those who wish to know them the principal events of Bolingbroke's career. There was no tolerable outline of them before, and in some respects this is a good one. Mr. Mac-

[1] *The Life of Henry St. John Viscount Bolingbroke, Secretary of State in the reign of Queen Anne.* By Thomas Macknight, author of the *History of the Life and Times of Edmund Burke.*

knight's style is clear, though often ponderous; his remarks
are sensible, and he has the great merit of not being imposed
on by great names and traditional reputations.    The defect of
the book is, that he takes too literary a view of politics and
politicians; that he has not looked closely and for himself at
real political life; that he therefore misses the guiding traits
which show what in Queen Anne's time was so like our present
politics, and what so wholly unlike.    We shall venture in the
course of this article to supply some general outline of the
controversies that were to be then decided, and of the political
forces which decided them; for unless these are distinctly
imagined, a reader of the present day cannot comprehend why
such a man as Bolingbroke was at one moment the most conspicuous and influential of English statesmen, and then for
years an exile and a wanderer.

We must own, however, that it is not the intrinsic interest
even of events once so very important as the war of the Grand
Alliance and the peace of Utrecht which tempts us to write
this article.    It is the interest of Bolingbroke's own character.
He tried a great experiment.    There lurks about the fancies of
many men and women an imaginary conception of an ideal
statesman, resembling the character of which Alcibiades has
been the recognised type for centuries.    There is a sort of
intellectual luxury in the idea which fascinates the human
mind.    We like to fancy a young man, in the first vigour of
body and in the first vigour of mind, who is full of bounding
enjoyment, who is fond of irregular luxury, who is the favourite
of society, who excels all rivals at masculine feats, who gains
the love of women by a magic attraction, but who is also a
powerful statesman, who regulates great events, who settles
great measures, who guides a great nation.    We seem to outstep
the *mœnia mundi,* the recognised limits of human nature,
when we conceive a man in the pride of youth to have dominion over the pursuits of age, to rule both the light things of
women and the grave things of men.    Human imagination so

much loves to surpass human power, that we shall never be able to extirpate the conception. But we may examine the approximations to it in life. We see in Bolingbroke's case that a life of brilliant license is really compatible with a life of brilliant statesmanship; that license itself may even be thought to quicken the imagination for oratorical efforts; that an intellect similarly aroused may, at exciting conjunctures, perceive possibilities which are hidden from duller men; that the favourite of society will be able to use his companionship with men and his power over women so as much to aid his strokes of policy, but, on the other hand, that these secondary aids and occasional advantages are purchased by the total sacrifice of a primary necessity; that a life of great excitement is incompatible with the calm circumspection and the sound estimate of probability essential to great affairs; that though the excited hero may perceive distant things which others overlook, he will overlook near things that others see; that though he may be stimulated to great speeches which others could not make, he will also be irritated to petty speeches which others would not; that he will attract enmities, but not confidence; that he will not observe how few and plain are the alternatives of common business, and how little even genius can enlarge them; that his prosperity will be a wild dream of unattainable possibilities, and his adversity a long regret that those possibilities have departed. At any rate, such was Bolingbroke's career. We have better evidence about him than about any similar statesman, for the events in which he was concerned were large, and he has given us a narrative of them from his own hand. A summary retrospect of his career will not be worthless, if it show what sudden brilliancy and what incurable ruin such a life as his, with such a genius as his, was calculated to ensure.

Bolingbroke's father was a type of his generation. He was a rake of the Restoration. Charles II. is the only king of England who has had both the social qualities which fitted him

to be the head of society, and the immoral qualities which
fitted him to corrupt society.  His easy talk, his good anecdotes, his happy manners, his conversancy with various life,
made Whitehall the 'best club' of that time.  What sort of
life he encouraged men to lead there we all know.  Bolingbroke's father learned of him all the evil which he could learn.
It was not singular that he committed excesses of dissipation,
but it was rather singular that he committed what was thought
to be murder.  He stabbed a man in a drunken broil, and if
Burnet can be trusted, only escaped from the gallows by a
great bribe.  He dawdled on at the coffee-houses far into Queen
Anne's time, a monument of extinct profligacy, and a spectacle
and a wonder to a graver generation.

Bolingbroke's mother was a daughter of the Earl of War-
wick; but she died early, and his father married again, so that
we hear very little about her.  If the silence of his biographers
may be trusted as evidence, she exercised but little influence
upon his infancy or upon his life.

The most influential preceptors of Bolingbroke's boyhood
were his grandfather and grandmother, who also were not unusual characters in their generation.  The former was a serious
and moderate Royalist, the latter was a serious but moderate
Puritan.  Bolingbroke's father apparently did not much like
keeping house: it must have interfered with his pleasures,
and marred the life of coffee-houses.  The whole direction of
Bolingbroke's mind was given to his grave grandfather and
grandmother.  In after-times, when he was a prominent Tory
and a professed high-churchman, satirists used to say that he
was brought up among 'Dissenters.'  And it is probable that
his grandmother, who was the daughter of the celebrated
Oliver St. John, the great parliamentary lawyer and chief
justice, was far from being in opinion what a high Anglican
divine would term a 'Churchwoman.'  Bolingbroke himself
used to relate terrible stories of having been compelled to read
the sermons of Puritan divines.  But, as far as our slight

information goes, he did not suffer more than in any moderately ' serious ' family of our own time. All serious families were then thought to have a little taint of Dissent, and Bolingbroke was probably very sensitive to the partial dulness of a semi-puritanical religion.

At any rate, we have no doubt it was said (and that his elder relatives much grieved at it) that 'the boy was gone wrong, like his father.' When he came out into the world, he astonished his associates by his license. He had been at Eton and Oxford, but he had not learnt, what is often learned there, a decorum in profligacy. To what precise enormities his license extended is immaterial, and cannot now be known. Goldsmith had talked to an old gentleman who related that Bolingbroke and his companions, in a drunken frolic, ran ' naked through the Park.' But this is hardly credible ; and probably Goldsmith's informant was one of the many old people who believe that the more wonderful the stories they tell, the more wonderful they themselves become. But at any rate his outrages attracted censure. He did not, like his father, belong to his generation. The age of King William tolerated much that we tolerate no longer, but it was not like the first years of Charles II. There was no longer a headlong recoil from Puritan strictness, and the Crown was on the side of at least apparent morality. As is usual in England, grave decorum and obvious morals had a substantial influence, and against these Bolingbroke offended.

He wrote poetry too, and the sort of poetry can only be appreciated by reading Locke's celebrated warning against that art, and the connections which it occasions. Bolingbroke's verses are addressed to a Clara A—, an orange-girl, who pretended to sell that fruit near the Court of Requests, but who really had other objects. She was a lady of what may be called mutable connections ; and the object of Bolingbroke's verses is to induce her to give them up and adhere to him only. He says :—

> No, Clara, no ; that person and that mind
> Were formed by Nature, and by Heaven designed
> For nobler ends : to these return, though late ;
> Return to these, and so avert thy fate.
> Think, Clara, think ; nor will that thought be vain ;
> Thy slave, thy Harry, doom'd to drag his chain
> Of love ill-treated and abused, that he
> From more inglorious chains might rescue thee :
> Thy drooping health restored by his fond care,
> Once more thy beauty its full lustre wear ;
> Moved by his love, by his example taught,
> Soon shall thy soul, once more with virtue fraught,
> With kind and generous truth thy bosom warm,
> And thy fair mind, like thy fair person, charm.
> To virtue thus and to thyself restored,
> By all admired, by one alone adored,
> Be to thy Harry ever kind and true,
> And live for him who more than dies for you.

One would like to know what the orange-girl thought of all this, but it would seem he was lavish of money as well as of verses.

At twenty-two he married. We do not know much about his money matters ; and, as his father and grandfather were both alive, his means could not have been at all large, especially as his expenses had been great. But his wife had certainly a considerable fortune. She was descended from a clothier called Jack of Newbury, who had made a fortune several generations before, and was one of the coheiresses of Sir Henry Winchescomb, who had large property. What sort of person she was does not very clearly appear. But it does appear that the match was an unhappy one. He said she had a bad temper, with what truth we cannot ascertain now ; and she said he was a bad husband, which was unquestionably true. He had been a rake before marriage, and did not cease afterwards. He could drink more wine than anyone in London, and continued that habit too. A kind of connection was kept up between them for many years, but it was a dubious and unhappy connection.

We may suppose, however, that when he was a great statesman she derived some glory, if little happiness, from him; and
he certainly received a large income from her property during
very many years.

At the age of twenty-eight Bolingbroke entered the House
of Commons. Before that time he had done nothing to prove
himself a man of great ability. At school and college he had
done well, and had laid up perhaps a greater store of classical
knowledge than those around him knew of. When abroad for
a year or so, he had learned to speak French unusually well and
unusually easily. But since he had been of age and in the
world, his vices had been great, and he had not done much
to compensate for them. Probably his boon companions considered him very clever; but then sober men rated very low
the judgment of those companions. His skill in writing poetry
had not been greater than most people's, and his choice of subjects had been worse. Until now he had had no opportunity of
showing great talents, and much opportunity of showing considerable vices.

In the House of Commons it was otherwise. His handsome person, long descent, and aristocratic mien set off a very
remarkable eloquence, which seems to have been very ready
even at the first. Years afterwards he was the model to whom
Lord Chesterfield pointed in all the arts of manner and expression. 'Lord Bolingbroke,' he tells us, 'without the least
trouble, talked all day long full as elegantly as he wrote. He
adorned whatever subject he either spoke or wrote upon by the
most splendid eloquence; not a studied and laboured eloquence,
but by such a flowing happiness of diction which (from care
perhaps at first) was become so habitual to him, that even his
most familiar conversations, if taken down in writing, would
have borne the press without the least correction either as to
method or style.' 'He had the most elegant politeness and
good-breeding which ever any courtier or man of the world was
blessed with.'

Nor did he neglect matter in the pursuit of manner. In later life he wrote some characters of the two great orators of antiquity, which showed how acutely he had studied them. He turned aside from the commonplace topics, from their language and their manner, to comment on their acquaintance with all the topics of their time, and on the practical style in which they discuss practical questions. No one can read those delineations without perceiving that the writer is speaking of an art which he has himself practised. Those who knew how little studious Bolingbroke's habits were, appear to have been surprised at the information he displayed. But his excitable life rather promoted than forbad brief crises of keen study. His parts were quick, his language vague, though imposing, and he could always talk very happily on subjects of which he only knew a very little.

The time was favourable to a great orator. The Tory party was exactly in the state in which it has been in our own time. It had many votes and no tongue. Our county system tends to prevent our county magnates from ruling England. Stringent limitations are laid down which narrow the electoral choice, and tend to exclude available talent. It is wise and natural that the landed interest should choose to be represented by landed gentlemen; a community of nature between it and its representatives is desirable and inevitable. But our counties are more exacting than this : each county requires that the member shall have land within the county, and as in each the number of candidates thus limited is but small, unsuitable ones must be chosen. We have left off expecting eloquence from a county member. Grave files of speechless men have always represented the land of England. In Queen Anne's time too, as in our own time, a lingering prejudice haunted rural minds, and inclined them to prefer stupid magnates who shared it to clever ones who were emancipated from it. Bolingbroke, like Mr. Disraeli, found the Tory party in a state of dumb power; like him, too, he became its spokesman and obtained its power.

Bolingbroke came into Parliament just at the end of King
William's reign, and was at once forced into contact with the two
subjects which were to occupy almost exclusively his active life.
The reign of King William, which was about to end, and that
of Queen Anne, which was just about to begin, were filled by
two of the greatest topics which can occupy a period. The first
of these was a question of dynasty. Our revolution has been
called the 'minimum of a revolution,' and in the eyes of a political philosopher so it is. It altered but little in the substance
of our institutions and in our positive law. But to common
people, when it happened, the change was great. Even now the
detail of our parliamentary system is not much understood by
the poorer part of the public, and they care for it but little ; the
Queen and her family, and the Prince of Wales and the Princess
Alexandra, mainly interest them. The person of the sovereign
embodies to them constitution, law, power. But our revolution
changed the sovereign. The only political name and idea
known to rural hamlets were taken away, and another name and
idea were substituted in their stead. Jacobites went about saying that there was one king whom God had made, and another
king whom Parliament had made. At this moment, though the
dogma of hereditary right has been confuted for ages, though
it has been laughed at for ages, though parliaments have condemned it, though divines have been impeached for preaching
it, though it is a misdemeanour to maintain it, the tenet still
lives in ordinary minds. In Somersetshire and half the quiet
counties the inhabitants would say that Queen Victoria ruled
by the right of birth and the grace of God, and not by virtue
of an Act of Parliament. They still think that she has a divine
right to the crown, and not a right by statute only. If the old
creed of the Jacobites is still so powerful, what must have been
its force in Queen Anne's time ? That generation had seen the
change from 'God's king' to 'man's king,' and very many of
them did not like it. Shrewd men said that England was
prosperous under the revolutionary government ; common sense

said that an ill-born king who governed well was better than
a well-born king who governed ill; Whigs said that England
was free after the revolution, and would have been enslaved
but for the revolution; yet on the simple superstition of many
natural minds the force of these arguments was lost.    They
admitted the advantage of liberty and of prosperity, but they
would not renounce ' the Lord's anointed for a mess of pottage.'
Happily this political feeling was counteracted by a religious
feeling.    The hatred to Popery supported the successful and
rebellious king, who was a Protestant, against the unsuccessful and legitimate king, who was a Papist.    But the strength
so obtained was precarious; it might cease at any time.    The
'Pretender' might change his religion, and reports were
continually circulated that he had done so, or was to do so.
The existing dynasty could not be strong while its best support
in the most natural minds was the continued  profession of one
religion  by a  person  who had  very strong motives to profess
another.

The question of dynasty was the prominent question in
Bolingbroke's age; such a question must always be the first
where it exists.    The question, who shall be king, can never be
secondary.    But it had a formidable rival.    All through King
William's and all through Queen Anne's time, the English mind
was occupied with almost the only question which could compete
with the question who should be king of England—the question
whether there ought or ought not to be war with France.    Frequent battles, daily hopes of battles, daily arguments whether
there should be battles or not, kept even the greatest domestic
question out of our thoughts.

On both these subjects Bolingbroke was compelled to critical action in his first parliament.    The question of dynasty was
in a very odd and very English state of complexity.    It might
have been thought to be a question of bare alternatives, and to
have been susceptible of no compromise.    *Either* Parliament had
no power to choose a sovereign upon grounds of expediency, or it

might choose any sovereign who was expedient. If King James
might be expelled at all, it could only be because he was a bad
king, and in order to put in a better king. On principle, Parliament was either powerless or omnipotent. But this clear decisive logic has never suited Englishmen. As for King William,
indeed, no one could say he was any sort of king except a parliamentary king, but his heir was the Princess Anne. ' Surely,
it was thought, she and her children had *some* divine right—a
little, if not much ? She had no right by birth certainly, for
her father and her brother came before her; she was not the
nearest heir, but she was the nearest Protestant heir ; she was
not the eldest son of the last king, but she was his eldest
daughter that was living.' These facts do not seem to be
very material to us now, but at the time they were critically
material. Half the population probably believed that it would
be right—not merely expedient, but right in some high mystic
sense—to obey Anne and her children. They were not only
ready, but were anxious, to take her for the root of a new
dynasty. But the Fates seemed capriciously determined to
defeat their wishes. Anne had thirteen children, and all the
thirteen died. At the death of the Duke of Gloucester, who was
the last of them, some further settlement was necessary, and
what it should be was decided in Bolingbroke's first parliament.

On this subject he ought to have been a Whig of the Whigs.
His writings are full of such expressions as the ' chimera of
prerogative ;' ' the slavish principles of passive obedience and
non-resistance which had skulked ' in old books till the reign of
James I. And he has stated the Whig conception of the revolution as well as anyone, if not better. ' If,' he says, ' a divine,
indefeasible, hereditary right to govern a community be once
acknowledged ; a right independent of the community, and
which vests in every successive prince immediately on the
death of his predecessor, and previously to any engagement
taken on his part towards the people ; if the people once
acknowledge themselves bound to such princes by the ties of

passive obedience and non-resistance, by an allegiance unconditional, and not reciprocal to protection; if a kind of oral law,
or mysterious cabbala, which pharisees of the black gown and
the long robe are always at hand to report and interpret as a
prince desires, be once added, like a supplemental code, to the
known laws of the land : then, I say, such princes have the
power, if not the right, given them of commencing tyrants;
and princes who have the power, are prone to think that they
have the right.   Such was the state of king and people before
the revolution.'   He could have no horror of Popery, for he regarded all the historical forms of Christianity with an impartial
scepticism ; he probably thought it more gentlemanly than
Presbyterianism, and not more absurd than Anglicanism.   He
ought to have been ready to obey whatever king was most
eligible upon grounds of rational expediency.

The proposal of the Whigs, too, was as moderate as it was
possible for it to be.   As public opinion required, they selected
the next Protestant heir.   They passed over all the children of
James II., who were Catholics, the descendants of Henrietta,
daughter of Charles I., who were Catholics, the elder descendants
of Elizabeth, the daughter of James I., who were Catholics, and
found the Princess Sophia, a younger daughter of Elizabeth, who
was a very clever and accomplished lady, and who, if she had any
religion, was a Protestant.   All the reasonable and prudent part
of the nation were in favour of this scheme.   The Whigs were
of course in favour of it, for it was their scheme.   Harley, at the
head of the moderate Tories, strenuously supported it.   But
it was not popular with the unthinking masses, and perhaps
could not be.   Half or more than half the believers in divine
right were ready, as we have explained, to pay obedience to
Queen Anne as a sort of consecrated queen ; she was at any
rate a princess born of a real king and queen in real England ;
we had always been used to her.   But a search in Germany for
the sort of Protestants we were likely to find there was not
pleasant to the mass of Englishmen ; and of the strong-minded

old lady who had been discovered nothing whatever was
commonly known. After all, too, there was no certainty that
in future we should be obeying the nearest Protestant heir.
We were passing over several Catholic families; and if hereafter any one of them were to become a Protestant—according
to *principle*, or what was called such, we must obey him as our
king.

Though the choice of the Hanoverian family as heirs to the
crown was prudent, wise and statesmanlike, there was no strong
popular sentiment on which it was firmly based, and no neat
popular phrase by which it could in argument be precisely supported. In a word, unthinking people of the common sort did
not much like the House of Hanover, and a mass of ill-defined
prejudice accumulated against it. Of this prejudice Bolingbroke made himself the organ. He did not share it or try to
share it. But, finding a large and speechless party, he thought
he could become at once politically important by saying for
them that which they could not say for themselves. The
scheme was successful. He became at once important in Parliament, because he was the eloquent spokesman of many in-
audible persons.

In foreign policy, Bolingbroke's tactics were the same. The
aggression of France was the natural terror of lovers of liberty
at that time. Louis XIV. was as ready to use his power without scruple against free nations as Napoleon ; and his power,
though not equal to that of Napoleon at his zenith, was greater
than that of Napoleon at most times, and than that of any other
French sovereign at any time. The King of Spain, too, was
about to die; it was to be feared that he would name as his
heir Philip, the grandson of Louis, and few doubted but that
Louis, notwithstanding an express renunciation of all such claims
by treaty, would permit his grandson to accept the throne.
Nor was the Spain of 1700 merely the Spain of our time. She
was much more powerful. She possessed the 'California' of
that age, a vast empire in South America, producing gold and

silver, which were then thought to be magically potent substances, for the whole civilised world. She possessed, too, Sicily, and Naples, and Milan, and Belgium ; and the popular imagination, which ever clings to decaying grandeur, still believed that Spain itself was a nation of great power—was still able, as in former generations, to obtain ascendency in Europe. The *terror*, for such it was, of liberal politicians then was, that this vast inheritance would practically fall into the dominion of Louis XIV.—that it would belong to a Bourbon prince brought up under his eye, and slavishly in subjection to him. The Whigs contended that this calamity should be prevented, if possible, by an amicable partition of Spain, by giving France as little as possible, and that little in places as little important as possible. If no such amicable arrangement were possible, they said, it must be prevented by a war. The Tories did not like war, did not like partition treaties. They did not love France, but they were not anxious to oppose France. In that age we were uneducated in foreign policy ; the mass of men had no distinct conception of continental transactions, nor was reason reinforced very distinctly by antipathy. We hated France, it is true, but we hated Holland also ; she was our rival in commerce, and our enemy—sometimes our successful enemy—in naval warfare ; and to vanquish the French by the aid of the Dutch did not greatly gratify our animosity. The anti-revolutionary part of the nation did not care for liberty, for that was the code of the Whigs and the basis of the revolution. In a word, though there was little distinct or rational opinion opposed to a war with France, there was much indistinct and crude prejudice. Of this too Bolingbroke became the organ.

In the later part of his life he did not attempt to defend his first notion of foreign policy. He says: ' I have sometimes considered, in reflecting on these passages, what I should have done if I had sat in parliament at that time ; and have been forced to own myself that I should have voted for disbanding

the army then, as I voted in the following parliament for cen-
suring the partition treaties.   I am forced to own this, because
I remember how imperfect my notions were of the situation of
Europe in that extraordinary crisis, and how much I saw the
true interest of my own country in a half light.   But, my lords,
I own it with some shame, because in truth nothing could be
more absurd than the conduct we held.   What! because we
had not reduced the power of France by the war, nor excluded
the house of Bourbon from the Spanish succession, nor com-
pounded with her upon it by the peace ; and because the house
of Austria had not helped herself, nor put it into our power to
help her with more advantage and better prospect of success—
were we to leave that whole succession open to the invasions of
France, and to suffer even the contingency to subsist of seeing
those monarchies united ?   What! because it was become extravagant, after the trials so lately made, to think ourselves
any longer engaged by treaty, or obliged by good policy, to
put the house of Austria in possession of the whole Spanish
monarchy, and to defend her in this possession by force of
arms, were we to leave the whole at the mercy of France ?   If
we were not to do so, if we were not to do one of the three
things that I said above remained to be done, and if the Emperor put it out of our power to do another of them with advantage ; were we to put it still more out of our power, and to
wait unarmed for the death of the king of Spain ?   In fine, if
we had not the prospect of disputing with France, so successfully as we might have had it, the Spanish succession whenever it should be open ; were we not only to show by disarm-
ing, that we would not dispute it at all, but to censure likewise the second of the three things mentioned above, and
which King William put in practice, the compounding with
France, to prevent if possible a war, in which we were averse
to engage ? '   The truth doubtless is, that Bolingbroke never
believed, or much believed, these absurdities.   As he was the
spokesman of the Tories, he advocated, and was compelled to

advocate, the vague notions which they not unnaturally held, and these were prejudices imbibed by habit, not opinions elaborated by effort.

That his mode of advocacy was very skilful, we may easily believe. His speeches have perished, but their merit may be conjectured. He is in his writings a great master of *specious* statement. Accessory arguments and subordinate facts seem of themselves to fall precisely where they should fall. He has the knack of never *making* a case; the case always seems made for him; he seems to be giving it its most suitable expression, but to be doing no more. In the greater part of his writings which were written late in life, except when he defends the peace of Utrecht, he had no tenet to defend in which he took a keen interest. He had not the habits suitable to abstract thought, nor the genius for it. He is apt, therefore, to embody meagre thoughts in excellent words, to develop long arguments from sparse facts. He had a pleasure in writing, and he had little to say. But when his passions were eager, when his interest was vivid, when the very dissipation of his life quickened his excitability, when the topic of discussion was critically important to himself—we may well believe his advocacy to have been effective. He could ever say what he pleased, and in early life he had much to say which he well knew and for which he much cared.

A blunder of Louis' for several years simplified English politics. At the death of James II. he acknowledged his son, the 'Pretender,' as king of England, and he could have done him no greater harm. The English people were not very sure of abstract rights, but they were very sure of practical applications. Whether they had a right to choose a king for themselves might be doubtful, but it was clear that the king of France had no such right. Whoever might be our king, it certainly should not be his *protégé*. War with France became popular. The king of Spain was dead; as was feared, he had left the vast inheritance of Spain to Louis' grandson,

and war with France became expedient. It was declared
accordingly.

The death of William simplified politics still further. Bolingbroke himself may explain this. ' The alliances,' he tells
us, ' were concluded, the quotas were settled, and the season
for taking the field approached, when King William died. The
event could not fail to occasion some consternation on one side,
and to give some hopes on the other; for, notwithstanding the
ill success with which he made war generally, he was looked
upon as the sole centre of union that could keep together the
great confederacy then forming; and how much the French
feared from his life had appeared a few years before, in the
entravagant and indecent joy they expressed on a false report
of his death. A short time showed how vain the fears of some,
and the hopes of others, were. By his death, the Duke of
Marlborough was raised to the head of the army, and indeed
of the confederacy; where he, a new, a private man, a subject,
acquired by merit and by management a more deciding influence than high birth, confirmed authority, and even the
crown of Great Britain, had given to King William. Not only
all the parts of that vast machine, the grand alliance, were
kept more compact and entire, but a more rapid and vigorous
motion was given to the whole; and, instead of languishing or
disastrous campaigns, we saw every scene of the war full of
action. All those wherein he appeared, and many of those
wherein he was not then an actor—but abettor, however, of
their action—were crowned with the most triumphant success.
I take with pleasure this opportunity of doing justice to that
great man, whose faults I knew, whose virtues I admired, and
whose memory, as the greatest general and as the greatest
minister that our country or perhaps any other has produced, I
honour.' The war absorbed England for several years. For
the first time in our history we were the centre of a great
confederacy, and our general was the victorious leader, in great
battles, of miscellaneous armies. It was then that we first

acquired that great name as a military people, which, notwithstanding our small numbers and small armies, we have since
supported, and that a great foresight, a minute diligence, and
a splendid courage in modern war, were first combined in an
Englishman.   Marlborough was in one respect more fortunate
than Wellington.   Napoleon must always be the first military
figure of his generation, but throughout the last century the
whole Continent talked of the wars of Marlborough, for he
was the most fascinating as well as the most successful general
in them.

During the first eight years of Marlborough's wars, the
English nation was nearly united.   A war always unites a
people ; the objector to it becomes a kind of traitor to his
country ; he seems to be a favourer of the enemy, even though
he is not.   Not only Harley, a moderate Tory, but Bolingbroke,
an extreme Tory, took office in the war ministry.   It is true
there was no dereliction of party principle in their doing so,
either as such principle was then understood, or as it is understood now.   Marlborough himself had never been a Whig ;
and Godolphin, the head of the treasury and first minister for
the home administration, had ever been a Tory.   But though
plain party ties might not be violated by a Tory support of
Marlborough's wars, a sort of sentiment was violated.   The
war was a Whig war, and could only be carried on by Whig
support.   Ere long Godolphin and Marlborough were compelled
to give the Whigs a large share in the actual administration.
The ministry became a composite one.   Though many Tories
remained in it, yet its essence and its spirit were Whig.   It
was carrying on the sort of war which one party in the State
had extolled for years, and which the antagonist party had
deprecated for years.   It has been called after its cause.   It
has been called the Whig Ministry of Godolphin and Marlborough, the two leading Tories of the age.

The place which Bolingbroke accepted was that of Secretary at War, which brought him into contact with the best

business of the time, with that sort of business upon which most depended. As far as appears, he did it well, and the official experience he then acquired must have been inestimable to him afterwards. There is much which no statesman can in truth know, and much more which he will not be thought to know, unless he has gone through a certain necessary official education, and learned to use certain conventional official expressions. This sort of knowledge Bolingbroke now acquired. But it was not by success or failure in office desk-work that the movements of his life were to be regulated.

The Whigs naturally did not quite like the subordinate position which they occupied in a ministry which was carrying out a Whig policy. They thought it hard that Tories should be paid for Whig measures ; that the glory of delivering Europe should be given, not to Whigs, who had striven to deliver her, but to Tories, who would have liked not to deliver her. Their support was necessary to Godolphin and to Marlborough, and they gradually raised the price of that support. Early in 1708 most of the remaining Tories were turned out, and Bolingbroke among them. Except the two chiefs, Godolphin and Marlborough, the ministry became a Whig ministry almost exclusively.

That Bolingbroke did not like to be turned out is probable, but he professed to like it. He sought refuge in retirement ; he professed to study philosophy, and passed much of his time in the country, and in reading. Such professions from a man of great ambition and lax life were ridiculed. A friend suggested that he should write this motto over his favourite rural retreat :—

> From business and the noisy world retired,
> Nor vexed by love, nor by ambition fired,
> Gently I wait the call of Charon's boat,
> Still drinking like a fish, and amorous like a goat.

And Swift says he could hardly bear the jest, for he was a man rather sensitive to ridicule. And though satirists might laugh at his meditations and his studies, and though he permitted them to derange very little his pleasure or his vices, there is no doubt but that they were real, and that they were valuable. Doubtless, too, though he was only twenty-eight, he was a little tired of subordinate office. His disposition was very impatient, and his sense of personal dignity very considerable. Even so patient a pattern of routine diligence as Sir Robert Peel rejoiced as a young man to be for a year or so out of office. His mind, he acknowledged, widened, and his capacity to think for himself improved. If Peel, who was made to toil in the furrow, felt this, Bolingbroke, who was made to exult in the desert, might well feel it. During three years he really read much and thought much.

But a great change was at hand. The war with France was still successful and still popular, but it might be doubted if it was still necessary. We had weakened France so much, that it might be questionable if she wanted weakening more. Our victories had destroyed her prestige, and the results of these victories had weakened her vigour. Sensible men began to inquire what was to be the time, what the occasion, and what the terms of peace.

The ministry, indeed, appeared to be firm, but it was firm in appearance only. The conditions of ministerial continuance differed in that age in a most material respect from the present conditions. Now the House of Commons, in almost all cases, prescribes imperatively not only what measures shall be taken, but what men shall take them: it chooses both policy and ministers. In Queen Anne's time Parliament had acquired an almost complete ascendency in policy; it could fix precisely whether there should be war or no war, peace or no peace; it had acquired a perfect control upon legislation, and a nearly perfect control upon internal administration. But it had no choice, or but little, in the selection of persons. *What* was to be done Parliament settled, but *who* was to do it the Queen settled.

Queen Anne had done so at her accession. Though she was engaged in a Whig war, she removed the Whig ministers

whom she found in office. She appointed as supreme general-
issimo over the war abroad, and real prime minister over matters of state at home, the Duke of Marlborough, not because of
his discretion or his acquaintance with business, or his military
genius, but because his wife was her early friend and her special
favourite. As the Duke of Wellington justly observed, the
Duke of Marlborough *was* the English government; he was not
liable to be thwarted, or misconstrued, or neglected; his operations in Flanders were never cramped by the home government, as the operations of the Duke of Wellington in Spain were
cramped. He appointed the lord high treasurer Godolphin;
he placed the treasury, then even more than now the supreme
internal office, in Godolphin's hands, because he was connected
with him by domestic ties, because they had long acted together,
because he had great confidence in his financial ability. The
Duke of Marlborough was not only great because of his wife,
but absolute because of his wife.

By a kind of compensation the source of his power was the
cause also of his downfall. The Queen and the duchess quarrelled, as was natural. The duchess was virulent and obtrusive,
and the Queen was sensitive and sullen. The Queen had a
strong sense of personal dignity, which the duchess used to out-
rage. The duchess, who was clever, thought the Queen a fool,
and scarcely forbore to look and say so. From early habit the
friendship lasted much longer than could have been thought
likely, but it could not last for ever. As it was breaking up,
a small force produced a large effect. The Queen, Swift says,
had not a 'stock of amity' for more than one person at a time:
she commonly cared but little for anybody save one; but she
required one. The duchess had placed at court a poor relative
of her own, a Miss Hill, whom both she and the Queen regarded
as a petty dependant, a *real* maid, who would be useful and lie
on the floor when peeresses and young ladies of quality were
useless and went to bed. As she was humble and artful, she
acquired influence: she was never in the way and never out

of the way. She was always pleasant to the Queen, and the duchess was commonly unpleasant. The consequence was certain. The abject new favourite soon supplanted the querulous old favourite.

A very curious man took advantage of this. Wits and satirists have been fond of describing Robert Harley, but perhaps they have not described him very well. They have made a heap of incongruities of him. They have told us that, being bred a Puritan, and retaining till his death much of the Puritan phraseology, he yet became the favourite leader of high churchmen and Tories; that being a muddle-headed dawdler, he gained a great reputation for the transaction of business; that having an incapacity for intelligible speech, he became an influential orator in Parliament; that being a puzzle-headed man, of less than average ability, and less than average activity, he long ruled a great party, for years ruled the court, and was at last prime minister of England.

It is very natural that brilliant and vehement men should depreciate Harley, for he had nothing which they possess, but had everything which they commonly do not possess. He was by nature a moderate man. In that age they called such a man a trimmer, but they called him ill. Such a man does not consciously shift or purposely trim his course. He firmly believes that he is substantially consistent. 'I do not wish in this house,' he would say in our age, 'to be a party to any extreme course. Mr. Gladstone brings forward a great many things which I cannot understand; I assure you he does. There is more in that bill of his about tobacco than he thinks; I am confident there is. Money is a serious thing, a *very* serious thing. And I am sorry to say Mr. Disraeli commits the party very much. He avows sentiments which are injudicious. I cannot go along with him, nor can Sir John. He was not taught the Catechism; I know he was not. There is a want in him of sound and sober religion—and Sir John agrees with me—which would keep him from distressing the clergy, who are very important. Great orators are very well; but, as I said, how is the revenue? And the point is, not to be led away and to be moderate, and not to go to an extreme. As soon as it seems *very* clear, then I begin to doubt. I have been many years in parliament, and *that* is my experience.' We may laugh at such speeches, but there have been plenty of them in every English parliament. A great English divine has been described as always leaving out the principle upon which his arguments rested; even if it was stated to him, he regarded it as far-fetched and extravagant. Any politician who has this temper of mind will always have many followers; and he may be nearly sure that all great measures will be passed more nearly as he wishes them to be passed than as great orators wish. Harley had this temper, and he enjoyed its results. He always had a certain influence over moderate Whigs when he was a Tory, and over moderate Tories when he was a Whig. Nine-tenths of mankind are more afraid of violence than of anything else; and inconsistent moderation is always popular, because of all qualities it is most opposite to violence—most likely to preserve the present safe existence.

Harley's moderation, which was influential because it was unaffected, was assisted by two powers which brilliant people despise, because in general they do not share them. Harley excelled in the forms of business. There is distinct evidence that official persons preferred his management of the treasury to that of Lord Godolphin, who preceded him, or Sir R. Walpole, who succeeded him. In real judgment and substantial knowledge of affairs, there was doubtless no comparison. Godolphin was the best financier of his generation, and Walpole was the best not only of his own but of many which came after him. But the ultimate issue of business is not the part of it which most impresses the officials of a department. They understand how business is conducted better than what comes of it. The statesman who gives them no trouble—who coincides with that which they recommend—who thinks of the things which they think of, is more satisfactory to his mere subordinates than a real ruler, who has plans which others do not share, and whose mind is occupied by large considerations, which only a few can appreciate, and only experience can test. In his own time, both with the Tory party and with moderate Whigs, Harley's reputation as a man of business was a means of influence which, on the same scene and in our own day, could hardly be surpassed.

But it was surpassed in his own day. In personal questions, as we have explained, the Parliament in Queen Anne's time was only a subordinate power; the court was the principal and the determining power. Now the faculty of business is but secondary in all courts; the faculty of intrigue is the main source of real influence. To be able to manage men, to know with whom to be silent, to know with whom to say how much, to be able to drop casual observations, to have a sense of that which others mean, though they do not say—to be aware what Lady A. is in secret planning, though she says the very opposite—to know that Lord B. has no influence, though he seems most potent—to know that little C. is a wire-puller, and can get you anything, though he looks mean and though no one knows; in a word, to understand, to feel, to be unable to help feeling, the *by-play* of life, is the principal necessity for success in courts. It is the instinct of management which is not to be shown even in conversation, far less in writing or speculation, but yet which rules all small societies. Harley possessed it, and the obscure but potent talents of business also; and we need seek no farther explanation why he was one of the most successful men in his own time.

Harley was some sort of relative to Miss Hill (or Mrs. Masham, for she married), the rising favourite of Queen Anne's time. He was the favourite leader of all moderate Tories; and, on the whole, though not without grumblings from extreme men, the most important leader of the Tory party. He had been turned out when Bolingbroke was turned out, and he wished to return. The fly was brought to the spider. Mrs.

Masham, the new favourite, asked Harley what counsel she should give the Queen. He said, 'Turn out the Whigs;' and meant, 'Bring *me* in.'

The Queen was inert, for that was her nature; and the evident popularity and the glorious success of the Whig war naturally staggered her. But the Whigs made an error. The high-church and semi-high-church party had enormous power in the nation; they had always advocated non-resistance before the revolution, and though they had taken the oaths to King William's government, they did not like to think that they were supporting a government which was conspicuously rebellious, which began in resistance to legitimate authority. Of course the fact was so. King William invaded England with Dutch troops, and was joined by English rebels; but the divine right of princes, and the duty of unconditional obedience, retained much influence over most of the clergy and over many of the laity. If the Whigs had been wise, they would have offended this powerful sentiment as little as possible. High churchmen were certainly powerful, but were necessarily inert; they had no distinct course to recommend; they *would* have done much, but they *could* do nothing. They had assented to the existing government, and though their assent might be unwilling and ungracious, the existing government should have let them alone. The Whigs adopted the reverse course. A foolish parson expressed with unusual folly the sentiments of the great majority of his order. The Commons, at the instigation of the Whigs, actually impeached him at the bar of the Lords. In their folly they used against a pious and innocuous fool the extreme remedy which the constitution provides for the final punishment of impious and dangerous traitors. The country was in a ferment; the Tory party were active; the moderate classes were alarmed; the clergy were incensed; the Whigs became unpopular.

Harley seized the opportunity. He persuaded Mrs. Masham to persuade the Queen that now was the moment to gratify her new antipathy to her old favourite; that now she should punish the Duchess of Marlborough; that now she should dismiss the Whig ministry. She did so. He came in himself, and made Bolingbroke a secretary of state, and the first member in the House of Commons.

It has been said, and is very likely, that Harley would have preferred to retain in office the quiet and moderate Whigs, and not to bring in Bolingbroke, an extreme and unquiet Tory. The Whig party, however, was compact, and held together; it must be expelled as a whole, or retained as a whole. If it had been wholly retained, Harley could not have come in, and he was therefore obliged to ally himself with the aggravated Tories and with Bolingbroke, who had made himself their mouthpiece. It only completes the mingled character of Bolingbroke to repeat the legend of the time, that his acceptance of office was heard with gladness, not only in grave manor-houses, and by severe high-churchmen, but in more unmentionable places and by more questionable persons. Some ladies of much beauty and little virtue, so runs the legend, were heard to say, ' Bolingbroke is minister. He has six thousand guineas a year. Six thousand guineas, and all for us.' The auspices of such a ministry were not good.

The public aspect of affairs was, however, in the most critical particular very favourable. While the French War lasted, indeed, the new ministry must be perplexed. They must either retain the Duke of Marlborough as general-in-chief, which was not pleasant, as he was the chief of the party opposed to them, and since probably Mrs. Masham did not wish it; or they must dismiss the duke in the midst of victory, and find a new general, who might be defeated. But this painful alternative was temporary only. The English nation had been sated with sieges and victories, and more than sated with taxes and with debt; it was disposed to peace. The new ministry came therefore into the enjoyment of a great inheritance, the greatest that has ever fallen to a new ministry. France had been so reduced by

Marlborough's victories that she was ready to consent to a peace which a few years before she would have thought most shameful, which a few years before we should have thought most honourable. The new ministry were to make that peace.

The preliminary difficulty soon assumed its worst shape. It became necessary to dismiss the Duke of Marlborough ; and, as might be expected, the Duke of Ormond, who succeeded him, was much less successful. There was happily no great defeat, but there were minor disasters, which were magnified by the contrast with past glories. We had been used to a great exploit every year, and we were now asked to be thankful for not being defeated very much. The contrast was painful, and the necessity of making peace became greater than ever.

Up to this time Bolingbroke had been the most successful politician of his age, and almost of any age, in England. He had, it is true, no influence at court. Queen Anne distrusted him ; she liked decorous men of regulated life. But, though little over thirty, he was the leader of the House of Commons ; the first orator there ; the second minister in the cabinet ; the favourite minister of the most ardent section of his party—a section just strengthened by an election. The fame of his oratory filled London, and the fame of his genius filled the country. Mr. Pitt excepted, no Englishman has risen so high and so rapidly under our parliamentary system. It was at this crisis that his eager nature and his life of excitement began to prepare his downfall, as they had prepared his rise.

The official management of the foreign negotiations was in the hands of Bolingbroke. Lord Dartmouth, the other secretary of state, could speak no French, and Harley, the prime minister, could speak but little ; but Bolingbroke spoke it well. Harley, too, had no directing ability. He had the defects of the late Lord Aberdeen : he was moderate and useful and judicious. But he could not upon the spur of the moment strike out a

distinct policy.   Other statesmen must create before he could
decide on their creations.   Bolingbroke was to devise how a
peace should be made.

A plain and strongheaded statesman—such a statesman as
Walpole or as Palmerston—would have had little difficulty.
France was most anxious to make peace, and it mattered but
little for England or for Europe what were the precise conditions
of it.   There are occasions when a war itself does its own work,
and does it better than any pacification.   The Crimean War was
an instance of this.   That war thoroughly destroyed the prestige
of Russia and the pernicious predominance of Russia.   At the
end of it, what were to be the conditions of peace was almost
immaterial.   The wars of Marlborough had done their work also.
We had gone to war to prevent the acquisition of overbearing
power by Louis XIV.   If a grandson who was devoted to him
had succeeded to Spain and the Spanish empire while France
was unexhausted he would have been a despot in Europe; he
would have been terrible to us as Napoleon was terrible.   But
nine years of continuous defeat had exhausted France, and
Louis XIV. was now a vanquished and decayed old man.   At
his death the crown of France would pass to Louis XV., who
was an infant; it was not much to be feared that the policy of
France and the policy of Spain would be dangerously connected
because their kings were second cousins.   Possibly, indeed,
Louis XV. might die, and the King of Spain might come to
the throne of France.   But this was a remote and contingent
danger; it would have been unwise in our ancestors to lavish
blood and spend treasure because a prince might have died
young who really lived to be extremely old.   The true object
of the war had been accomplished by the war itself, and the
substantial task of making a peace was therefore very easy.

The accessories of the task, too, it would seem, were easy
also.   As we had been victorious in a first-rate war, it was
right that we should be dignified in the final pacification.   It
was right that we should be ready, that we should even be

anxious, to make peace; but, at any rate, France, who was vanquished, ought to seem equally anxious. Since, in part, the war was a war to reduce her influence over the European imagination, the manner of making peace was at least as material as the terms of it. We were principal members of a great league, and we had stirred up a part of Spain to resist the French king of Spain. We were bound to keep clear faith with our allies, and bound not to desert brave provinces who had relied principally on our protection.

Bolingbroke was too eager to perceive these plain considerations. He sent a man to Paris to ask for peace; and the French minister was so astounded that he would hardly believe the man. He owned afterwards that, when he was asked the preliminary question, 'Do you want a peace?' it seemed to him like asking a lingering invalid whether he wanted to recover. He could hardly bring himself to believe that Bolingbroke's messenger was duly authorised.

The previous life of that messenger certainly was not such as to gain him credit. He was a French abbé named Gaultier, who had been a French spy, and perhaps still was so, in England. He was an acute, plausible person, very fat, and not very respectable, and altogether as unlikely a person to be sent from a victorious nation to a defeated nation as could be imagined.

Nevertheless the Abbé Gaultier was so sent. He said to Torcy, the French minister, 'Do you want a peace? I bring you the means of treating independently of the Dutch, who are unworthy of his Majesty's kindness and the honour he has done them in addressing himself to them so many times to restore peace to Europe.' In an ordinary alliance, such a clandestine reconciliation with the enemy, and such a secret desertion of allies, would have been plainly dishonest. There would have been little to say for it, and very few would have been willing to say that little. But the Grand Alliance was not an ordinary one. Its acute framers had perceived the difficulty of their task.  They had foreseen the difficulty of retaining in firm cohesion a miscellaneous league of scattered states.  They had adopted the best expedient at their disposal : they had prohibited the very commencement of exclusive negotiation by individual states.  Their words are as clear as words can be.  They are these : 'Neutri partium fas sit, Bello semel suscepto, de Pace cum Hoste tractare nisi conjunctim et communicatis conciliis cum altera Parte.'  These words expressly forbid such secret missions as those of Gaultier, and were inserted expressly to forbid them.

The separate treaty with Holland was even more express : it said that ' no negotiation shall be set on foot by one of the allies without the concurrence of the other ; and that each ally shall continually, and from time to time, impart to the other everything which passes in the said negotiation.'  And yet it was especially from Holland that Bolingbroke was anxious, by every secret disguise, and every diplomatic artifice, to conceal his negotiation.  He hoped, by a separate and secret peace, to obtain commercial advantages for the English, in which the Dutch should have no share.

Even after the first mission of Gaultier had terminated, there was an intricate series of secret negotiations, in which he and Prior were employed for us, and Mesnager for the French.  Prior expressly required on our behalf 'that the secret should be inviolably kept till allowed by both parties to be divulged ;' and the French minister wrote to Bolingbroke : ' It wholly depends upon the secrecy and good use you will make of the entire confidence he testifies to the Queen of Great Britain ; and the King of France extols the firmness of the Queen, and sees with great pleasure the new marks of resolution she shows.'  It was impossible to desert our allies more absolutely or more dishonourably.  It was impossible to violate an express treaty more audaciously or more corruptly.

Nor was the secret negotiation a mere crime ; it was also a miserable blunder.  Diplomacy could hardly commit a greater.

There was a splendid, a nearly unexampled power of compelling France to make a good peace. There was a great coalition against her, which had always been victorious under Eugene and Marlborough; which had obtained such successes as no Englishman had imagined; which had reduced France to a pitch of shame, degradation, and weakness, that surprised her most sanguine enemies, and depressed her most sanguine friends. So long as the coalition was compact, the coalition was all powerful. But by the mere act of commencing a separate negotiation, Bolingbroke dissolved the coalition. There could be no mutual trust after that. The principal member of the league deserted the league, and its bond was immediately disunited. We all know what would have been the consequences if England had acted thus in the great war. Suppose Lords Grey and Grenville had come in before the campaign of 1814; suppose that they had sent a secret emissary to Napoleon; suppose that they had offered a separate peace without Spain, or Austria, or Russia. We know that Napoleon would again have been a principal potentate in Europe, for the coalition which alone could extirpate him would have been dissolved.

The truth of these remarks is written on the very face of the treaty of Utrecht, and is obvious in every part of the negotiation of it. A few months before Louis had been willing to abandon Spain and to abandon his grandson. He had said, 'If you can take Spain from him, take it; I will not help him.' But the allies were not content. They required that Louis should compel his grandson to resign, and this he considered dishonourable. But at Utrecht it was not even proposed that Philip should abandon Spain; that the House of Bourbon should possess Spain, was a conceded and admitted principle. We had dissolved the European confederacy, and we could not hope to attain its objects.

Nor was the desertion of the other powers combined with us in the Grand Alliance our only desertion, or our worst. All

these powers were states of some magnitude, and some were
states of great magnitude.  They would be able to go on as they
had always gone on—to shift for themselves, as they had
always shifted.  But we also deserted others who were not so
independent.  We had incited the Catalans in the north-east
of Spain to resist the French king of Spain ; we had promised
them in express terms our support and aid ; for a long time we
had given them that aid.  But at the peace of Utrecht we
deserted them.  The Catalans made a brave resistance, but a
small province could do nothing against a great nation.  The
Catalans were soon overcome, and deprived of all their liberties.
Throughout Europe, and doubtless throughout England also,
there were many murmurs against our policy.  We had encouraged a brave people to rebel ; we had even threatened them
if they did not rebel ; and when they did rebel, we deserted
them.  If, at present, France and England were to incite the
Poles to rebel against Russia, they hardly *could* desert them :
the public opinion of the world is now so powerful ; in Queen
Anne's time public opinion could only murmur, but it did
murmur.  The peace of Utrecht, men said, was a base crime as
well as a gross blunder.

But why, it will be asked, did Bolingbroke commit so gross
a blunder ?  What reasons could have rendered it plausible to
him.  The principal answer is the principal key to his character.  With many splendid gifts, he was exceedingly defective
in cool and plain judgment.  He failed where in all ages such
men as Alcibiades have failed.  Whether by nature he was
much gifted with judgment we cannot tell ; the probability is
that he was about as well gifted as other men.  But his life
was such as to render a cool judgment impossible.  ' His fine
imagination,' says Lord Chesterfield, ' was often heated and exhausted with his body in celebrating and almost deifying the
prostitute of the night ; and his convivial joys were pushed to
all the extravagancy of frantic bacchanals.'  Swift tells graphic
stories of his drinking till his associates could drink no longer,

and his being left at three in the morning calling for 't'other flask.' Many men may lead gross lives and keep cool heads, but such are not men of Bolingbroke's temperament. A man like Walpole, or a man like Louis Napoleon, is protected by an unsensitive nature from intellectual destruction. But such a man as Bolingbroke, whose nature is warm and whose imagination is excitable, imbibes the eager poison into the very heart of his mind. Such is our protection against the possibilities of an Alcibiades. No one who has not a vivid imagination can succeed in such a career; and any man of vivid imagination that career would burn away and destroy. Cold men may be wild in life and not wild in mind. But warm and eager men, fit to be the favourites of society, and fit to be great orators, will be erratic not only in conduct but in judgment. They will see men 'like trees walking.'

Bolingbroke's excitement did not prevent his working. He laboured many hours and wrote many letters. He often complains of the number of hours he has been at his desk, and of the labours which were thrown upon him. But his work probably only excited him the more; for a time *vires acquirit eundo* is the law of such wild strength. In the course of the negotiations he went to Paris, became the idol of society there, and used his social advantages efficiently for political purposes. To dazzle people more, he learned or pretended to learn, the Spanish language, to read such diplomatic documents as were written in it. But such minor excellences could not mend the incurable badness of a peace commenced by a surrender of the best we had to surrender, by a dissolution of our alliance. A plain strong-headed man would have left alone the accessory advantages, and succeeded in the main point. Without Spanish and without French, Walpole would have made a good peace; Bolingbroke could not do so with both.

Bolingbroke, too, had a scheme, as imaginative and excited men will have. He knew that in relinquishing Spain to the house of Bourbon, he was giving the opponents of peace a

great argumentative advantage. The mass of mankind, who
judge by visible symbols, considered that a peace by which the
king whom we had opposed should reign in Spain, and by
which the king whom we had proposed did not reign there,
was a gross failure. In sound argument, it was probably right
for us to concede. As we have explained, the war had accomplished its own work ; France was excessively weakened, and
there was little fear of present danger from her. If, by a possible death, the crown of France should fall to the king of
Spain, it would be time enough then to prevent the same person from reigning in the two kingdoms. The treaty of Utrecht
provides that the same prince shall not reign in both ; and,
if necessary, we could go to war to enforce the treaty. The
Bourbon king was popular in Spain, and was preferred by the
Spaniards to anyone else. It would have been hard to dis-
lodge him. But Bolingbroke did not like to rely on these
plain arguments. He hoped to make the peace popular by an
appeal to our commercial jealousy, by gaining mercantile advantages for ourselves which our rivals the Dutch did not
share. He obtained for us the celebrated Assiento contract,
giving us the right of carrying Negro slaves to the West Indies,
and also certain privileges which would have given our manufacturers great advantage in the French markets. He hoped
this commercial bribe would silence the national conscience—
that it would induce us to forget our treachery to our allies, our
desertion of the Catalans, and the establishment of the House
of Bourbon in Spain. He hoped it would make the peace
popular.

He was disappointed. The reception of that peace by the
nation, and especially by the Tory party, was very like the reception of Mr. Disraeli's great budget of 1852. A great secret had
been long paraded of something which was to please everybody :
it was divulged, and it pleased nobody. Bolingbroke may himself describe the effect that his work produced on the more
moderate portion of his party : —

The whimsical or the Hanover Tories continued zealous in appearance with us till the peace was signed. I saw no people so eager for the conclusion of it. Some of them were in such haste, that they thought any peace preferable to the least delay, and omitted no instances to quicken their friends who were actors in it. As soon as the treaties were perfected and laid before the Parliament, the scheme of these gentlemen began to disclose itself entirely. Their love of the peace, like other passions, cooled by enjoyment. They grew nice about the construction of the articles, could come up to no direct approbation, and, being let into the secret of what was to happen, would not preclude themselves from the glorious advantage of rising on the ruins of their friends and of their party.

Nothing could be more natural than their conduct. The moderate Tory party, and most sensible men, wished for a satisfactory peace made in a satisfactory manner: they wished for dignity in diplomacy, and desirable results. They were disappointed. After a war which everyone was proud of, we concluded a peace which nobody was proud of, in a manner that everyone was ashamed of.

The commercial treaties on which Bolingbroke relied, so far from helping him, were a hindrance to him. The right of taking slaves to the West Indies was indeed popular: the day for anti-slavery scruples had not commenced. But, in return for the privileges which the French gave to our manufacturers, we had given many privileges to them. We had established an approximation to free trade, and everyone was aghast. The English producer clamoured for protection, and he has seldom clamoured in vain. The commercial treaties required the consent of Parliament, and were rejected. If Bolingbroke had been a free-trader upon principle, his convictions might have consoled him. But he professed to know nothing of commerce, and did know nothing. His books are full of nonsense on such topics: he hated the City because they were Whigs, and he hated the Dutch because he had deserted them; and these were his cardinal sentiments on mercantile affairs. He speaks of ' matters, such as that of commerce, which the negotiators of

the peace of Utrecht could not be supposed to understand.'
Certainly he did not understand them.  He only directed his
subordinates to get out of the French as much for ourselves,
and as little for the Dutch, as possible.

Instead of gathering strength (says Bolingbroke), either as a
ministry or as a party, we grew weaker every day.  The peace had
been judged with reason to be the only solid foundation whereupon
we could erect a Tory system ; and yet when it was made, we found
ourselves at a full stand.  Nay, the very work, which ought to have
been the basis of our strength, was in part demolished before our eyes
and we were stoned with the ruins of it.

In our time he would have been really stoned.  The fierce
warlike disposition of the English people would not have endured such dishonour.  We may doubt if it would have endured
any peace.  It certainly would not have endured the best peace,
unless it were made with dignity and with honesty.  We should
have been wildly elated by Marlborough's victories, and little in
a mood to bear shame and to be guilty of desertion.  The English people has been much the same for centuries.  In country
manor-houses, where a son had been killed for the cause which
was sacrificed—in alehouses, where men were used to hear of
glorious victories—in large towns, where the wrongs of injured
races like the Catalans were understood—through a whole nation, which has ever been proud, brave, and honourable, a mean
peace, effected by desertion, must have been abhorred.  It was
merely endured because it was made, and because in those days,
when communication was slow, public opinion, as in America
now, did not distinctly form itself till the crisis for action was
over.  But though for the moment endured, it was long abhorred.  For very many years half our political talk was
coloured by it.  It was to the Tories what the coalition between
Lord North and Fox was to the Whigs—a principal operating
cause in excluding them from office during fifty years.

And, what for the time was worse, the Tory ministry of the
moment was disunited.  'Whilst this was doing,' says Boling-

broke, ' Harley looked on, as if he had not been a party to all which had passed ; broke now and then a jest, which savoured of the Inns of Court, and the bad company in which he had been bred ; and on those occasions where his station obliged him to speak of business, was absolutely unintelligible.' In reality Harley disliked his position. He had always been a moderate man, respected by moderate men ; he had the reputation of a man of care and judgment, and he had thriven by that reputation. On a sudden he became a party to a disreputable peace, at which even moderate Whigs were frantic, for which even moderate Tories could not vote. That the negotiations had commenced by artifice and deceit did not horrify him much, for he was a man much given to stratagem. But he knew also that the negotiation had ended in conspicuous meanness and unpopular concessions ; he felt that his reputation for judgment was weakened. All shrewd observers knew that there would soon be disunion between Harley, the old head of the moderate Tories, and Bolingbroke, the present head of the extreme Tories. Swift, who was a very shrewd observer, and who was close at hand, knew that here was already disunion.

Before the treaties had been discussed by, and the commercial part of them rejected in, the House of Commons, Bolingbroke made another error. He left the House of Commons. Harley had been created Earl of Oxford, and he could not endure to be inferior to him. There was much delay in conferring the peerage, and he was very angry at it. He was, Oxford says, ' in the utmost rage against the Treasurer, Lady Masham, and without sparing the greatest,' and made ' outrageous speeches.' A wise friend would have observed to him that no greater kindness could have been done him than to refuse him a peerage altogether. The great but gradual revolution which was consummated in the time of Walpole was then beginning to be apparent. Before Queen Anne's time our most conspicuous statesmen had been, during the most important part of their lives, members of the House of Lords ; since Queen Anne's

time they have at similar periods been usually members of
the House of Commons.   There are several causes for this, but
the principle is one on which Bolingbroke has often commented.
From time immemorial the Commons have been the guardians
of the public purse ; and whenever the public purse was to be
touched, they have always been the first body in the State.   But
before the revolution they were seldom wanted.   They granted
the king, at the commencement of his reign, an estimated revenue, which was supposed to be adequate to the estimated expenditure in time of peace.   As our wealth was rapidly increasing,
it was often more than sufficient.   In time of war the House of
Commons must be applied to ; new money was needful for new
expenses ; but the ordinary expenditure went on every year
without their being consulted or required.   The expense of
William's wars and Queen Anne's wars made a great change :
taxation became larger than it had ever been, though very small
as it seems to us now.   Since that time the estimated revenue
which the crown yearly enjoyed, without additional parliamentary aid, has scarcely ever been adequate to the estimated
expenditure.   There has yearly been a budget, and yearly a recourse to the House of Commons.   The position of a minister
in the House of Commons has therefore greatly risen.   Nine
years out of ten the nation could at present dispense with a
House of Lords—though a useful it is an auxiliary power ; but
every year we want a House of Commons, for it has to grant
funds of primary necessity.   The minister who can manage the
Commons, and extract from them the necessary moneys, has
then become our most necessary minister.

The change was just beginning ; for Walpole, Bolingbroke's
schoolfellow and parliamentary rival, ruled his generation by
his parliamentary and financial abilities.   But Bolingbroke was
too eager and impetuous to foresee the action of this powerful
but obscure cause.   The tradition had been, that the Peers were
superior to the Commons, and he adhered to this tradition.   He
was angry till he obtained his peerage.

Nor was he satisfied when he did obtain it. He was made a Viscount only, and Harley had been made an Earl. He could not bear to be inferior to him in anything, especially as there was an extinct earldom in his own family. He was vexed, angry, and dissatisfied. Once he went out of town, and would attend to no business for days. He was angry too with the press. The peace of Utrecht was attacked and assailed, and it was his peace. It is true that Bolingbroke should have been able to bear literary comments, even when rather bitter. He was himself through life an unscrupulous writer, using the press without reluctance and without cessation. He was then employing Swift, the most bitter writer of libels, both political and personal, that can be conceived. He lived with Swift in intimacy, and printed his libels. He gave him political information and ideas, and praised him when he used them so as most to hurt his adversaries. He ought to have been able to bear anything, yet he could bear nothing. He prosecuted many more persons than it was usual to prosecute then, and far more than have been prosecuted since. He thought, with a continental wit, that 'a press is free when government newspapers are licentious.' He thought that everything should be said for him, and that nothing should be said against him. The copyists of Alcibiades are commonly irritable, for neither their nature nor their habits teach them forbearance.

But neither Bolingbroke's disunion with his principal colleague, nor the attacks of the press, were his greatest danger. He was in the worst political position which can be imagined. As we have explained, the principal question of the age was a question of dynasty: after the peace with France it was the sole great question; it is in the nature of a topic so absorbing to swallow up every subject of minor interest. There were only two solutions of the problem possible. The law prescribed one, and a sort of superstition prescribed another. The Act of Settlement said that the House of Hanover was to succeed Queen Anne; the doctrine of non-resistance said that the Pretender was to succeed her. The Jacobites adhered to the doctrine of non-resistance. The Whigs adhered to the Act of Parliament. Both these parties had a definite solution of the principal topic of the hour. But between these fluctuated the great mass of the Tory party, who did not like the House of Hanover because it had no hereditary right, who did not like the Pretender because he was a Roman Catholic. This party objected to both possible solutions: they lived in the vague hope that the Pretender might turn Protestant—that some unforeseen circumstance would intervene—that Queen Anne would last their time. For persons in a private station such a state of mind was very possible and very natural. But it was of this very party that Bolingbroke was the spokesman and the leader, and he was a minister. He could not well remain without a distinct policy. Queen Anne, though not old, was often ill. She was suspected to be, and we now know she was, very near her death. He must make a choice.

Yet which king was Bolingbroke to choose? If he chose the House of Hanover, he himself ought not to be minister. This was the Whig candidate, this was the candidate whom his party disliked—at whom they murmured—whom they declined to support. A Tory ministry which should bring in the House of Hanover was like a Derbyite ministry that should propose free-trade or reform of Parliament. It was a ministry which tried to maintain its existence by denying its party tenets. Probably in those times a Tory ministry could not have done what we have seen them do in our own time. Party spirit ran much stronger in Queen Anne's time than in ours. The political contentions of London were like the contests at a borough election now. At three o'clock on the polling day it is very difficult to change your politics and keep your character. So it was in London then. A fierce strife raged. Whig society and Tory society were separated like two hostile camps, and a deserter from one to the other was sure of contemptuous hatred from those he left, and of contemptuous patronage from those

to whom he came.  Bolingbroke could not do even once that
which Mr. Disraeli has done twice.

Bolingbroke's enemies have been very anxious to fix on him
a formed design to bring in the Pretender.  He would doubtless have been very glad to do so, if he could have formed a
coherent scheme.  But he could not.  Oxford was far too
moderate and timid a man to break the law, or to plan to break
it.  He had himself supported the Act of Settlement.  He
knew that the Hanoverian succession, though not popular to
the imagination of any class, was acceptable to the reason of
the most thinking class.  He knew that the aristocracy, the
large towns, and all the cultivated part of the community, were
in favour of it.  He knew that, as the aristocratic classes had the
command of the House of Lords, of the small boroughs, and of
very many counties, as the great towns were of themselves
favourable, the House of Hanover was sure of a majority in
Parliament.  He knew that the general vulgar, and especially
the rural vulgar, who were favourable to the House of Stuart,
though numerically strong, were but weak in parliamentary
representation.  He was probably a party to some covert
intrigues, for intrigue was intrinsically agreeable to him ; but,
in reality, he was too timid to abandon the plain and legal
course for a tortuous and illegal one.  Bolingbroke had, on the
other hand, a constitutional predilection for violent courses,
and no particular objection to an illegal course.  If he could
have turned out Oxford—if he could have carried his party
with him, he would certainly have contrived some scheme for
proclaiming the Pretender at Queen Anne's death.  But even
he was not mad enough to commit himself to a definite plan
before he knew that he should have the power to execute it.
In the meantime 'Tom Harley,' the prime minister's brother,
exactly expressed the position of the ministry.  'We ought,'
he said, 'to be better or worse with Hanover than we are.'
The case, as men saw it then, was simple.  The Queen was
daily approaching the grave.  The ministry in power were

uncertain what to do in the event of her death. They had 'no settled intention' of breaking the law, Bolingbroke tells us; but he does not venture to contend that they had a settled intention of obeying it. They were drifting to a crisis without a plan.

Nor was Bolingbroke comfortable while the Queen lived. She herself did not like him. A smaller person has never been placed by the caprice of fate amid great affairs than the 'good Queen Anne.' She had not, Swift says, 'a sufficient stock of amity' for more than one person at a time; she was always choosing a favourite upon whom to concentrate her affections exclusively. Her comprehension was as limited as her affections. She seriously objected, it is said, to one minister for appearing before her in a tie-wig instead of a full-bottom; and even if this anecdote has been exaggerated by continual narration, it expresses the sort of objections which ruled her mind and determined her conduct. She had a strong objection to all license; decorum was a sort of morality to her, as to most great ladies; she would have been much puzzled to fix where manners ended and where morals began. Bolingbroke was license personified; and therefore she distrusted and disliked him. She did not altogether approve, either, of the peace of Utrecht. She probably did not understand the details, but she evidently understood that it was a 'perplexing matter,' and 'not the sort of thing to which she had been accustomed under Lord Marlborough.' The original strength of the Tory ministry had been in the Queen's predilection for Miss Hill, afterwards Lady Masham; Harley ruled Miss Hill, and Miss Hill ruled the Queen. But the Queen was not quite sure about Miss Hill. One of her tastes was a taste for aristocracy; and she was half ashamed of having taken a great liking to a waiting-maid who had been placed about her. She had an old predilection also for the Duchess of Somerset, by birth the last of the Percies, whose husband was a Whig. Swift was never easy as to the effect of this friendship. He said, the 'Duchess of

Somerset is a proud woman, but I will pull her down;' so he
libelled her, which did not make her more propitious to him or
his masters. There was always a danger that the ex-waiting-
maid, on whom all depended, should be discarded, as the
Duchess of Marlborough had been discarded; that the Duchess
of Somerset might become prime favourite in her stead; that
the policy of the government, and all the persons of our rulers,
should be again changed by the inexplicable caprice of a quiet
old lady.

And Bolingbroke had another difficulty. The distrust of
him was not confined to Queen Anne. It extended through
his party, and was an inevitable result of his peculiar position.
He was an eloquent man without prejudices, speaking the prejudices of men who could not speak. But the speechless client
and the eloquent advocate differ in nature so much that they
can never much like or well understand the other. The Tory
party knew that when Bolingbroke expressed their favourable
conviction, he did not himself believe a word of what he was
saying. And they could not tell what he did believe. And,
being for the most part regular men of middle life from the
agricultural counties, they did not much like to trust as their
leader a young man of loose life about town. After the peace
of Utrecht especially, he could not tell what they would think,
and they could not tell what he would do. They could never
have anticipated his doing anything so mean as that, and he
could never understand what disgrace there was in so obvious a
diplomatic stratagem as breach of faith. In our own time, it is
easy to vex Tories. You have only to ask, 'What is Dizzy's
next move?' Such short words would not have suited our formal ancestors. But many a courteous Whig, doubtless, asked
many a Tory, 'What is to be my Lord Bolingbroke's next
fine stroke of policy?' and the Tory could not have known
what to say. So long as Oxford was at the head of affairs
common men felt that there was still something ordinary about
the government. But if Bolingbroke were to become sole

minister, or chief minister, we should be subjected to the bold schemes of undiluted genius.

In this difficult position Bolingbroke showed great ability. He could not, indeed, remove its irremovable defects. He could not declare for the House of Hanover; and he could not declare for the House of Stuart. He could not remove the dislike which a dull queen, and a dull party, felt for a brilliant man. But what could be done he did. He showed great parliamentary ability, and was ever ready with wonderful eloquence. He pleased his party by a schism bill, agreeable to High Churchmen, and disagreeable to Dissenters. He obtained the favour of the waiting-maid, if he could not obtain that of the Queen, her mistress. Miss Hill (or Lady Masham, as she now was) was a sort of relation of Oxford's; and this had first brought them together. For a long time the union was firm; he gave her much counsel and some money, and she gave him much power. But Oxford had a conscience, or vestiges of a conscience, in the use of public money. He was not ready to give Miss Hill, or Miss Hill's brother, all that they wanted. Swift puts it that he was too careful of the public interest for the corruption of the time; or, as we should put it, he would not bribe without limit against the public interest out of the public treasury. But Bolingbroke had no scruples: he bid higher; he gave Miss Hill and 'Jack Hill' all he could, and promised that they should have more if they would make him first minister and maintain him as such. He himself may tell the result: 'The Earl of Oxford was removed on Tuesday; the Queen died on Sunday. What a world is this, and how our fortune banters us!' Such was the close of three years of intrigue. He had bribed the waiting-maid just when the mistress was no more.

Nor at the moment was this the worst. The Queen's distrust of Bolingbroke had lasted till her death. The white staff —the 'magic wand,' as Bolingbroke calls it, long disused in English politics, but then the symbol of the lord high treasurer and of the prime minister—had been taken from Oxford, but it had not been given to anyone. Bolingbroke could not gain it for himself. It was arranged that the treasury should be put into commission, as it had been in King William's time, and as it always now is. Bolingbroke was to continue secretary of state, and be in fact principal minister; yet he was not to have the indefinite power of the lord treasurer—the mystic power of the white staff. But on her death-bed Queen Anne felt that Bolingbroke could not be trusted even so far. She was dying, and knew that she was dying. She doubtless felt it was her duty to place the administration in the hands of some one who would obey the law on her death. She did not like the family of Hanover; she had the most keen repugnance to the presence of any of them in England during her life. She could not endure to see her successor close at hand, and it probably never struck her as a matter of duty to save the country from a possible convulsion of civil war. She was a very little-minded woman, but at the same time she was a decorous woman, and a well-meaning woman. She would not have planned or dared or wished to break the law which she had passed. As death was coming upon her, she knew that the practical premiership of Bolingbroke would endanger the security of the Act of Settlement. Of all statesmen he was least likely to obey it, and therefore most unfit to be prime minister when it was of critical importance to obey it. Obscurely, perhaps, but effectually, Queen Anne felt this. She gave the white staff to Shrewsbury, and Bolingbroke's three days of premiership were at an end.

Probably Bolingbroke felt the disaster the more that he was obliged to seem to assent to it. Shrewsbury had been acting as confidential adviser to the Queen for some time, to Bolingbroke's dismay. He knew, he said, how he stood with Oxford —that was open war; but how he stood with Shrewsbury, he did not know. As soon as the Queen was despaired of, the privy council was summoned, and by ordinary rule only those summoned should attend; a ministry thus secures a privy council of chosen friends. But at this meeting two Whig dukes, the Duke of Somerset and the Duke of Argyle, attended, though not summoned, and by their influence the council was induced to ask the Queen to make Shrewsbury high treasurer; and Bolingbroke was obliged to assent. Neither in the nation, nor at the court, had he substantial influence or effectual power.

He had in truth no alternative. A frantic bishop, Atterbury, bishop of Rochester, wanted him to proclaim the Pretender. But Bolingbroke, though a hot-headed statesman, had a notion of law and a perception of obvious consequences. He was not a hot-headed divine: he knew that by law George I. must be proclaimed at once; he knew that Shrewsbury, who wielded the white staff, which everyone would obey, would at once proclaim George I. He knew that he could not himself command the obedience of a watchman. All the force of government had at once passed from him, and he acquiesced in the new order of things. He assisted at the proclamation of George I.

The law had indicated the steps which should be taken in case of the Queen's death, and before her successor could be brought over from Germany. A document was produced by the Hanoverian minister, naming Lords Justices, who were to administer the government until the arrival of George I. Of these Lords Justices, Bolingbroke, of course, was not one. They were all sound Whigs, and steady friends to the House of Hanover. As Bolingbroke had for four years been wielding the force of government so as to give pain to them, they immediately began to exercise it so as to give pain to him. They appointed Addison as their secretary; desired all documents to be addressed to him; and, though Bolingbroke was still in high office, and had at the last moment been real prime minister, they kept him waiting at their door with studied circumstances of indignity, which were much remarked on then, and which much tried his philosophy.

It would, however, have been well for Bolingbroke if mere indignities like these had been all which was in store for him, or all which he deserved. When Parliament met, zealous Whigs naturally began to murmur a good deal as to the past. Bolingbroke had ruled them hardly during his reign. His ministry had removed Marlborough from his appointments; his ministry had expelled Walpole from the House of Commons. Walpole would most likely have said that the Whig 'innings' had arrived, and that the actions of their predecessors must be scrutinised. Bolingbroke for a time affected to fear nothing. Oxford went to and fro in London, and Bolingbroke followed his example. All at once he changed his policy. He appeared at the theatre in state, and took pains while there to attract attention; went home, changed his dress, and fled to France.

In truth, he was thoroughly frightened. He declared that 'his blood was,' he understood, 'to have been the cement of a new alliance,' between the moderate Tories and the Whigs. Some have traced this notion to the hints of Marlborough, but it was most likely due as much to Bolingbroke's own conscience. He knew well that the secret negotiations prior to the peace of Utrecht would not bear even fair scrutiny. He knew that they were now to be subjected to hostile scrutiny. Even from impartial judges he could only expect condemnation, and his case would now be tried by his enemies. His life, indeed, was in no danger. Neither the nation, nor the party opposed to him, were inclined to bloodshed; but he felt he was in danger of something. His guilty conscience magnified the possibilities of punishment; to escape them, he did exactly what was worst for his reputation. Though it was as much as pleading guilty, he fled.

He was attainted as a traitor in his absence, and there may be legal doubt as to whether the attainder was deserved. That a minister who advises his sovereign to violate a treaty, and who violates it accordingly, is worthy of severe punishment, will be admitted by everyone ; and that Bolingbroke had done this is beyond question or dispute.   But this offence does not amount to high treason, and the details of an incidental transaction as to the town of Tournay had to be pressed into the service ; and it required much stretching to make these amount even to a constructive treason.   But whatever might be the legal correctness or the incorrectness of the precise punishment inflicted on Bolingbroke is scarcely material now.   He well deserved a bill of 'Pains and Penalties;' and whether he was or was not visited with the very penalty that was most suitable, does not matter much.

On Bolingbroke's arrival in France, he looked about him for awhile.   He was at once solicited by the emissaries of the Pretender, but he deliberated for some time, and it would have been wiser for him to have deliberated longer.   He well knew that, though there was much latent Jacobite sentiment in England, there was no good material for a Jacobite rebellion.   Many squires and rectors and peasants would have been glad to see the legitimate king restored ; but their zeal was not very active ; it belonged to the region of traditional sentiment and vague prejudice rather than to that of practical and vigorous life.   The House of Hanover had the force of the government and the *sense* of the country in its favour.   It was in possession, and Bolingbroke was aware that the Jacobites could not expel it from possession.   He knew all this well, but his passions were too strong for his judgment ; from excitability, restlessness, and rage, he joined the Pretender.   He could not help being busy, and hoped, or half-hoped, to be revenged on his enemies.

He could not, however, long agree with his new associates. The descent from actual office to imaginary office was too sudden ; to many men it was pleasing to be secretary of state to a mock king, but it was very painful to one who had just been secretary to a real queen.   His contempt, too, for the Irish associates of the Pretender was unbounded.   He saw that they were hot-headed and ignorant men—who knew nothing of the country which they hoped to rule—whom that country would not endure for a day. He knew that the Roman Catholics in England were a small and unpopular body, and their aid more dangerous than their enmity. The genuine Jacobites distrusted him also. He said that they were untrustworthy because they were fools, and they said that he was untrustworthy because he was a traitor. This could not last; after a brief interval, he left the Pretender and his court: they began to slander him, and he began to speak much evil of them.

With his secession from the Jacobites Bolingbroke's active career ends. He was afterwards only an aspirant for a career. He was, after several years, permitted to return to England, and to enjoy his estate though he was an attainted traitor; but the attainder was not reversed, and while it was in force he could not take his seat in the House of Lords, or hold any office whatever. He wrote much against Walpole, but he did not turn out Walpole. On one occasion he was much mortified because Pulteney and the practical opponents of Walpole said that the support of his name rather weakened than strengthened them. He gave in a long memorial of suggestions to George I.; but the King said they were 'bagatelles.' He then fancied that he should become minister because of the support of Lady Suffolk, George II.'s mistress; but Lady Suffolk had no influence, and Queen Caroline, who had predominant influence, supported Walpole. He then hoped to be minister under the Prince of Wales, George II.'s son, and wrote a treatise on a 'Patriot King' for that prince's use. But George II. outlived his son; and he was saved the mortification of seeing how little that small prince would have carried out his great ideas. Though he survived Queen Anne more than thirty years, he never after her death attained to a day's power in England. Three years of eager unwise power, and thirty-five of sickly longing and impotent regret—such, or something like it, will ever be in this cold modern world the fate of an Alcibiades.

## SIR GEORGE CORNEWALL LEWIS.

### [1863.]

FEW more curious sights were, not long since, to be seen in London than that of Sir G. C. Lewis at the War Office. What is now a melancholy recollection was, when we used to see it, an odd mixture of amusing anomalies. The accidental and bit-by-bit way in which all minor business is managed in England has drifted our public offices into scattered, strange, and miscellaneous places. It has drifted the war minister into the large drawing-room of an old mansion, which is splendid enough to receive fashionable people, and large enough to receive a hundred people. In this great and gorgeous apartment sat, a few months since, a homely scholar in spectacles, whose face bore traces of sedentary labour, and whose figure was bent into the student-stoop. Such a plain man looked odd enough in such a splendid place. But it was much more odd to think that that man in that place supremely regulated the War Department of England. The place should have been a pacific drawing-room, and the man was a pacific student. He looked like a conveyancer over deeds, like a scholar among treatises, like a jurist making a code; he looked like the last man to preside over martial pomp and military expeditions.

So *unique* a man as Sir George Lewis has, in truth, rarely been lost to this country. Most men, most politicians especially, fall easily into some ready-made classification; belong to one of the recognised groups of ordinary character. Political

¹ *A Dialogue on the Best Form of Government.* By the Right Hon. Sir G. C. Lewis, Bart. M.P. London, 1863.

life has gone on so long that we have ascertained the principal
species of statesmen, and have a fixed name ready for each. But
Sir George Lewis, as all who knew him in the least well will testify, did not belong exactly to any received type. People were
puzzled how to classify a man who wrote on the Astronomy of
the Ancients, the Fables of Babrius, and Roman History *before*
there was history, and who was yet able to fill three difficult
cabinet offices in quick succession. He wrote what most cabinet ministers would think it too much and too hard to read.
No German professor, from the smoke and study of many silent
years, has ever put forth books more bristling with recondite
references, more exact in every technicality of scholarship, more
rich in matured reflection, than Sir George Lewis found time,
mind, and scholarlike curiosity, to write in the very thick of
eager English life. And yet he was never very busy, or never
seemed so. In the extremity of the *Trent* difficulty, when, as
he was inclined to think, a war with America was impending,
when a war minister might be pardoned for having no time for
general reflection, Sir George Lewis found time, at three o'clock
on a busy parliamentary day, to discuss with the writer of these
lines, for some twenty minutes, the comparative certainty, or
rather *un*certainty, of the physical and moral sciences. It was
difficult to know what to make of such a man.

The difficulty was the greater because he made no pretence
to be a marvel of versatile ability. When Lord Brougham was
chancellor, he was always doing—his enemies said for display,
his friends said from a certain overflow of miscellaneous activity
—many out-of-the-way matters. According to one legend, he
even wrote a treatise on hydrostatics for the Society of Useful
Knowledge which was so full of blunders that it could not be
published. Many statesmen have had the vanity of variety.
But if ever there was a plain man, an unpretending man, a man
who in matters of business affected to be *par negotiis neque
supra*, that man was Sir George Lewis. The objection to him
was that he was too prosaic, too anxiously safe, too suspicious

of everything showy. It was not possible for an enemy or for an opponent—for he had no enemies—to hint that Sir George Lewis's miscellaneous books were written from a love of display. They were written from a bent of nature—from the born love of dry truth.

To those, however, who had an opportunity of accurately observing Sir George Lewis there was no difficulty in making him out. He was so simple and natural that he explained himself. His principal qualities were all of a plain and homely species, and though it may not be possible to give a likeness of them, yet a brief description may easily give an idea and an approximation.

The specialty of his mind was a strong simplicity. He took a plain, obvious view of every subject which came before him. Ingenuities, refinements, and specious fallacies might be suggested around him in any number or in any variety, but his mind was complication-proof. He went steadily through each new ambiguity, each new distinction, as it presented itself. He said, in unadorned but apt English, 'The facts are these and these : the new theory concerning them is so and so : it accounts for facts Nos. 1, 2, and 3, but fails to account for facts Nos. 4, 5, and 6.' Of course he was not uniformly right. We shall show that there were some kinds of facts, and some sorts of events, which he was by mental constitution not able wholly to appreciate. But his view of every subject, though it might not be adequate, though it might be limited, was always lucid. His mind was like a registering machine with a patent index. It took in all the data, specified, enumerated them, and then indicated with unmistakable precision what their sum-total of effect precisely was. The index might be wrong, though it pretty generally was right ; but nobody could ever mistake for a moment what it meant and where it was.

Few men ever kept apart, in civil matters, so well what, in medical matters, would be called the diagnosis and the prescription. Most men mix, even to themselves, their view of what is with their suggestion of what should be. You could not have made Sir George Lewis mix the two. His mind on such points was almost a tedious formality. He would say, ' The facts proved are so and so ; from these there are the following probable inferences. If you wish to alter the present circumstances and to produce others, you must do so and so.' When a man came to him with a plan, he asked, ' What is your object ? ' Until he got a plain answer to that, and a proof that the object was good, he never looked at the plan. All this in theory may seem very obvious and very trite. Nothing is so easy as to be sensible on paper. The only true theory of transacting business is a simple matter which has been known for hundreds of years. Any part of that theory in print looks stupid, and not worth saying. Yet in real life, especially in political life, how few great actors are there ! In politics the issues to be determined are for the most part plain and simple ; but they are exciting, are embedded in rhetoric, and overlaid with irrelevant matter. A certain strong simplicity sweeps away all these outside matters. Talking to Sir George Lewis on a pending political matter was like reading a chapter of Aristotle's Politics—you might think the view incomplete, but there were the same pregnant strength and matter-of-fact simplicity.

One great advantage of this sort of mind Sir George Lewis noted in an article in the ' Edinburgh Review,' which, though when published anonymous, may now be quoted as his : ' When Demosthenes was asked what was the first and second and third qualification of an orator, he answered, " Delivery ; " in like manner, if we were asked what is the first and second and third qualification of an English statesman, we would answer, " Intelligibility." As in oratory the most eloquent words and the wisest counsels will avail but little if they are not impressed by voice and manner upon the minds of an audience : so integrity and public spirit will fail to command confidence, if the course

adopted is intricate or inextricable.' Sir George Lewis could
not have described his own sort of mind better if he had been
trying to do so; he *could* not be intricate or perplexed. On
those rare occasions in politics when it is useful to be ambiguous he failed. When he was Home Secretary he could not
diffuse that useful mist over delicate difficulties which was now
and then desirable, and in which Sir George Grey has succeeded.
An unbroken fluency in indefinite half-truths was simply impossible to Sir George Lewis. He could not be said to fail in
it, for he did not attempt it. His mind was unsuited to
ambiguity, whether artful or natural. But on those all but
universal occasions when only a plain intelligible statement of
an important proposition was required, his solid vigour was
appropriate. He could never have appealed to the people by
the felicitous attraction of his words, but he had an even surer
source of popularity in the certain intelligibility of his plans.

The last words of his last book show the sort of grave moderation with which he regarded politics, as wise as any of which
he ever made use. They are the judgment in which the reflec-
tive man of the world sums up the arguments of the advocates
of different forms of government.

Each one of you, in to-day's discussion, has been able to show
specious, perhaps strong, grounds in favour of his opinion. Monar-
chicus can say with truth that the testimony of experience is in his
favour; that the vast majority of nations, now and at all former
periods of time, have been governed by monarchs; and that a plural
or republican government is an intricate machine, difficult to work,
and constantly tending to relapse into monarchy. Aristocraticus
can argue that aristocracy is the government of intelligence and
virtue; and that it is a just medium between the two extremes of
monarchy and democracy; while Democraticus can dwell upon the
splendid vision of a community bound together by the ties of frater-
nity, liberty, and equality, exempt from hereditary privilege, giving
all things to merit, and presided over by a government in which all the
national interests are faithfully represented. But even if I were to
decide in favour of one of these forms, and against the two others, I
should not find myself nearer the solution of the practical problem.

A nation does not change the form of its government with the same
facility that a man changes his coat. A nation in general only
changes the form of its government by means of a violent revolution.
This is not a moment when reason is in the ascendent, and when the
claims of force can be safely disregarded. The party which is upper-
most in the revolution dictates the form of government, and pays
little attention to abstract theories, unless it be those which coincide
with its own views. The past history of a nation, its present interests,
its present passions and antipathies, the advice of favourite leaders,
the intervention of foreign governments, all exercise a powerful influence at such a crisis in determining the national decision. Such is
the rude process by which one form of government is actually converted into another; very unlike the gentle and rational method
which is assumed by the constructors of Utopias. Besides, the
political preferences of a people are in general determined by habit
and mental association; and though the newly introduced constitution may be intrinsically better than its predecessor, yet the
people may dislike it, and refuse it the benefit of a fair trial. It
may therefore fail, not from its own defectiveness, but through the
ill-will and reluctance of those by whom it is worked.

There are some rare cases in which a nation has profited by a
revolution. Such was the English revolution of 1688, in which the
form of the government underwent no alteration, and the person of
the king was alone changed. It was the very minimum of a revolution; it was remarkable for the absence of those accompaniments
which make a revolution perilous, and which subsequently draw
upon it a vindictive reactionary movement. The late Italian revolution has likewise been successful; by it the Italian people have
gained a better government, and have improved their political condition. It was brought about by foreign intervention; but its success
has been mainly owing to the moderation of the leaders in whom the
people had the wisdom to confide, and who have steadily refrained
from all revolutionary excesses.

The history of forcible attempts to improve governments is not,
however, cheering. Looking back upon the course of revolutionary
movements, and upon the character of their consequences, the practical
conclusion which I draw is, that it is the part of wisdom and prudence
to acquiesce in any form of government which is tolerably well
administered, and affords tolerable security to person and property.
I would not, indeed, yield to apathetic despair, or acquiesce in the
persuasion that a merely tolerable government is incapable of im-

provement. I would form an individual model, suited to the character, disposition, wants, and circumstances of the country, and I would make all exertions, whether by action or by writing, within the limits of the existing law, for ameliorating its existing condition, and bringing it nearer to the model selected for imitation; but I should consider the problem of the best form of government as purely ideal, and as unconnected with practice; and should abstain from taking a ticket in the lottery of revolution, unless there was a well-founded expectation that it would come out a prize.

This sober simplicity is not to the taste of many people. Many wish to find in politics a sort of excitement. They wish that public affairs should be managed in a rather theatrical way, in order that they themselves may have the pleasure of reading a stimulating series of brilliant events. People who went to Sir George Lewis for excitement were very likely to be disappointed. He was sure to knock the gloss off things. 'People,' he would observe, 'who know how things are managed, know that the oftener cabinets meet the better. Ignorant persons fancy that when cabinets meet often there is something wrong; but that is a mistake. It is in the long vacation and in the country that some ministers do something brilliant and extraordinary that is much objected to. When ministers get together, they can agree on something plain and satisfactory.' He always talked of the cabinet as if it were a homely sort of committee.

At bottom, perhaps, he did not much object to be thought a little commonplace. 'In *my* opinion,' he said (and perhaps there is no harm in adding that it was in reference to the Suez canal), 'in nine cases out of ten, cure is better than prevention. If it be ever necessary to hold Egypt, then fight for Egypt. By looking forward to all possible evils, we waste the strength that had best be concentrated in curing the *one* evil which happens.' Those who wish that the foreign affairs of England should be managed according to a far-seeing and elaborate policy will not like such voluntary shortsightedness; but the

English people themselves rather like to have the national course fixed by evident, palpable, and temporary circumstances.

Some people thought Sir George Lewis obstinate, and in one sense he was so. No one was a better colleague ; no one, after full discussion, was readier to take a share in the responsibility for measures of which he did not entirely approve the whole. But though he gave up his proposals, he did not alter his opinion. It may be said of him that he could not alter it. Most men's conclusions are framed upon fluctuating considerations, some of which are very indistinctly present to their minds, and most of which it would puzzle them to state shortly. Sir George Lewis knew exactly what were the facts upon which he grounded his opinion, and what his inference from those facts. Unless you gave him new facts, he could not help drawing the same inference. This was one of the comforts of dealing with him. You always knew exactly where you would find his mind. Unless the data had altered, you might be sure his inference from the data would be unchanged.

It may be added that his inference was almost sure to be exactly sound. His *data* might be limited. As we shall show, there were some kinds of facts which, from a limitation of nature, he did not thoroughly appreciate. When such facts were in question, his conclusion was likely enough to be wrong; for he was arguing rightly on incomplete premisses. But no one could gainsay the correctness of his inference from what he did see. He was the soundest judge of probability we have ever known. The facts being admitted to be so and so, what will be the consequence of those facts ? Upon this question few judgments, if any, in England were better than that of Sir George Lewis.

It is this judgment of probability which makes the man of business. The data of life are accessible ; their inference uncertain : a sound judgment on these data is the secret of success to him who possesses it, and the reason why others trust him. It is this that men call a *sound* understanding ; it is this that

Napoleon had in mind when he said that a man should be *carré à la base.*

To this straightforward simplicity of understanding, Sir George Lewis added the most complete education perhaps of any man of his time. He did not believe in what has been called *speciality* ; at least he confined it to the lower grades of practical life and literary labour. He has observed : ' The permanent officers of a department are the depositories of the official traditions, they are generally referred to by the political head of the office for information upon questions of official practice ; and knowledge of this sort acquired in one department would be useless in another. If, for example, the chief clerk of the criminal department of the Home Office were to be transferred to the Foreign Office or to the Admiralty, the special experience which he has acquired in the Home Office, and which is in daily and hourly requisition for the assistance of the Home Secretary, would be utterly valueless to the Foreign Secretary or to the First Lord of the Admiralty. . . . . The same person may be successively at the head of the Home Office, the Foreign Office, the Colonial Office, and the Admiralty ; he may be successively President of the Board of Trade and Chancellor of the Exchequer ; but to transfer an experienced clerk from one office to another would in general be like transferring a skilful naval officer to the army, or appointing a military engineer officer to command a ship of war. A similar distinction may be observed in other branches of practical life ; thus an architect may direct the execution of different classes of buildings ; he may give plans for palaces, churches, courts of justice, bridges, private dwellings ; but the subordinate workmen whom he employs retain their separate functions unchanged—a carpenter does not become a mason, a painter or glazier does not become an ironmonger or plasterer.'

He sincerely believed (and perhaps acted to excess on the belief) that a well-educated man was competent to undertake any office and to write on any subject. He would have acknow-

ledged the truth of the saying, that the end of education was
to make a good *learner*. He was at the day of his death
perhaps the best learner in England; there was no sort of
definite information, whether relating to public business or to
books, which he did not know how to acquire and where to find.
Some public men may know where to find as much political
information; some scholars may know where to find as much
learned information; but what other man knows so precisely
the best sources of both kinds of knowledge?

He had a nearly perfect mastery over the keys of knowledge. He derived from Eton and Oxford a perfect knowledge
of the classical languages, and he extended it to the day of his
death. An article published in 'Notes and Queries' within a
week or two of that time showed that he had read Mr. Freeman's
history—a rather formidable work, relating to the Ætolian and
other Greek leagues, which was only then just published,
and which is as much as many busy men read in ten years.
Many English statesmen have been good classical scholars,
and it is happily not difficult for those who have once well
learned the languages of antiquity to retain a familiarity with
its masterpieces. The very business of life, indeed, adds to
these masterpieces an additional charm, for it reveals touches
of discerning thought, and traits of external human knowledge, which the writers learned from experience, and which
no one can appreciate without it. Mr. Pitt, Mr. Canning,
Lord Grenville, the Marquis Wellesley, and many others of
our conspicuous statesmen, have had this sort of scholarship.
The knowledge of the Classics was to them an intellectual
luxury. But Sir George Lewis had a far more laborious
scholarship than this. He had read and knew, not only the
classical writers themselves, but also terrific German treatises,
in many volumes and upon the worst paper, *about* the
Classics, which no intellectual voluptuary would touch or
look at.

In addition to his Eton and Oxford scholarship, Sir George

Lewis was excellently well acquainted with modern languages, and had a fair knowledge of mathematics. But a mere enumeration of this kind does not in the least give a notion of the sort of knowledge he had—a phrase, not of the purest English, alone expresses it : it was a knowledge which 'turned up' everywhere. Hardly a subject could be started on which he could not throw an unexpected light, and to which he could not add some new fact. The sort of way in which this happened is aptly enough illustrated by Lord Stanhope's 'Miscellanies,' published last year : 'Mr. Windham,' writes Lord Stanhope, 'in his speech of December 9, 1803, observes of the Martello towers that they were so called from a place of that name in Corsica; and I have quoted that sentence from him in my "Life of Pitt." Since my own publication, however, there has been suggested to me, by a very high authority upon all such subjects, a derivation far more probable than Mr. Windham's, and certainly, as I conceive, the right one.                                    S.

*Right Hon. Sir George C. Lewis to Earl Stanhope.*

[Extract]                                    April 2, 1862.

The origin of Martello towers I believe to have been that when piracy was common in the Mediterranean, and pirates like the Danes made plundering descents upon the coasts, the Italians built towers near the sea in order to keep watch and give warning if a pirate ship was seen to approach the land. This warning was given by striking on a bell with a hammer; and hence these towers were called *Torri da Martello.*

*The same to the same.*

May 7, 1862.

I think that I have discovered, with the assistance of a friend, the origin of Windham's statement respecting Martello towers. An attack was made on the tower of Mortella, in Corsica, by the British forces both by sea and land, in February 1794. The tower was taken after an obstinate defence, but the two attacking ships were beaten off. The circumstance is likely to have given rise to the confusion between Martello towers generally and this tower of Mortella.'

And Lord Stanhope adds some additional facts showing that the derivation suggested by Sir George C. Lewis was correct. Again, in p. 40, Lord Stanhope gives an extract from a letter of Sir George Lewis:—

'Lord Grenville told my father that Pitt had formed a plan for abolishing all Customs Duties, and that he would have carried it into effect, if the war of the French Revolution had not broken out, which defeated all his financial and commercial schemes. Lord Grenville said that the amount of the public expenditure at that time rendered such a plan quite feasible.'

These are two instances casually occurring in one little volume. But anyone who knew Sir George Lewis would know that miscellaneous odd facts of this sort were accumulated in his memory, to what seemed an infinite number, and were at once brought out when they could be useful in illustrating anything.

As a writer this great knowledge, especially when connected with the strong love of bare truth which led him to acquire that knowledge, was not advantageous to him. He gave a mistaken credit to his readers; he fancied they loved fact and truth as much as he did. 'Woe to the writer,' goes a wise saying, 'that exhausts his subject; his readers are exhausted first.' Sir George Lewis always exhausted his subject if he could, and you could not have persuaded him not to do so. In proposing the dowry of the Princess Royal he amused the House of Commons by an elaborate reference, not only to the dowry of George III.'s daughters, who seemed quite far enough back for an impatient audience that wanted its dinner, but also to a perfectly forgotten Princess Royal who was George III.'s aunt. Most of his books are too full of citations and explanations; and to the last he would have been more read and more influential if he had thought often of Sidney Smith's precept, 'Now, remember Noah, and be *quick.*'

But though a tendency to overlay a subject with superfluous erudition was one of Sir George Lewis's defects, the

possession of that available erudition was one of his greatest
powers.   In the present day, the usefulness of a public man is
largely measured by the number of subjects which he can get
up—Sir George Lewis could get up any subject.   There was
no probable topic on which he could not form, from the very
best sources, with ease and pleasure, a clear, determinate, and
exact opinion.   His memory helped him.   It has been compared to Macaulay's—not that it was equal to such marvellous
displays, but that it contained as much, or nearly as much,
miscellaneous knowledge.   And there was this peculiarity in
it.   Macaulay's memory, like Niebuhr's, undoubtedly confounded not unfrequently inference and fact: it exaggerated;
it gave, not what was in the book, but what a vivid imagination inferred from the book.   Sir George Lewis had none of
this defect: his memory was a dry memory, just as his mind
was a dry light; if he said a thing was at page 10, you might
be sure it was at page 10.   Somebody called him a 'sagacious
dictionary,' and there was felicity in the expression.

Apart from this massive simplicity of understanding, and
this immense accumulation of exact knowledge, there was nothing *very* remarkable in Sir George Lewis.   It would be the
greatest injustice to his memory, and be the very last thing
which he would have desired, to mar the picturesque outlines
of his character by concealing its limitations.   He had, as we
explained, some great qualities in an extraordinary measure,
but in other respects he was no more than an ordinary man,
and in some he was even less than one.

There was a want of brisk enthusiasm about him, both in
appearance and in reality.   He looked like a scholar, a thinker,
and a man of business; he did not look like—he was not—a
buoyant ruler or a popular orator.   He was quite conscious of
this himself, and would sometimes allude to it.   The late Mr.
Wilson—a very vivacious and active man—who was Secretary
of the Treasury when Sir George Lewis was Chancellor of the
Exchequer, used to relate, that when he once was urging some-

thing rather strongly, Sir George answered: ' No ; I can't do
it.  The fact is, Wilson, you are an animal, and I am a vege-
table.'  Taken literally, this would have been a satire on himself, but it indicated his main defect.  He had always, or nearly
always, sufficient judgment for a great statesman, but he had
not always sufficient impulse.

He was *puzzled* about the passions of mankind ; he had so
little passion himself that it seemed to him an unknown force
which might take men to a distance which it was impossible to
foresee, and in a direction that could not be calculated.  ' When,'
we have heard him say, ' you know a man will act for his own
interest, you know how to deal with him ; but if he is likely to
be guided by feeling, it is impossible to predict his course.'
Such extreme calmness of mind is not favourable to a statesman ; it is good to be without vices, but it is not good to be
without temptations.  It would always have been a difficulty
to Sir George Lewis, that he did not share the impetuous part
of human nature, whether for good or evil.  He was ever liable
to impute to a settled design and intellectual self-interest what
was in fact owing to an impulse of philanthropy or a gust of
mere passion.  He was apt to be thought cynical in opinion,
though good-natured in manner and action—and in some sense
he was so.  He took too external a view of human nature,
and ascribed to consistent selfishness what was really produced by mixed motives and a close combination of good and
evil.

He was so defective in the more conspicuous sorts of imagination, that he was often thought to have no imagination.
But this was an error.  He could conceive well the working of
a polity, the operation of a scheme, the details of a plan.  His
criticism on the working, say of the American constitution,
would show great power of conceiving distant causes, and of
predicting and analysing strange effects.  He had the business
imagination.  But he had no other.  He could not imagine
great passions, or overwhelming desires, or involved character ;

he knew that there were such things, but he had no image of
them in his mind and no picture. He was like a man on the
edge of a volcano, who dreaded an eruption, but had no vision
of the flames. He was thus apt to be out of sympathy with,
and even to be impatient of, some elements in ordinary men's
judgment. He was a little too critical of public opinion, too
critical, that is, for a parliamentary statesman, for one who
should try to sympathise with the master whom he must obey.
Sir George Lewis hated exaggeration as much as he could hate
anything—and popular opinion is always exaggerated. 'There
is,' said Sir Stafford Northcote, 'no quality for which Sir George
Lewis is more remarkable than for a quiet courage, which
emboldens him to give utterance from time to time, and sometimes without any apparent necessity for his doing so, to propositions of the most alarmingly unpopular nature.' And such
courage is admirable. In this day it is much to have a statesman who, on any occasion and for any object, will withstand
public opinion. But such opposition should be reserved for
great occasions, and too much must not be expected from the
mass of men. A vague tendency and loose approximation to
what is right is all we can hope for from miscellaneous popular
opinion ; and it is not wise in a statesman to criticise too
nicely, or to attempt to give to the rough practical judgment
of men a fine accuracy which it can never in fact possess. Sir
George Lewis was the antithesis of a demagogue ; he could not
take a test without a qualification ; he was sure to distrust, and
apt to despise, a popular dogma.

A slight survey—and we have only space or powers for a
very slight one—will show that these qualities were as conspicuous in Sir George Lewis's writings as in his political career.
Indeed, if there ever was a man whose mind was always and
everywhere one and the same, Sir George was that man. He
had not really a versatile mind, though his pursuits were varied.
He was far too modest and wise to aim at what was impossible
to him, and nature had given him sharp limitations. It was

said by the 'Times' of Lord Brougham, 'that he might have been any *one* of ten first-rate kinds of men, but that he had tried to be *all* ten, and had failed.' Sir George Lewis had none of this flexibility, and none of this vanity. He never tried to be a great poet or a great orator, or to be anything else but what nature made him—a shrewd and solid thinker. He had a great faculty of research, but his matter is everywhere of the same sort. It is the same imperturbable homely sense upon finance in his Budgets, upon the Egyptology of Baron Bunsen in his Ancient Astronomy.

Sir George Lewis's principal writings may be divided into two classes, the historical and the speculative; and it is hardly too much to say that the whole of the historical are developments in many forms of one central idea. He always devotes himself to the refutation of an hypothesis: some previous writer has elaborated a theory which, Sir George Lewis maintains, rests on no basis of evidence, and which he wishes to dispel. Some one has seen a *mirage*, and related it as a fact; Sir George Lewis wishes to dispel the *mirage*.

His earliest work of this sort was the 'Origin and Formation of the Romance Language.' M. Raynouard, a distinguished French scholar, had expounded a very curious and remarkable theory as to the breaking-up of the Latin language. It is certain that good Latin was once spoken at Rome; it is certain that the Romans conquered the rest of Italy, France, and Spain; it is certain that in each of these countries a modern language, analogous to the Latin, and derived from the Latin, is now spoken. How, then, did the Latin break up? How, then, were the new languages formed? M. Raynouard maintained that they were formed by means of an intermediate language. He held that the Romance language, which was purely spoken in the times of the Troubadours, and which is still corruptly spoken in Provence, was a language once used in the same form all over Europe; that it was the same tongue in France, in Portugal, in Italy, and in Spain; and that as a person who

spoke Latin would have been universally intelligible at one
time, so a person who spoke Romance would have been universally understood at a subsequent time.   This idea of a single
diffused Middle Age language Sir George Lewis undertakes to
dispel ; he thinks it a dream and a theory.   He says that the
Latin broke up under different circumstances, with different
velocities, and in different modifications, in the different states
of Europe.   There was a certain general resemblance, he holds,
in the changes which were in progress, whether in Italy or
Spain, France or Portugal, because those changes in all these
countries were produced by the same causes.   The invasion of
the barbarians, the fall of the Roman Empire, and the somewhat mysterious movement which tends to break up the old
rhetorical and synthetic languages, and replace them by analytic
and conversational languages, were common causes, operating
alike in all countries where Latin had been spoken.   But
though the change in all the languages was in the same general
direction, it was not at the same rate, nor was it identical in
details.   There has, according to Sir G. Lewis, never been a
single vernacular language spoken through Europe since Latin
was so spoken.   The theory of Raynouard is, according to Sir
George Lewis's characteristic language, an 'unsupported and
imaginary hypothesis.'

This essay on the Romance language was republished by Sir
George within a few months of his death, and is worth reading
as an illustration of his mode of thought and argument.   The
burden of proof is upon Raynouard.   He says there was a common language at a certain date ; where, then, is that language ?
what were its parts of speech, its verbs, its pronouns, and its
substantives ?   Let us look at them in the different countries
of Europe at the time in question, and prove that the language
was uniform by the identity of its forms.   Accordingly, Sir
George Lewis goes through the earliest known forms of the
Italian, Spanish, Provençal, and French languages, and he
shows that at the earliest stage they were *not* identical.   He

characteristically says, ' The importance and interest of the philological problem which is treated in the following pages are much increased by the fact that it lies entirely within the historical period ; and that not only the original and the derivative languages, but also the circumstances attending the transition, are known by authentic evidence and by an unbroken tradition. It is therefore a problem which admits of solution by demonstrative arguments, and without recourse to a series of hypotheses and conjectures, weakening as the chain lengthens.' Sir George Lewis revels, we may almost say, in the plentifulness of the evidence.   He has lists of the ' tenses and inflexions of Romance nouns,' ' new Romance nouns formed by affixes,' of the degrees of comparison, pronouns, and numerals, in the Romance language, with endless similar information.   He elaborately compares the earliest stages of the Italian, Spanish, and French languages with the earliest form of the Provençal ; and he shows clearly and fully, what was probable enough in itself, that the earliest forms of these languages differ ; that they have pursued a different history ; that the Provençal is only one of the derived languages, with a history of its own ; that there never was any one derived language generally diffused through Europe ; that as soon as the use of Latin ended, distinctions of speech began.   A very close political observer, who did not himself easily relinquish anything, once described Sir George Lewis as the most pertinacious man he had ever known : ' He returns,' it was added, ' to the charge again and again, and he hardly ever fails.'   This was said by one who seldom read anything, who had read very little of Sir George Lewis's writing, who assuredly had never opened the treatise on the Romance languages.   But if he had studied the treatise, he could not have described it better.   Sir George returns again and again, with verbs and pronouns, to the charge, and he hardly ever fails.   A student who continued to believe Raynouard's theory must be impervious to argument and detail-proof.

The largest of all Sir George Lewis's writings, and his

acutest, strikes with the same tactics at a nobler game upon a larger field. The reception of Niebuhr's ' History of Rome ' is one of the most curious of recent literary phenomena. Though he really is a bold theorist on Roman history, though his narrative is by admission constructed by the imagination, he has obtained something like the credit due to an almost contemporary authority—to a person who had some special information. He believed he had acquired, by long study and brooding, a special faculty, a peculiar divination. He tells us :

' All my faculties were directed to a single object for sixteen months, without any intermission except now and then for a few days. My sight grew dim in its passionate efforts to pierce into the obscurity of the subject, and unless I was to send forth an incomplete work, which sooner or later would have had to be wholly remodelled, I was compelled to wait for what Time might gradually bring forth. Nor has he been niggardly, but, though slowly, has granted me one discovery after another. . . . The true account, it must be owned, is not always the most probable. But when an inquirer, after gazing for years with ever renewed undeviating steadfastness, sees the history of mistaken, misrepresented, and forgotten events rise out of mists and darkness, and assume substance and shape, as the scarcely visible aerial form of the nymph in the Sclavonic tale takes the body of an earthly maiden beneath the yearning gaze of love—when by unwearied and conscientious examination he is continually gaining a clearer insight into the connexion of all its parts, and discerns that immediate expression of reality which emanates from life—he has a right to demand that others, who merely throw their looks by the way on the region where he lives and has taken up his home, should not deny the correctness of his views, because they perceive nothing of the kind. The learned naturalist, who has never left his native town, will not recognise the animal's track, by which the hunter is guided : and if any one, on going into Benvenuto's prison, when his eyes had for months been accustomed to see the objects around him, had asserted that Benvenuto like himself could not distinguish anything in the darkness, he would surely have been somewhat presumptuous.'

It is beautiful to see the heavy care and sluggish diligence with which Sir George Lewis reckons all this poetry back into mere prose.

' The history of Niebuhr (he tells us) ' has thus opened more questions than it has closed, and it has set in motion a large body of combatants, whose mutual variances are not at present likely to be settled by deference to a common authority, or by the recognition of any common principle.

' The main cause of the great multiplicity and wide divergence of opinions, which characterise the recent researches into early Roman history, is the defective method, which not only Niebuhr and his followers, but most of his opponents, have adopted. Instead of employing those tests of credibility which are consistently applied to modern history, they attempt to guide their judgment by the indications of internal evidence, and assume that the truth can be discovered by an occult faculty of historical divination. Hence, the task which they have undertaken resembles an inquiry into the internal structure of the earth, or into the question, whether the stars are inhabited. It is an attempt to solve a problem, for the solution of which no sufficient data exist.

' The consequence is, that ingenuity and labour can produce nothing but hypotheses and conjectures, which may be supported by analogies, and may sometimes appear specious and attractive, but can never rest on the solid foundation of proof. There will, therefore, be a series of such conjectural histories ; each successive writer will reject all or some of the guesses of his predecessors, and will propose some new hypotheses of his own. But the treatment of early Roman history, though it will be constantly moving, will not advance ; it will not be stationary, but neither will it be progressive; it will be unfixed and changeable, but without receiving any improvement ; and it will perpetually revolve in the same hopeless circle. Like the search after the philosopher's stone, or the elixir of life, it will be constantly varying its aspect, under the treatment of different professors of the futile science ; but truth and certainty, the aim of all rational employment of the intellect, will always be equally distant. Each new system of the early Roman constitution will be only (to use Paley's words) one guess among many ; whereas he alone discovers who proves. There is indeed no doubt that long habit, combined with a happy talent, may enable a person to discern the truth where it is invisible to ordinary minds, possessing no peculiar advantages. This may be observed, not only in historical researches, but in every other department of knowledge. In order, however, that the truth so perceived should recommend itself to the convictions of others, it is a necessary condition that it should admit of proof which they can understand. Newton might have perceived, by a rapid and intuitive sagacity, the connexion between the fall of an apple and the attraction of the earth to the sun; but unless he could have demonstrated that connexion by arguments which were intelligible and satisfactory to the scientific world, his discovery would have been useless, except as a mere suggestion. In like manner, we may rejoice that the ingenuity and learning of Niebuhr should have enabled him to advance many novel hypotheses and conjectures respecting events in the early history, and respecting the form of the early constitution, of Rome. But unless he can support those hypotheses by sufficient evidence, they are not entitled to our belief. It is not enough for a historian to claim the possession of a retrospective second-sight, which is denied to the rest of the world; of a mysterious doctrine, revealed only to the initiated. Unless he can prove as well as guess; unless he can produce evidence of the fact, after he has intuitively perceived its existence, his historical system cannot be received. The oases of truth which he discerns amidst the trackless expanses of fiction and legend, may be real; but until their existence can be verified by positive testimony, we have no certainty that these "green spots in memory's waste" may not be mere mirage and optical delusion. It is an excellence in a historian of antiquity, who has sufficient data to proceed upon, that he should form a vivid conception of the events described; that he should live as it were among the persons whose acts he recounts; and that he should carry his reader back into the bygone times in which his drama is placed. On the other hand, it is a fault in the modern writers who first narrated Roman history that they should have related the events as if they had never happened. But when there is a want of solid evidence, we do not render the history true by treating the events as if they were real.'

Almost the whole of Sir George Lewis's two volumes are an expansion and development of this passage. He turns Niebuhr's revelations into fancies, and his divinations into mere guesses. Since Sir George Lewis's work on Roman history, no English scholar at least has ventured to defend Niebuhr's essentially arbitrary treatment of legendary history. A historian, it is now agreed, cannot accept one legend because it suits a preconceived hypothesis, and reject another because it is inconsistent with that hypothesis. He must take both or must reject both. We may not, and perhaps have not, attained to a complete and accepted theory of the value of traditional evidence ; there are many points on that subject which require much more delicate handling than they have received. But no one will ever revive Niebuhr's notion of an occult tact. A long acquaintance and a familiar meditation upon any sort of *truth*, does indeed give an instinctive sense with respect to that truth. A constant habit of comparing accurate truth with legendary versions of the same truth, would really give a student a verified knowledge, and even a quick instinctive idea to what sort of inventions popular tradition is prone. But Niebuhr had studied legends as to times of which there are only legends ; he had not compared truth with fiction, but fiction with fiction. He had not acquired a test of truth by a contact with truth ; but his hot brain had brooded so long on a favourite subject that he mistook its own fancies for realities. Sir George Lewis did not mistake them.

It is sometimes said that Sir George Lewis would accept no fact of which there was not contemporary evidence, and that he set no value whatever upon any tradition in any case. But this is a mischievous exaggeration. Sir George Lewis was not the most exacting of historical critics. He considered Polybius as too strict and sceptical. Polybius thought that a historian without books, and with only oral information, could not be sure of events more than twenty years before his own birth. Sir George Lewis held that a sort of memory of leading events, accurate in substance though probably inaccurate in detail, might be preserved by tradition for about a hundred years, and that special events from special circumstances might be remembered longer ; but that, in such cases, it was only the general outline which could be faintly traced, and only events of interest that would be preserved. After about a hundred years—after the period about which a man could hear from his grandfather—he thought, for the most part, there was no reliable knowledge.

Sir George Lewis's Ancient Astronomy might seem a deviation from his general studies. Astronomy is a physical science,

and Sir George, though well enough acquainted with such
sciences, did not profess to have made them a special study.
He was often enough heard to say, half in jest but still with a
certain meaning, ' On matters of practical interest the physical
sciences are less certain than the moral : as long as you are
dealing with abstractions, with perfectly elastic beams and a
world without fiction, physical science is quite certain ; but as
soon as you introduce the actual conditions of life, and talk of
the real world in which we live, most physical sciences become
as uncertain as any moral science.   Take, for example, physic.
If you will question your medical man, you will find that, if he
cures you, it will not be by the goodness of his *arguments*.   A
great deal of what is set down upon that subject in grave treatises appears to me to be inconsistent rubbish.   And my experience at the War Office shows me that scientific evidence
may be accumulated in almost any quantity for any given invention and against any given invention.'   A man who talked in
this spirit was scarcely likely to devote many hours out of the
scanty leisure of English public life to the history of physical
science.   Nor was Sir George Lewis attracted to the subject by
its abstract scientific interest.   He is at great pains to explain
that he makes no pretension to such abstract mathematical
knowledge as was possessed by Delambre and others, his predecessors, and that astronomy is conversant with obvious realities
which have always excited human curiosity.   In truth, he
encountered ancient astronomy in his investigations of ancient
history.   He found many pretensions to ancient scientific
knowledge which it was much in his way to scrutinise and dis-
believe ; he was in all his inquiries compelled to deal with
ancient chronology, which is not to be understood except with
reference to the astronomical notions of those who framed it.
Such questions as, ' Was there a Roman year of ten months ? '
met him at every step.   He was thus led to write a clear, com-
pendious, ard popular account of the rise of astronomical science
in ancient Greece.   It is not exhaustive, as most of his treatises

are exhaustive ; it is not, like his other treatises, supported by an available accumulation of all appropriate knowledge, for he was in some places cramped by the deficiency of his mathematics. It is not, therefore, one of the works on which his fame as a great scholar will hereafter rest. But it is a very clear, sensible, and interesting account of the interesting subject to which it relates.

Bound up with the history of Ancient Astronomy, and having but a very slender relation to it, are three essays: one on the Early History and Chronology of the Egyptians ; another on the Early History and Chronology of the Assyrians; and a third on the Navigation of the Phœnicians. Here Sir George Lewis is all himself, dealing with the subjects which he liked best, and dealing with them as he liked best. Anybody who wishes to know the sort of mind he had may read—and it is not unamusing reading—his criticism on the Egyptian history of Baron Bunsen. At the risk of tediousness we will condense a little of it :—

'The principal manipulator' (says Sir George Lewis) 'of the ancient Egyptian chronology is Baron Bunsen, who, in his recent work on Egypt, has avowedly applied the method of Niebuhr to Egyptian antiquity. Now the method with which Niebuhr treated the early history of Rome, was to reject the historical narrative handed down by ancient, and generally received by modern writers ; and to substitute for it a new narrative reconstructed on an arbitrary hypothetical basis of his own. Everything that is original and peculiar in Niebuhr's historical method, and in its results, is indeed unsound. But it possessed advantages, when employed in the transmutation of Roman antiquity, which are wanting to it when applied to Egyptian antiquity. The early Roman history, whatever may be its authenticity, presents at least a full and continuous narrative, most parts of which are related in discordant versions by different classical writers. As not one of these versions rests on an ascertained foundation, or can be traced to coeval attestation, great facility is afforded for ingenious conjecture, for bold and startling combinations, for hypothetical reconstruction by means of specious analogies, and for the display of imposing paradox and dazzling erudition. But the so-called history of ancient Egypt consists of little more than chronology. It is, for the most part, merely a string of royal names.  Now this is a most unattractive field for the hypothetical historian; he is condemned to make bricks without straw.  Instead of demolishing and rebuilding constitutions, instead of creating new states of society out of obscure fragments of lost writers, he is reduced to a mere arithmetical process.  Accordingly, the operations of Bunsen and other modern critics upon the ancient history of Egypt rather resemble the manipulation of the balance-sheet of an insolvent company by a dexterous accountant (who, by transfers of capital to income, by the suppression or transposition of items, and by the alteration of bad into good debts, can convert a deficiency into a surplus), than the conjectures of a speculative historian who undertakes to transmute legend into history.

'Egyptology has a historical method of its own.  It recognises none of the ordinary rules of evidence; the extent of its demands upon our credulity is almost unbounded.  Even the writers on ancient Italian ethnology are modest and tame in their hypotheses, compared with the Egyptologists.  Under their potent logic all identity disappears; everything is subject to become anything but itself.  Successive dynasties become contemporary dynasties; one king becomes another king, or several other kings, or a fraction of another king; one name becomes another name; one number becomes another number; one place becomes another place.

'In order to support and illustrate these remarks, it would be necessary to analyse Bunsen's reconstruction of the scheme of Egyptian chronology.  Such an analysis would be inconsistent with the main object of the present work : but a few examples will serve to characterise his method.

'Sesostris is the great name of Egyptian antiquity.  Even the builders of the pyramids and of the labyrinth sink into insignificance by the side of this mighty conqueror.  Nevertheless, his historical identity is not proof against the dissolving and recompounding processes of the Egyptological method.  Bunsen distributes him into portions, and identifies each portion with a different king.  Sesostris, as we have already stated, stands in Manetho's list as third king of the twelfth dynasty, at 3320 B.C., and a notice is appended to his name clearly identifying him with the Sesostris of Herodotus.  Bunsen first takes a portion of him, and identifies it with Tosorthrus (written Sesorthus by Eusebius), the second king of the third dynasty, whose date is 5119 B.C., being a difference in the dates of 1799 years —about the same interval as between Augustus Cæsar and Napoleon;

he then takes another portion, and identifies it with Sesonchosis, a king of the twelfth dynasty ; a third portion of Sesostris is finally assigned to himself. It seems that these three fragments make up the entire Sesostris ; who, in this plural unity, belongs to the Ancient Empire ; but it is added that the Greeks confound him with Ramesses, or Ramses, of the New Empire, a king of the nineteenth dynasty, whose date is 1255 B.C. ; who, again, was confounded with his father, Sethos, which name again was transmuted into Sethosis and Sesosis.

' Lepsius agrees with Bunsen that Sesostris in the Manethonian list, who stands in the twelfth dynasty, at 3320 B.C., is not Sesostris ; but, instead of elevating him to the third dynasty, brings him down to the nineteenth dynasty, and identifies him with Sethos, 1326 B.C. ; chiefly on account of a statement of Manetho, preserved by Josephus, that Sethos first subjugated Cyprus and Phœnicia, and afterwards Assyria and Media, with other countries further to the east. Lepsius, moreover, holds that Ramses, the son of Sethos, was, like his father, a great conqueror, but that the Greeks confounded both father and son under the name of Sesostris.

' We therefore see that the two leading Egyptologists, Bunsen and Lepsius, differing in other respects, agree in thinking that Sesostris is not Sesostris. The notice appended to his name in Manetho, which identifies him with the Sesostris of Herodotus, Diodorus, and other Greek writers, is regarded by Lepsius as spurious. But here their agreement stops. One assigns Sesostris to what is called the Old, the other to what is called the New Empire, separating his respective dates by an interval of 3793 years. What should we think, if a new school of writers on the history of France, entitling themselves Fran-cologists, were to arise, in which one of the leading critics were to deny that Louis XIV. lived in the seventeenth century, and were to identify him with Hercules, or Romulus, or Cyrus, or Alexander the Great, or Cæsar or Charlemagne ; while another leading critic of the same school, agreeing in the rejection of the received hypothesis as to his being the successor of Louis XIII., were to identify him with Napoleon I. and Louis Napoleon ? '

It is well known that all these conjectures on early Egyptian history are supported by the recent discovery of the true meaning of the long-unintelligible hieroglyphic inscriptions. But Sir George Lewis does not believe they have discovered their meaning. He states the problem certainly with formidable force.   It is something like this: 'Here you have inscriptions composed in a lost *language*, and written down in a *character* which is also lost.   Is it to be believed that the imagination of man can first guess rightly the system of written symbols, and then guess the meaning too ?   It is the old story; you have to interpret the dream without knowing what it is.   Even supposing that you have found out, as you think, one set of written symbols, and made a language in these symbols which you can read, who will assure us that some other person will not find another set of symbols with another set of meanings in a new imaginary language ?'   'The question,' says Sir George Lewis, ' as to the possibility of interpreting a language whose tradition has been lost, is further confused by a deceptive analogy derived from the process of deciphering.   A cipher is a contrivance for disguising the alphabetical writing of a known language by a conventional change of characters.   The explanation of this conventional change is called the *Key*.   If a document written in cipher falls into the possession of a stranger ignorant of the Key, and if he can conjecture with tolerable certainty the language in which it is written, he can proceed to apply to it the rules for deciphering, which are founded upon the comparative frequency of certain letters and certain words in the given language.   This process, if the document be tolerably long, is almost infallible.   It is difficult to devise a cipher, sufficiently simple for frequent use, which cannot be deciphered by a skilful and experienced decipherer.   But this operation supposes the language to be understood ; it is a merely alphabetical process ; it does not determine the meaning of a single word ; it merely strips the disguise off a word, and reproduces it in its ordinary orthography.   No process similar to deciphering can afford the smallest assistance towards discovering the signification of an unknown word, written in known alphabetical characters.   The united ingenuity of the most skilful decipherers in Europe could not throw any light upon an Etruscan or Lycian inscription, or interpret a single sentence of the Eugubine Tables.

In like manner, assuming an Egyptian hieroglyphical text to be correctly read into alphabetical characters, no process of deciphering could detect the meaning of the several words.'

It is possible, for example, that Champollion may have discovered, by comparison on some proper names, some phonetic characters, and it is also possible that the ancient Egyptian may have had some analogy with the modern Coptic—the same sort of analogy, perhaps, which Italian bears to Latin. But it is very difficult to be satisfied that any great knowledge could be derived from the spelling of a few letters, and the guessing of a few words as expressed in these letters. 'Where,' says Sir George Lewis, ' the tradition of a language is lost, but its affinity with a known language is ascertained or presumed, the attempts to restore the significations of words proceed upon the hypothesis that the etymology of the word can be determined by its resemblance, more or less close, to a word in the known language, and that the etymology of the word is a certain guide to its meaning. But although there is a close affinity between etymology and meaning, yet etymology alone cannot be taken as a sure index to meaning. When the signification of a word is ascertained, it is often difficult to determine the etymology. The Lexilogus of Buttmann, the Romance Dictionary of Diez—in fact, any good etymological vocabulary —will furnish ample evidence of this truth. But when the process is inverted, and it is proposed to determine the signification of the words of an entire language from etymological guesses, unassisted by any other knowledge, the process is necessarily uncertain and inconclusive, and can be satisfactory only to a person who has already made up his mind to accept *some* system of interpretation.

' Thus in Italian the word *troja* signifies a sow. Diez refers the origin of this word to the old Latin expression *porcus Trojanus,* which meant a pig stuffed with other animals and served for the table ; the name being an allusion to the Trojan horse. He conceives that this phrase first became *porco di troja,* and afterwards *troja* simply, with the signification of a pregnant sow. Assuming this etymology to be true, what possible ingenuity could have enabled anybody to invert the process, and to discover the meaning by the etymology, if the meaning were unknown ?'

The alphabet of Baron Bunsen is very complicated. He has four classes and an extra, or later class. He has more than 1000 characters altogether:

| | |
|---|---:|
| Ideographics . . . . . . | 620 |
| Determinatives . . . . . . | 164 |
| Phonetics . . . . . . . | 130 |
| Mixed . . . . . . . . | 55 |
| Later alphabet . . . . . . | 100 |
| | 1069 |

And he can read a very large number of words; but we are not surprised to hear that 'the system of reading the hieroglyphic characters as expounded by the Egyptologists, is flexible and arbitrary. It involves the hypothesis of homophones; that is to say of a plurality of signs for the same sound. It likewise involves a mixture of ideographic and phonetic symbols.'

Altogether, though Sir George Lewis may not be right in his bold assertion that *no* early Egyptian history is possible, he is clearly successful in proving that Baron Bunsen's history is untrue. As he expelled the conjectures of Niebuhr from Roman history, so he has expelled the conjectures of Niebuhr's great pupil from Egyptian history. Nobody who reads Sir George Lewis can doubt that Bunsen, for the most part, indulges in conjecture as to the language, as to the written character, and as to the history of ancient Egypt. *His* theories in future will not be accepted as facts. A better feat of iconoclasm has seldom been performed.

These historical works might well have exhausted the leisure of a man almost always occupied in civil business. But Sir George Lewis wrote another long series of books on philosophical politics also. We have not left ourselves much space to speak of them at length, and we do not think that they need be spoken of at such great length as his historical works. We think that they represent less perfectly the best parts of his mind, and that they bear more marks of his deficiencies.

The earliest and among the most curious is an essay on the ' Use and Abuse of certain Political terms,' published in 1832. It is curiously characteristic of Sir George Lewis that, at a time when England was convulsed by the almost revolutionary struggle of the Reform Bill, when all Europe still gazed with wonder at the prosperous effect of the most happy of French revolutions, Sir George Lewis should have sat down to write, not on the facts of political revolution, but on the *words* of political science. After he became a practical statesman he became more alive to political passions and less occupied with political terms ; but to the last he was too apt to wonder at great conflicts, and to be pleased with verbal inquiries. In 1833 he was under the mastery of a remarkable teacher. The late Mr. Austin had little fame in his lifetime, and was so discouraged by neglect that he could not nerve himself to complete great works, of which he had finished what most men would consider the difficult part, and had only to add that which most people would think the easy part. He in this point resembled Coleridge. That great thinker has left no work which embodies his philosophy, and yet his philosophy has permeated his generation. Mr. Austin seized hold, some thirty years ago, of several strong minds, and by the help of these great minds he greatly influenced his time. You will find thoughts distinctly traceable to him far away among people who never heard of him. His few lectures and his years of conversation were a peculiar source of nice expression and accurate thought for more than half a century ; a little bit of just though almost pedantic thought cropped suddenly up in our crude and hasty English life. Thirty years ago Mr. Austin, at the London University, explained what may be called the necessary part of political science, and illustrated it by the best of all illustrations—Roman law. He analysed not a particular government, but what is common to all governments; not one law, but what is common to all laws; not political communities in their features of diversity, but political communities in their features of necessary resemblance. He gave politics not an interesting aspect, but a new aspect; for by giving men a steady view of what political communities *must* be, he nipped in the bud many questions as to what they ought to be, or ought not to be. As a gymnastic of the intellect, and as a purifier, Mr. Austin's philosophy is to this day admirable—even in its imperfect remains; a young man who will study it will find that he has gained something which he wanted, but something which he did not *know* that he wanted; he has clarified a part of his mind which he did not know needed clarifying. Sir George Lewis was deeply penetrated by this abstract teaching; to the last day of his life, in the unphilosophical atmosphere of the War Office, he would use the phrases of, and would like allusions to, this philosophy. One source of his power as a political thinker was, that he had, under Mr. Austin's guidance, studied political questions as it were in their skeleton. Once a jurist, always a jurist. The vast and easy command of the whole sources of juridical literature which Sir George Lewis showed in his essay 'On Foreign Jurisdiction, and the Extradition of Criminals,' and elsewhere, is largely due to his early studies. Yet it may be doubted whether Mr. Austin's influence was entirely favourable for him. A certain school of thinkers magnify the effects of human language. Calm and simple-minded students, when they see the hasty world of human beings using inaccurate and vague words, are apt to ascribe all their errors to those words, and to believe that, if you could put human language right, you would set the world in order. There is no greater mistake. Men are mainly deceived by their passions and their interests; they care but little for abstract truth, and rush forward to small, petty, but concrete, objects. They catch hastily at any sort of word that justifies what they wish to do, and if it sounds well, care little for fallacies and ambiguities. The language is inaccurate, no doubt, but it is a symptom only of a mental disease. You cannot calm the passions of men by defining their words. Mr. Austin's school was apt to forget this. The early treatise of Sir George Lewis on the ' Use and Abuse of Political Terms,' and some of his later treatises too, are not exempt from this defect, though his strong sense and really practical turn of mind always kept it in check. A person wishing to watch his intellectual history, should look carefully at this book ; it is a series of exercises in Mr. Austin's class-room.

A more serious defect mars the popularity of Sir George Lewis's writings, and we think Mr. Austin is partly to blame for that too. Mr. Austin was always talking of the 'formidable community of fools ;' he had no popularity; little wish for popularity; little respect for popular judgment. This is a great error. The world is often wiser than any philosopher. ' There is some one,' said a great man of the world, ' wiser than Voltaire, and wiser than Napoleon, *c'est tout le monde.'* Popular judgment on popular matters is crude and vague, but it is right. And it is even more certain that a great writer on morals and politics ought not to adopt a mode of writing which excludes him from popularity. Mr. Austin's mere style did this for him. He wrote on the principle that people would be sure to comprehend what was completely expressed, but could never be trusted to supply a *hiatus* in what was incompletely expressed. His writings accordingly read like a legal document ; every possible case is provided for, every ambiguity is guarded against, and— hardly any one can read them. The ordinary human mind cannot bear that method of expressing everything ; it is more puzzled by such elaborate precision than by anything else. Sir George Lewis did not err in mere language, but he erred in treatment. Mr. Austin expands all thoughts, new and old, at just the same length ; and he taught Sir George Lewis to do so also. In the present state of the moral sciences, this is absurd.

Much of them is very well, though a little vaguely, understood
by the world at large. It is often of great consequence to
reduce them to a principle; it is often of great importance to
add new truths, and to give a new edge to old truth. But it
is not advisable to begin with a principle and to work steadily
through all its possible applications at the *same* length. If
you do, the reader will say, 'How this man *does* prose! why, I
knew that;' and he did know it. Some of the applications of
a principle are new, and should be treated at length; some are
of pressing importance, and should be treated at length too;
but all the consequences should not be worked out like a sum.
An atmosphere of commonplace hangs over long moral didac-
tics, and an equal expansion of what the world knows and what
it does not know will not be read by the world.

Sir George Lewis did his fame serious harm by neglecting
this maxim. He wrote, for example, 'An Essay on the Influence
of Authority in Matters of Opinion,' which was described by a
hasty thinker as a book to prove that when 'you wanted to
know anything, you asked someone who knew something about
it.' The essay certainly abounds in acute remarks and interesting illustrations, and if these remarks and these illustrations
had been printed separately, it would have been a good book.
But the systematic treatment has been fatal to it. The different kinds and cases of authority are so systematically enumerated, that the reader yawns and forgets.

The case is even worse with his great treatise 'On the
Methods of Observation and Reasoning in Politics,' in two large
volumes. Scarcely any one has read these volumes, and those
who have are sure that their bulk was a mistake. They are
written upon the principle that 'two and two make four' is as
much unknown to the mass of men as the integral calculus.
Easy things are explained exactly with the same care as difficult things, and in consequence very few people read the explanations. There are many admirable parts and essays in the
book. It contains an account and criticism of 'political induc-

tion' as described by Mr. Mill, and an account and criticism
of jurisprudence as described and understood by Mr. Austin.
Both these discussions are very good, and the speculations of
the two thinkers are well spliced together; but they are overlaid with long explanations of what requires no explanation,
and discussions of what need never have been discussed.
Charles Fox used to say of a very dull but able speaker, ' I
always listen to that man, and then speak his speech over
again.' A dishonest writer might well do so with Sir George
Lewis's writings. There are many thoughts, and a million facts
in them, which the world would be glad to hear, though it cannot
extract them from the rest. A writer of this sort naturally
did not look for profit from his laborious writings; few men
have done more gratuitous work. He was disposed to agree
with Mr. Mill, that the notion of ' thinkers giving out doctrines
for bread was a mistake,' and even to hold that speculators
should *pay* for the opportunity of placing their opinions before
the world.

We own that we much regret this misconception of the
conditions of modern writing, now that Sir George Lewis's career
has been cut short in the midst. When he had life before him,
it seemed less important that he should throw away fame; but
now that all is over, we wish he had desired popularity more,
for he would have been remembered better. He really had
considerable powers of pointed writing. The little treatise at
the head of this article shows that when he did not aim at com-
pleteness he could write easily that which would be easily read.
He had not, indeed, the powers of a great literary artist; it was
not in his way to look at style as an alluring art. He wanted to
express his opinion, and cared for nothing else. He had no
literary vanity; and without the vanity that loves applause, few
indeed cultivate the tact that gains applause. ' If you can do
without the world,' says the cynic, ' the world can do without
you;' and it is as true to say that few, if any, gain literary
fame who do not long and hunger after it.

As a sort of compensation, Sir George Lewis rose more rapidly as a parliamentary statesman than any of his contemporaries. He was in the first rank of the Liberal party, yet he entered parliament five years after Mr. Cardwell, fifteen years after Mr. Gladstone, nineteen years after Sir Charles Wood, and forty years after Lord Palmerston. It is curious at first sight that he should have done so. He was not an attractive speaker, he wanted animal spirits, and detested an approach to anything theatrical. He had very considerable command of exact language, but he had no impulse to use it. If it was his duty to speak, he spoke ; but he did not want to speak when it was not his duty. Silence was no pain, and oratory no pleasure to him. If mere speaking were the main qualification for an influence in Parliament—if, as is often said, parliamentary government be a synonym for the government of talkers and *avocats*—Sir George Lewis would have had no influence, would never have been a parliamentary ruler. Yet we once heard a close and good observer say : ' George Lewis's influence in the House is something wonderful ; whatever he proposes has an excellent chance of being carried. He excites no opposition, and he commands great respect, and generally he carries his plan.' The House of Commons, according to the saying, is wiser than any one in it. There is an elective affinity for solid sense in a practical assembly of educated Englishmen which always operates, and which rarely errs. Sir George Lewis's influence was great, not only on his own side of the House, but on the other. He had, indeed, probably more real weight with moderate Conservatives than with extreme Liberals. Enterprise neither seemed to be nor was his forte, and bold men thought him rather tame. His influence was like that of Lord Palmerston : he was liked by the moderate members, whether Whigs or Tories, who think just alike, whatever they call themselves ; and who are likely nowadays to rule the country, whatever name the party in power may chance to bear. He was a safe man, a fair man, and an unselfish man. He had a faculty of ' patient labour,'

which, as he himself remarked, '*was as sure* to be appreciated
when Englishmen meet together to transact business, as wit or
eloquence;' and therefore it was that he had great influence in
the House of Commons; and therefore it was that he rose rapidly.

He filled three cabinet offices; the first was that of Chancellor of the Exchequer, and this was the one which he liked
best, and for which he conceived himself best qualified. He
had no easy time, however, during his actual tenure of the
office. He had to find money for the Crimean War, the heaviest
draft on the resources of the exchequer since Waterloo; he had
to break the 'fundamental law of the currency,' as he called it,
Peel's Act, in the unexpected panic of 1857. He gave universal satisfaction as finance minister, and especial satisfaction
in the City. He was clear, considerate, and it was at once felt
that argument would move him if good argument could be
found. He had to borrow much money, and he so managed as
to be able to borrow it without undue charge to the state, and
with that immediate success which sustains the credit of the
state, and secures a *prestige* in the money-market. It is scarcely
possible to speak of him as finance minister without alluding to
his differences with Mr. Gladstone in the cabinet and out of it.
Yet it is not possible to discuss the subject accurately. Mr.
Gladstone's views of the budget of 1860, we all know; but Sir
George Lewis's views have never been set forth at length, and
it is not wise to base an argument on scraps of oral conversations. It may be as well, however, to point out that, in addition
to their intrinsic and considerable differences of temperament
and character, they approached finance from two different and
even opposite points of view. Mr. Gladstone is the successor,
the legitimate inheritor of the policy of Sir Robert Peel. He
made his reputation as a financier and as a statesman by the
budget of 1853, in which the prominent object is to remove old
taxes that cramp and harass industry. He regards the public
purse as donative, out of which trade may be augmented and
industry developed. Sir Robert Peel used the public purse in

that manner, and Mr. Gladstone has done so also. Sir George
Lewis was led, perhaps from temperament, and certainly from
circumstances, to take a stricter and simpler view of finance.
He came into office on a sudden, during a great war, and he had
to find the resources for that war. He had to consider, not how
taxation could be adjusted so as to help trade, but how the
exchequer could be filled to pay soldiers. On all financial
matters he looked solely at the balance of the account, Will
there be a deficit, or will there not be? Forms of account,
and all minor matters, were in his mind of very small importance; he looked to the simple question, How much will there
be in the till at the end of the year? With two such different
prepossessions as these, it is no wonder that men so intrinsically
different as Sir George Lewis and Mr. Gladstone did not very
well agree upon finance; it is rather a wonder that they could
act together at all. There is no use, over Sir George Lewis's
grave, in reviving financial controversies; everybody will now
admit that while he was in office and responsible, he was a
sound and sure Chancellor of the Exchequer.

In the panic of 1857, we have heard, he was even amusing.
His perfect impassivity and collectedness contrasted much with
the excitement of eager men, and in a panic most men are eager.
A deputation of Scotch bankers attended at the Treasury to
ask Sir George to induce the Bank of England to make advances to them in certain possible cases. Sir George said, ' Ah,
gentlemen, if I were to interfere with the discretion of the Bank,
there would be a run upon me much greater than any which
there has ever been upon you.' He was a man who probably
*could* not lose his head.

At the Home Office he had the opportunity of displaying
great judicial faculties. The Home Office is the high court of
appeal in cases of criminal justice. When any one is to be hanged,
it is almost always argued before the Home Secretary that he
should not be hanged. If Sir George Lewis had practised at the
bar, for which he studied, he would have been a bad advocate;

his mind was not fertile in ambiguous fallacies, and was incapable of artificial belief; and a great pleader should excel in these. One of the greatest judges of our generation, when at the bar, could only state the point once, and when the court did not understand him, could only mutter, 'What fools they are ! awful fools ! infernal fools !' Sir George Lewis would not have indulged in these epithets, but he would have been nearly as little able to invent ingenious suggestions and out-of-the-way arguments. He probably would have said, 'I have explained the matter. If the court *will* not comprehend it, *I* cannot make them.' But no man was fitter for a judge than himself. He would never have shirked labour—which is not unknown even among judges—and his lucid exposition of substantial reasons would have been consulted by students for years. At the Home Office he could not display all these qualities, but he was able to display some of them.

At the War Office he shone far less. It did not suit his previous pursuits ; and no other man with such pursuits would have taken it, or, indeed, would have been asked to take it. He pushed the notion too far in this case, that an able and educated man can master any subject, and is fit for any office. The constitutional habit in England of making a civilian supreme over military matters, though we believe a most wise habit, has its objections, and may easily look absurd. It *did* look rather absurd when the most pacific of the pacific, the most erudite of the erudite, Sir George Lewis, was placed at the head of the War Department. In great matters, it cannot be denied, he did well. When the capture of the *Trent* made a war with the Federal States a pressing probability, the arrangements were admitted to be admirable. Much of the credit must belong in such a case to military and other subordinates—all the details must be managed by them ; but the superior minister must have his credit too. He brought to a *focus* all which was done ; he summed-up the whole ; he could say distinctly why everything which was done was done, and why everything left undone was left undone.   He would have been ready with a plain intelligible reason on all these matters in Parliament and elsewhere.   And this was not an easy matter for a civilian after a few months of office.   But on minor matters Sir George Lewis was not so good at the War Department as at the Exchequer or the Home Office.   He had been apprenticed to the Home Office as Under-Secretary, and to the Exchequer as Financial Secretary to the Treasury; but he had never been apprenticed to the War Office.   On matters of detail he was obliged to rely on others.   He held, and justly, that a parliamentary chief of temporary, perhaps *very* temporary, tenure of office should be very cautious not to interfere too much with the minor business of his department.   He should govern, but he should govern through others.   But the due application of this maxim requires that the chief minister should know, as it were by intuition and instinct, which points are important and which are not important.   And no civilian introduced at once to a new department like that of War can at once tell this.   He *must* be in the hands of others.   In the House of Commons, too, Sir George Lewis could never answer questions of detail on war matters in an offhand manner.   He had to say, 'I will inquire, and inform the honourable member.'   At the Home Office he could have answered at once and of himself.   It was an act of self-denial in him to go to the War Office.   He felt himself out of place there, and was sure that his administration of military matters would not add to his reputation.   But he was told it was for the interest of the Government that he should accept the office, and he accepted it.   Perhaps he was wrong.   The reputation of a first-rate public man is a great public power, and he should be careful not to diminish it.   The weight of the greatest men is diminished by their being seen to do daily that which they do not do particularly well.   A cold and cynical wisdom particularly disapproves of most men's *best* actions. Few men were less exposed to the censure of such wisdom than Sir George Lewis; but his acceptance of the War Office was a sacrifice of himself to the public, which injured him more than it advantaged the public—which it would have been better not to have made.

The usefulness of men like Sir George Lewis is not to be measured by their usefulness in mere office. It is in the cabinet that they are of *most* use. Sir George Lewis was made to discuss business with other men. ' If,' we have heard one who did much business with him say, ' if there is any fault in what you say, he will find it out.' In council, in the practical discussions of pending questions, a simple masculine intellect like that of Sir George Lewis finds its greatest pleasure and its best use. He was *made* to be a cabinet minister.

The briefest notice of Sir George Lewis should not omit to mention one of his most agreeable, and not one of his least rare, peculiarities—his good-natured use of great knowledge. It would have been easy for a man with such a memory as his, and such studious habits as his, to become most unpopular by cutting up the casual blunders of others. On the contrary, he was a most popular man, for he used his knowledge with a view to amend the ignorance of others, and not with a view to expose it. His conversation was superior either to his speeches or his writings. It had—what is perhaps rarer among parliamentary statesmen than among most people—the flavour of exact thought. It is hardly possible for men to pass their lives in oratorical efforts without losing some part of the taste for close-fitting words. Well-sounding words which are not specially apt, which are not very precise, are as good or better for a popular assembly. Sir George Lewis's words in political conversation were as good as words could be; they might have gone to the press at once. We have compared it to hearing a chapter in Aristotle's Politics, and perhaps that may give an idea that it was dull. But pointed thought on great matters is a very pleasant thing to hear, though, after many ages and changes, it is sometimes a hard thing to read. The conversation of the ' Dialogue ' at the end of his treatise on the ' Best Form of Government,' has been admired, but it is very inferior to the conversation of the writer. There was a delicate flavour of satire lurking in the precise thought which could not be written down, and which is now gone and irrecoverable.

'When,' says Lord Brougham, commenting on the death of a statesman once celebrated and now forgotten—'when a subject presented itself so large and shapeless, and dry and thorny, that few men's fortitude could face, and no one's patience could grapple with it ; or an emergency occurred demanding on the sudden, access to stores of learning, the collection of many long years, but arranged so as to be made available at the shortest notice— *then* it was men asked where Lawrence was.' And now, not only when information is wanted, but when counsel is needed—when parties are confused—when few public men are trusted—when wisdom, always rare, is rarer even than usual—many may ask, in no long time, ' Where is Lewis now ?'[1]

---

[1] I have given in the *Addenda* (page 330) a shorter article, written in the *Economist* newspaper by Mr. Bagehot, on occasion of the unveiling of the memorial to Sir George Lewis at Hereford in the autumn of 1864. This article, which appeared on the 10th September in that year, seems to me either supplementary to, or a very interesting expansion and illustration of, the longer paper.—EDITORS.

## ADAM SMITH AS A PERSON.

### [1876.]

OF Adam Smith's Political Economy almost an infinite quantity has been said, but very little has been said as to Adam Smith himself. And yet not only was he one of the most curious of human beings, but his books can hardly be understood without having some notion of what manner of man he was. There certainly are economical treatises that go straight on, and that might have been written by a calculating machine. But the 'Wealth of Nations' is not one of these. Anyone who would explain what is in it, and what is not in it, must apply the 'historical method,' and state what was the experience of its author and how he worked up that experience. Perhaps, therefore, now that there is a sort of centenary of Adam Smith, it may not be amiss to give a slight sketch of him and of his life, and especially of the peculiar points in them that led him to write the book which still in its effects, even more than in its theory, occupies mankind.

The Founder of the science of business was one of the most unbusinesslike of mankind. He was an awkward Scotch professor, apparently choked with books and absorbed in abstractions. He was never engaged in any sort of trade, and would probably never have made sixpence by any if he had been. His absence of mind was amazing. On one occasion, having to sign his name to an official document, he produced not his own signature, but an elaborate imitation of the signature of the person who signed before him; on another, a sentinel on duty having saluted him in military fashion, he astounded and offended the man by acknowledging it with a copy—a very clumsy copy no doubt—of the same gestures. And Lord Brougham preserves other similar traditions. ' It is related,' he says, ' by old people in Edinburgh that while he moved through the Fishmarket in his accustomed attitude—that is with his hands behind his back, and his head in the air—a female of the trade exclaimed, taking him for an idiot broken loose, " Hech, sirs, to see the like o' him to be aboot. And yet he is weel eneugh put on " (dressed). It was often so too in society. Once, during a dinner at Dalkeith, he broke out into a lecture on some politics of the day, and was bestowing a variety of severe epithets on a statesman, when he suddenly perceived the nearest relative of the politician he was criticizing, sitting opposite, and stopped ; but he was heard to go on muttering, " Deil care, Deil care, it's all true." ' And these are only specimens of a crowd of anecdotes.

The wonder that such a man should have composed the ' Wealth of Nations,' which shows so profound a knowledge of the real occupations of mankind, is enhanced by the mode in which it was written. It was not the exclusive product of a lifelong study, such as an absent man might, while in seeming abstraction, be really making of the affairs of the world. On the contrary, it was in the mind of its author only one of many books, or rather a single part of a great book, which he intended to write. A vast scheme floated before him much like the dream of the late Mr. Buckle as to a ' History of Civilisation,' and he spent his life accordingly, in studying the origin and progress of the sciences, the laws, the politics, and all the other aids and forces which have raised man from the savage to the civilised state. The plan of Adam Smith was indeed more comprehensive even than this. He wanted to trace not only the progress of the race, but also of the individual ; he wanted to show how each man being born (as he thought) with few faculties, came to attain to many and great faculties. He wanted to answer the question, how did man—race or individual—come to be what he is ? These immense dreams are among the commonest phenomena of literary history ; and, as a rule, the vaster the intention, the less the result. The musings of the author are

too miscellaneous, his studies too scattered, his attempts too
incoherent, for him to think out anything valuable, or to pro
duce anything connected.   But in Adam Smith's case the very
contrary is true ; he produced an enduring particular result in
consequence of a comprehensive and diffused ambition.   He
discovered the laws of wealth in looking for ' the natural progress of opulence ; ' and he investigated the progress of opulence
as part of the growth and progress of all things.

The best way to get a distinct notion of Adam Smith's
scheme is to look at the other works which he published
besides the ' Wealth of Nations.'   The greatest, and the one
which made his original reputation, was the ' Theory of Moral
Sentiments,' in which he builds up the whole moral nature of
man out of a single primitive emotion—sympathy, and in which
he gives a history of ethical philosophy besides.   With this are
commonly bound up some ' Considerations concerning the first
Formation of Languages,' which discuss how ' two savages who
had never been taught to speak, but had been bred up remote
from the society of man, would naturally begin their converse.'
Then there is a very curious ' History of Astronomy,' left imperfect ; and another fragment on the ' History of Ancient
Physics,' which is a kind of sequel to that part of the ' History
of Astronomy ' which relates to the ancient astronomy ; then a
similar essay on ' Ancient Logic and Metaphysics ; ' then another
on the nature and development of the Fine, or, as he calls them,
' The Imitative Arts, Painting, Poetry, and Music,' in which was
meant to have been included a history of the Theatre—all
forming part, his executors tell us, ' of a plan he had once
formed for giving a connected history of the liberal and elegant
arts.'   And he destroyed before his death the remains of the
book, ' Lectures on Justice,' ' in which,' we are told by a student
who heard them, ' he followed Montesquieu in endeavouring to
trace the gradual progress of jurisprudence, both public and
private, from the rudest to the most refined ages, and to point
out the effects of those arts which contribute to subsistence

and to the accumulation of property in producing correspondent alterations in law and government;' or, as he himself announces it at the conclusion of the 'Moral Sentiments,' 'another discourse' in which he designs 'to endeavour to give an account of the general principles of law and government, and of the different revolutions they have undergone in the different ages and periods of society, not only in what concerns justice, but in what concerns police, revenue, and arms, and whatever else is the subject of law.' Scarcely any philosopher has imagined a vaster dream.

Undoubtedly it is a great literary marvel that so huge a scheme, on so many abstract subjects, should have produced anything valuable, and still more so that it should have produced what has been for a whole century a fundamental book on trade and money—at first sight, the least fit for a secluded man to treat at all, and which, if he did treat of them, would seem more than any other to require from him an absorbed and exclusive attention. A little study of the life of Adam Smith, however, in some degree lessens the wonder; because it shows how in the course of his universal studies he came to meet with this particular train of thought, and how he came to be able to pursue it effectually.

Adam Smith was born early in the first half of the eighteenth century, at Kirkcaldy in Scotland, on June 5, 1713. His father died before he was born; but his mother, who is said to have been a woman of unusual energy and ability, lived to be very old, and to see her son at the height of his reputation as a philosopher. He was educated at school in the usual Scotch way, and at the University of Glasgow; and at both he is said, doubtless truly, to have shown an unusual facility of acquisition, and an unusual interest in books and study. As we should also expect, a very strong memory, which he retained till the last, showed itself very early. Nothing, however, is known with precision as to the amount of knowledge he acquired in Scotland, nor as to his place among his contemporaries. The examination system, which nowadays in England discriminates both so accurately, has in Scotland never been equally developed, and in Adam Smith's time had never been heard of there at all.

His exceptional training begins at the next stage. There is at the University of Glasgow a certain endowment called the Snell exhibition, after the name of its founder, which enables the students selected for it to study for some years at the University of Oxford. Of these exhibitioners Adam Smith became one, and as such studied at Oxford for as many as seven years. As might be expected, he gives the worst account of the state of the university at that time. In the sketch of the history of education which forms so odd an episode in the 'Wealth of Nations,' he shows perpetually that he thought the system which he had seen at Oxford exceedingly bad, and its government excessively corrupt. 'If,' he says, 'the authority to which a teacher is subject resides in the body corporate of the college or university of which he is himself a member, and in which the greater part of the other members are, like himself, persons who either are or ought to be teachers, they are likely to make a common cause, to be all very indulgent to one another, and every man to consent that his neighbour may neglect his duty, provided he is himself allowed to neglect his own. In the University of Oxford the greater part of the public professors have for these many years given up altogether even the pretence of teaching.' And he adds, 'In England, the public schools are much less corrupted than the universities. In the schools, the youth are taught, or at least may be taught, Greek and Latin. That is everything which the masters pretend to teach, or which it is expected they should teach. In the universities, the youth neither are taught, nor can always find the means of being taught, the sciences which it is the business of these incorporated bodies to teach.' And he retained through life a fixed belief that endowments for education tended only to the 'ease' of the teacher, and not to

the advantage of the learner. But though he says he had the
means of learning little at Oxford, he certainly, in fact, learnt
much. 'Greek,' as Sydney Smith says, 'never crossed the
Tweed in any force;' but Adam Smith incessantly shows a real
familiarity with Greek books and a sound accumulation of
Greek learning. Very likely his erudition would not bear
much comparison with what is now carried away from Balliol.
If we compare him with a more recent Snell exhibitioner, Sir
William Hamilton, we shall see that Greek teaching has
enormously advanced in the time between them; but, on the
other hand, if we compare Adam Smith with Scotch philosophers, or purely Scotch education, say with Reid or Hume, we
cannot help seeing that his acquaintance with Greek things
belongs, both in quantity and in quality, to an order altogether
superior to theirs.

For the vast works which Adam Smith contemplated, a
sound knowledge of Greek was, as he must have felt, far more
necessary than any other kind of knowledge. The beginnings
of nine-tenths of all philosophy are to be found there, and the
rudiments of many other things. But for the purpose of the
great task which he actually performed, Adam Smith learned
at Oxford something much more valuable than Greek. He acquired there a kind of knowledge and sympathy with England, in
which the other eminent Scotchmen—especially literary Scotchmen—of his time were often very deficient. At that time the
recollection of the old rivalry between the two countries had by
no means died away; there was still a separate Scotch philosophy and a separate literature; and when it happened, as it
perpetually did, that Scotch writers were not thought so much
of in England as they thought they ought to be, they were apt
to impute their discredit to English prejudice, and to appeal to
France and Paris to correct the error. Half Hume's mind, or
more than half, was distorted by his hatred of England and his
love of France. He often could not speak of English things
with tolerable temper, and he always viewed French ones with

extravagant admiration. Whether Adam Smith altogether liked this country may perhaps be doubted—Englishmen then hated Scotchmen so much—but he had no kind of antagonism to her, and quite understood that in most economical respects she was then exceedingly superior to France. And this exceptional sympathy and knowledge we may fairly ascribe to a long and pleasant residence in England. For his great work no qualification was more necessary; the 'Wealth of Nations' would have been utterly spoiled if he had tried (as Hume incessantly would have tried) to show that, in industrial respects, England might not be better than France, or at any rate was not so very much better.

The Snell foundation at Oxford has often been an avenue to the English Church, and it seems to have been intended that Adam Smith should use it as such. The only anecdote which remains of his college life may be a clue to his reasons for not doing so. He is said to have been found by his tutor in the act of reading Hume's 'Philosophical Essays,' then lately published, and to have been reproved for it. And it is certain that anyone who at all sympathised with Hume's teaching in that book would have felt exceedingly little sympathy with the formularies of the Church of England, even as they were understood in the very Broad Church of that age. At any rate, for some reason or other, Adam Smith disappointed the wishes of his friends, gave up all idea of entering the Church of England, and returned to Scotland without fixed outlook or employment. He resided, we are told, two years with his mother, studying no doubt, but earning nothing, and visibly employed in nothing. In England such a career would probably have ended in his 'writing for the booksellers,' a fate of which he speaks in the 'Wealth of Nations' with contempt. But in Scotland there was a much better opening for philosophers. The Scotch universities had then, as now, several professorships very fairly paid, and very fairly distributed. The educated world in Scotland was probably stronger a century ago than it ever was before or since. The Union with England had removed the aristocracy of birth which over-shadowed it before, and commerce had not yet created the aristocracy of wealth which overshadows it now. Philosophical merit had therefore then in Scotland an excellent chance of being far better rewarded than it usually is in the world. There were educated people who cared for philosophy, and these people had prizes to give away. One of those prizes Adam Smith soon obtained. He read lectures, we are told, under the patronage of Lord Kames, an eminent lawyer who wrote books on philosophy that are still quoted, and who was no doubt deeply interested in Adam Smith's plans of books on the origin and growth of all arts and sciences, as these were the topics which he himself studied and handled. Contrary to what might have been expected, these lectures were very successful. Though silent and awkward in social life, Adam Smith possessed in considerable perfection the peculiarly Scotch gift of abstract oratory. Even in common conversation, when once moved, he expounded his favourite ideas very admirably. As a teacher in public he did even better; he wrote almost nothing, and though at the beginning of a lecture he often hesitated, we are told, and seemed 'not to be suffi-ciently possessed of the subject,' yet in a minute or two he became fluent, and poured out an interesting series of animated arguments. Commonly, indeed, the silent man, whose brain is loaded with unexpressed ideas, is more likely to be a success-ful public speaker than the brilliant talker who daily exhausts himself in sharp sayings. Adam Smith acquired great reputa-tion as a lecturer, and in consequence obtained two of the best prizes then given to philosophers in Scotland—first the pro-fessorship of logic, and then that of moral philosophy, in the University of Glasgow.

The rules, or at any rate the practice, of the Scotch univer-sities, seem at that time to have allowed a professor in either of these chairs great latitude in the choice of his subject. Adam

Smith during his first year lectured on rhetoric and *belles lettres* 'instead of on logic,' and in the chair of moral philosophy he expounded, besides the theory of duty, a great scheme of social evolution. The beginnings of the 'Wealth of Nations' made part of the course, but only as a fragment of the immense design of showing the origin and development of cultivation and law; or, as we may perhaps put it, not inappropriately, of saying how, from being a savage, man rose to be a Scotchman. This course of lectures seems to have been especially successful. So high, we are told, was his reputation as a professor, 'that a multitude of students from a great distance resorted to the university merely upon his account. Those branches of science which he taught became fashionable' in the city, 'and his opinions were the chief topics of discussion in clubs and literary societies. Even the small peculiarities of his pronunciation and manner of speaking became frequently the objects of imitation.' This is the partial recollection of an attached pupil in distant years;—it may be over-coloured a little—but even after a fair abatement it is certainly the record of a great temporary triumph and local success.

That the greater part of the lectures can have been of much intrinsic merit it is not easy now to believe. An historical account 'of the general principles of law and government, and of the different revolutions which they have undergone in the different ages and periods of society,' would be too great a task for a great scholar of the ripest years and with all the accumulated materials of the present time, and it was altogether beyond the strength of a young man a century ago;—not to say that he combined it with an account of the origin of the moral faculties, a theory of *belles lettres,* and other matters. The delivery of that part of the course which was concerned with wealth and revenue may have been useful to him, because it compelled him to bring his ideas on those subjects into a distinct form. Otherwise, being a bookish man, he might have been too absorbed in bookish matters, and neglected what can only be taught by life for that which is already to be learned from literature. But at the time this was only a minor merit; —the main design of the lectures was only an impossible aim at an unbounded task.

So complex, however, is life, that this Scotch professorship, though in a superficial view wasteful, and likely to exhaust and hurt his mind by demanding the constant efflux of inferior matter, was, nevertheless, on the whole exceedingly useful. It not only induced him to study as a part of his vast scheme the particular phenomena of wealth, but it gave him an excellent opportunity of seeing those phenomena and of learning how to explain them. It was situated at Glasgow, and Glasgow, though a petty place in comparison with its present magnitude, was nevertheless a considerable mercantile place according to the notions of those times. The Union with England had opened to it the trade with our West Indian colonies, as well as with the rest of the English empire, and it had in consequence grown rapidly and made large profits. That its size was small, as we should think now, was to a learner rather an aid than a disadvantage. A small commerce is more easily seen than an immense one; that of Liverpool or London now is so vast that it terrifies more than excites the imagination. And a small commerce, if varied, has almost as much to teach as a large one; the elements are the same though the figures are smaller, and the less the figures the easier are they to combine. An inspection of Liverpool now would not teach much more than an inspection of Glasgow a hundred years ago, and the lessons of modern Liverpool would be much more difficult to learn But the mere sight of the phenomena of Glasgow commerce was but a small part of the advantage to Adam Smith of a residence at Glasgow. The most characteristic and most valuable tenets of Adam Smith are, when examined, by no means of a very abstract and recondite sort. We are, indeed, in this generation not fully able to appreciate the difficulty of arriving at them. We have been bred up upon them; our disposition is

more to wonder how anyone could help seeing them, than to
appreciate the effort of discovering them. Experience shows
that many of them— the doctrine of free trade for example—are
very uncongenial to the untaught human mind. On political
economy the English-speaking race is undoubtedly the best
instructed part of mankind; and, nevertheless, in the United
States and in every English-speaking colony, protection is the
firm creed of the ruling classes, and free trade is but a heresy.
We must not fancy that any of the main doctrines of Adam
Smith were very easily arrived at by him because they seem
very obvious to us. But, on the other hand, although such
doctrines as his are too opposed to many interests and to many
first impressions to establish themselves easily as a dominant
creed, they are quite within the reach and quite congenial to
the taste of an intelligent dissenting minority. There was a
whole race of mercantile freetraders long before Adam Smith
was born; in his time the doctrine was in the air; it was not
accepted or established;—on the contrary, it was a tenet against
which a respectable parent would probably caution his son;—
still it was known as a tempting heresy, and one against which
a warning was needed. In Glasgow there were doubtless many
heretics. Probably in consequence of the firm belief in a rigid
theology, and of the incessant discussion of its technical tenets,
there has long been, and there is still, in the south of Scotland,
a strong tendency to abstract argument quite unknown in
England. Englishmen have been sometimes laughing at it,
and sometimes gravely criticising it for several generations:
Mr. Buckle wrote half a volume on it: Sydney Smith alleged
that he heard a Scotch girl answer in a quadrille, 'But, my
lord, as to what ye were saying as to love in the *aib*stract,' and
so on. Yet, in spite both of ridicule and argument, the
passion for doctrine is still strong in southern Scotland, and it
will take many years more to root it out. At Glasgow in Adam
Smith's time it had no doubt very great influence; a certain
number of hard-headed merchants were believers in free trade

and kindred tenets. One of these is still by chance known to us. Dr. Carlyle, whom Mr. Gladstone not unhappily described as a ' gentleman clergyman' of the Church of Scotland, tells us of a certain Provost Cochrane, to whom Adam Smith always acknowledged his obligations, and who was the founder and leading member of a club ' in which the express design was to inquire into the nature and principles of trade in all its branches, and to communicate their knowledge on that subject to each other.' From this club Adam Smith not only learned much which he would never have found in any book, but also in part perhaps acquired the influential and so to say practical way of explaining things which so much distinguishes the ' Wealth of Nations.' Mr. Mill says he learned from his intercourse with East India directors the habit of looking for, and the art of discovering, ' the mode of putting a thought which gives it easiest admittance into minds not prepared for it by habit; ' and Adam Smith probably gained something of this sort by living with the Glasgow merchants, for no other book written by a learned professor shows anything like the same power of expressing and illustrating arguments in a way likely to influence minds like theirs. And it is mainly by his systematic cultivation of this borderland between theory and practice that Adam Smith attained his pre-eminent place and influence.

But this usefulness of his Scotch professorship was only in the distant future. It was something for posterity to detect, but it could not have been known at the time. The only pages of his professorial work which Adam Smith then gave to the public were his lectures on Moral Philosophy, in what an Englishman would consider its more legitimate sense. These formed the once celebrated ' Theory of Moral Sentiments,' which, though we should now think them rather pompous, were then much praised and much read. For a great part, indeed, of Adam Smith's life they constituted his main title to reputation. The ' Wealth of Nations ' was not published till seventeen years later ; he wrote nothing else of any importance in the interval ;

and it is now curious to find that when the ' Wealth of Nations '
was published, many good judges thought it not so good as the
' Theory of Moral Sentiments,' and that the author himself was
by no means certain that they were not right.

The ' Theory of Moral Sentiments ' was, indeed, for many
years, exceedingly praised.  One sect of philosophers praised
it, as it seems to me, because they were glad of a celebrated
ally, and another because they were glad of a celebrated opponent : the first said, ' see that so great an authority as Adam
Smith concurs with us ; ' and the second replied, ' but see how
very weak his arguments are ; if so able an arguer as Adam
Smith can say so little for your doctrines, how destitute of
argumentative grounds those doctrines must be.'  Several
works in the history of philosophy have had a similar fate.
But a mere student of philosophy who cares for no sect, and
wants only to know the truth, will nowadays, I think, find
little to interest him in this celebrated book.   In Adam Smith's
mind, as I have said before, it was part of a whole ; he wanted
to begin with the origin of the faculties of each man, and then
build up that man—just as he wished to arrive at the origin of
human society, and then build up society.  His ' Theory of
Moral Sentiments ' builds them all out of one source, sympathy,
and in this way he has obtained praise from friends and
enemies.  His friends are the school of ' moral sense ' thinkers,
because he is on their side, and believes in a special moral
faculty, which he laboriously constructs from sympathy ; his
enemies are the Utilitarian school, who believe in no such
special faculty, and who set themselves to show that his labour
has been in vain, and that no such faculty has been so built up.
One party says the book is good to gain authority for the conclusion, and the other that you may gain credit by refuting its
arguments.  For unquestionably its arguments *are* very weak,
and attractive to refutation.   If the intuitive school had had no
better grounds than these, the Utilitarians would have vanquished them ages since.   There is a fundamental difficulty in

founding morals on sympathy; an obvious confusion of two familiar sentiments. We often sympathise where we cannot approve, and approve where we cannot sympathise. The special vice of party spirit is that it effaces the distinction between the two; we sympathise with our party, till we approve its actions. There is a story of a Radical wit in the last century who was standing for Parliament, and his opponent, of course a Tory, objected that he was always *against* the king whether right or wrong, upon which the wit retorted that on his own showing the Tory was exposed to equal objection, since he was always *for* the king whether right or wrong. And so it will always be. Even the wisest party men more or less sympathise with the errors of their own side; they would be powerless if they did not do so; they would gain no influence if they were not of like passions with those near them. Adam Smith could not help being aware of this obvious objection; he was far too able a reasoner to elaborate a theory without foreseeing what would be said against it. But the way in which he tries to meet the objection only shows that the objection is invincible. He sets up a supplementary theory—a little epicycle—that the sympathy which is to test good morals must be the sympathy of an 'impartial spectator.' But, then, who is to watch the watchman? Who is to say when the spectator is impartial, and when he is not? If he sympathises with one side, the other will always say that he is partial. As a moralist, the supposed spectator must warmly approve good actions and warmly disapprove bad actions; as an impartial person he must never do either the one or the other. He is a fiction of inconsistent halves; if he sympathises he is not impartial, and if he is impartial he does not sympathise. The radical vice of the theory is shown by its requiring this accessory invention of a being both hot and cold, because the essence of the theory is to identify the passion which loves with the sentiment which approves.

But although we may now believe the 'Theory of Moral

Sentiments' to be of inconsiderable philosophical value, and though it would at first sight seem very little likely to contribute to the production of the 'Wealth of Nations,' yet it was, in fact, in a curious way most useful to it. The education of young noblemen has always been a difficulty in the world, and many schemes have been invented to meet it. In Scotland, a hundred years ago, the most fashionable way was to send them to travel in Europe, and to send with them some scholar of repute to look after their morals and to superintend their general education. The guardians of the great border nobleman, the Duke of Buccleugh, were in want of such a tutor to take him such a tour, and it seems to have struck them that Adam Smith was the very person adapted for the purpose. To all appearance an odder selection could hardly have been made. Adam Smith was, as we have seen, the most absent of men, and an awkward Scotch professor, and he was utterly unacquainted with the Continent. He had never crossed the English Channel in his life, and if he had been left to himself would probably never have done so. But one of the guardians was Charles Townshend, who had married the young duke's mother. He was not much unlike Mr. Disraeli in character, and had great influence at that time. He read the 'Theory of Moral Sentiments,' and Hume writes to Adam Smith : 'Charles Townshend, who passes for the cleverest fellow in England, is so taken with the performance, that he said to Oswald he would put the duke under the author's care and would make it worth his while to accept of that charge. As soon as I heard this, I called on him twice with a view of talking with him about the matter, and of convincing him of the propriety of sending that young nobleman to Glasgow ; for I could not hope that he could offer you any terms which would tempt you to renounce your professorship. But I missed him. Mr. Townshend passes for being a little uncertain in his resolutions, so perhaps you need not build much on this sally.' Mr. Townshend was, however, this time in earnest, and the offer was made to Adam Smith. In

our time there would have been an insuperable difficulty.   He
was a professor of great repute, they were asking him to give
up a life-professorship that yielded a considerable income, and
they would have hardly been able to offer him anything equally
permanent.    But in the eighteenth century there was a way of
facilitating such arrangements that we do not now possess.
The family of Buccleugh had great political influence, and
Charles Townshend, the duke's step-father, at times possessed
more ; and accordingly the guardians of the young duke
agreed that they should pay Adam Smith 200*l.* a year till
they should get him an equal office of profit under the Crown.
A person apparently more unfit for the public service could
not easily have been found ; but in that age of sinecures and
pensions it was probably never expected that he should perform
any service ;—an arrangement more characteristic of the old
world, and more unlike our present world, could hardly have
been made.   The friends of the young duke might, not unnaturally, have had some fears about it ; but, in fact, for his
interests, it turned out very well.   Long afterwards, when Adam
Smith was dead, the duke wrote :—' In October, 1766, we
returned to London, after having spent near three years together without the slightest disagreement or coolness ; on my part
with every advantage that could be expected from the society of
such a man.   We continued to live in friendship till the hour
of his death ; and I shall always remain with the impression of
having lost a friend whom I loved and respected, not only for his
great talents, but for every private virtue.'   Very few of Charles
Townshend's caprices were as successful.   Through life there
was about Adam Smith a sort of lumbering *bonhomie* which
amused and endeared him to those around him.

   To Adam Smith the result was even better.   If it had not
been for this odd consequence of the ' Theory of Moral Sentiments,' he might have passed all his life in Scotland, delivering
similar lectures and clothing very questionable theories in
rather pompous words.   He said in after life that there was no

better way of compelling a man to master a science than by
setting him to teach it.   And this may be true of the definite
sciences.   But nothing can be conceived worse for a man of
inventive originality, than to set him to roam over huge subjects like law, morals, politics, and civilisation, particularly at a
time when few good data for sound theories on such subjects
are at hand for him to use.   In such a position the cleverer
the man, the worse are likely to be the consequences : the wider
his curiosity and the more fertile his mind, the surer he is to
pour out a series of gigantic conjectures of little use to himself
or to anyone.   A one-eyed man with a taste for one subject,
even at this disadvantage, may produce something good.   The
limitation of his mind may save him from being destroyed by
his position ; but a man of large interests will fail utterly.   As
Adam Smith had peculiarly wide interests, and as he was the
very reverse of a one-eyed man, he was in special danger ; and
the mere removal from his professorship was to him a gain of
the first magnitude.   It was of cardinal importance to him to be
delivered from the production of incessant words and to be
brought into contact with facts and the world.   And as it turned
out, the caprice of Charles Townshend had a singular further
felicity.   It not only brought him into contact with facts and
the world ; but with the most suitable sort of facts, and, for his
purpose, the best part of the world.

The greater part of his three years abroad was naturally
spent in France.   France was then by far the greatest country
on the Continent.   Germany was divided and had not yet risen ;
Spain had fallen; Italy was of little account.   In one respect,
indeed, France was relatively greater than even at the time of
her greatest elevation, the time of the first Napoleon.   The
political power of the first empire was almost unbounded, but
it had no intellectual power ; under it Paris had ceased to be an
important focus of thought and literature.   The vehement rule
which created the soldiers also stamped out the ideas.   But
under the mild government of the old *régime*, Paris was the

principal centre of European authorship. The deficiency of the old *régime* in eminent soldiers and statesmen only added to the eminence of its literary men. Paris was then queen of two worlds : of that of politics by a tradition from the past, and of literature by a force and life vigorously evidenced in the present. France therefore thus attracted the main attention of all travellers who cared for the existing life of the time ; Adam Smith and his pupil spent the greater part of their stay abroad there. And as a preparation for writing the ' Wealth of Nations ' he could nowhere else have been placed so well. Macaulay says that ' ancient abuses and new theories ' flourished together in France just before the meeting of the States-General in greater vigour than they had been seen to be combined before or since. And the description is quite as true economically as politically ; on all economical matters the France of that time was a sort of museum stocked with the most important errors.

By nature then, as now, France was fitted to be a great agricultural country, a great producer and exporter of corn and wine; but her legislators for several generations had endeavoured to counteract the aim of nature, and had tried to make her a manufacturing country and an exporter of her manufactures. Like most persons in those times, they had been prodigiously impressed by the high position which the maritime powers, as they were then called (the comparatively little powers of England and Holland), were able to take in the politics of Europe. They saw that this influence came from wealth, that this wealth was made in trade and manufacture, and therefore they determined that France should not be behindhand, but should have as much trade and manufacture as possible. Accordingly, they imposed prohibitive or deterring duties on the importation of foreign manufactures ; they gave bounties to the corresponding home manufactures. They tried, in opposition to the home-keeping bent of the French character, to found colonies abroad. These colonies were, according to the maxim then everywhere received, to be markets for the trade and nurseries for the commerce of

the mother country;—they were mostly forbidden to manufacture for themselves, and were compelled to import all the
manufactures and luxuries they required from Europe exclusively in French ships. Meanwhile, at home, agriculture was
neglected. There was not even a free passage for goods from
one part of the country to another. As Adam Smith himself
describes it :

'In France, the different revenue laws which take place in the
different provinces require a multitude of revenue-officers to sur-
round, not only the frontiers of the kingdom, but those of almost
each particular province, in order either to prevent the importation
of certain goods or to subject it to the payment of certain duties,
to the no small interruption of the interior commerce of the country.
Some provinces are allowed to compound for the gabelle or salt-tax.
Others are exempted from it altogether. Some provinces are exempted from the exclusive sale of tobacco, which the farmers-general
enjoy through the greater part of the kingdom. The *Aides*, which
correspond to the excise in England, are very different in different
provinces. Some provinces are exempted from them, and pay a composition or equivalent. In those in which they take place and are in
farm, there are many local duties which do not extend beyond a particular town or district. The *Traites*, which correspond to our
customs, divide the kingdom into three great parts: first, the provinces
subject to the tariff of 1664, which are called the provinces of the
five great farms, and under which are comprehended Picardy,
Normandy, and the greater part of the interior provinces of the kingdom; secondly, the provinces subject to the tariff of 1667, which are
called the provinces reckoned foreign, and under which are comprehended the greater part of the frontier provinces; and, thirdly, those
provinces which are said to be treated as foreign, or which because
they are allowed a free commerce with foreign countries are in their
commerce with the other provinces of France subjected to the same
duties as other foreign countries. These are Alsace, the three bishop-
rics of Metz, Toul, and Verdun, and the three cities of Dunkirk,
Bayonne, and Marseilles. Both in the provinces of the five great
farms (called so on account of an ancient division of the duties of
customs into five great branches, each of which was originally the
subject of a particular farm, though they are now all united into one),
and in those which are said to be reckoned foreign, there are many

local duties which do not extend beyond a particular town or district. There are some such even in the provinces which are said to be treated as foreign, particularly in the city of Marseilles. It is unnecessary to observe how much both the restraints upon the interior commerce of the country and the number of the revenue officers must be multiplied, in order to guard the frontiers of those different provinces and districts which are subject to such different systems of taxation.'

And there were numerous attendant errors, such as generally accompany a great protective legislation, but which need not be specified in detail.

In consequence, the people were exceedingly miserable. The system of taxation was often enough by itself to cause great misery. 'In the provinces,' says Adam Smith, 'where the personal *taille* on the farmer is imposed, the farmer is afraid to have a good team of horses or oxen, but endeavours to cultivate with the meanest and most wretched instruments of husbandry that he can.' The numerous imposts on the land due from the peasantry to the nobles had the same effect even then—most of the country was practically held in a kind of double ownership; the peasant cultivator had usually, by habit if not by law, a fixed hold upon the soil, but he was subject in the cultivation of it to innumerable exactions of varying kinds, which the lord could change pretty much as he chose. 'In France,' continues Adam Smith, so oddly contrary to everything which we should say now, 'the inferior ranks of the people must suffer patiently the usage which their superiors choose to inflict on them.' The country in Europe where there is now, perhaps, the most of social equality was then the one in which there was, perhaps, the least.

And side by side with this museum of economical errors there was a most vigorous political economy which exposed them. The doctrines of Free Trade had been before several times suggested by isolated thinkers, but by far the most powerful combined school of philosophers who incessantly inculcated them were the French *Économistes*. They delighted in proving that the whole structure of the French laws upon industry was utterly wrong; that prohibitions ought not to be imposed on the import of foreign manufactures; that bounties ought not to be given to native ones; that the exportation of corn ought to be free; that the whole country ought to be a fiscal unit; that there should be no duty between any province; and so on in other cases. No one could state the abstract doctrines on which they rested everything more clearly. 'Acheter, c'est vendre,' said Quesnay, the founder of the school, 'vendre, c'est acheter.' You cannot better express the doctrine of modern political economy that 'trade is barter.' 'Do not attempt,' Quesnay continues, ' to fix the price of your products, goods, or services; they will escape your rules. Competition alone can regulate prices with equity; it alone restricts them to a moderation which varies little; it alone attracts with certainty provisions where they are wanted or labour where it is required.' 'That which we call dearness is the only remedy of dearness : dearness causes plenty.' Any quantity of sensible remarks to this effect might be disinterred from these writers. They were not always equally wise.

As the prime maxim of the ruling policy was to encourage commerce and neglect agriculture, this sect set up a doctrine that agriculture was the only source of wealth, and that trade and commerce contributed nothing to it. The labour of artificers and merchants was sterile; that of agriculturists was alone truly productive. The way in which they arrived at this strange idea was, if I understand it, something like this : they took the whole agricultural produce of a country, worth say 5,000,000*l.* as it stood in the hands of the farmer, and applied it thus :—

First, as we should say, in repayment of capital spent
    in wages, &c. . . . . . . 3,000,000*l.*
Secondly, in payment of profit by way of hire of capital,
    say, or as subsistence to himself . . . 500,000*l.*

              Total outlay . . 3,500,000*l.*

But that outlay of 3,500,000*l.* has produced a value of 5,000,000*l.*; there is therefore an overplus over and above the outlay of 1,500,000*l.*; and this overplus, or *produit net* as the *Économistes* call it, goes to the landlord for rent, as we should call it. But no other employment yields any similar *produit net.* A cotton spinner only replaces his own capital, and obtains his profit on it; like the farmer (as they said), he pays the outlay, and he gains a profit or subsistence for himself. But he does no more. There is no extra overplus in farming; no balance, after paying wages and hiring capital; nothing to go to any landlord. In the same way commerce is, according to this system, transfer only—the expense of distribution is paid; the necessary number of capitalists and of labourers are maintained, but that is all; there is nothing beyond the wages and beyond the profit. In agriculture only is there a third element—a *produit net.*

From this doctrine the *Économistes* drew two inferences—one very agreeable to agriculturists, the other very disagreeable; but both exactly opposite to the practice of their government. *First,* they said, as agriculture was the exclusive source of all wealth, it was absurd to depress it or neglect it, or to encourage commerce and manufacture in place of it. They had no toleration for the system of finance and commercial legislation which they saw around them, of which the one object was to make France a trading and manufacturing country, when nature meant it to be an agricultural one. *Secondly,* they inferred that most, if not all, the existing taxes in France were wrong in principle. 'If,' they argued, 'agriculture is the only source of wealth, and if, as we know, wealth only can pay taxes, then all taxes should be imposed on agriculture.' They reasoned: 'In manufactures there is only a necessary hire of labour, and a similar hire of capital, at a cost which cannot be diminished; there is in them no available surplus for taxation. If you attempt to impose taxes on them, and if in name you make them pay such taxes, they will charge higher for their necessary work. They will in a roundabout way throw the burden of those taxes on agriculture. The *produit net* of the latter is the one real purse of the state; no other pursuit can truly pay anything, for it has no purse. And therefore,' they summed up, 'all taxes, save a single one on the *produit net,* were absurd. They only attempted to make those pay who could not pay; to extract money from fancied funds, in which there was no money.' All the then existing taxes in France, therefore, they proposed to abolish, and to replace them by a single tax on agriculture only.

As this system was so opposed to the practice of the government, one would have expected that it should have been discountenanced, if not persecuted, by the government. But, in fact, it was rather favoured by it. Quesnay, the founder of the system, had a place at Court, and was under the special protection of the king's mistress, who was then the king's government. M. de Lavergne has quoted a graphic description of him. 'Quesnay, writes Marmontel, well lodged in a small *appartement* in the *entresol* of Madame de Pompadour, only occupied himself from morning till night with political and agricultural economy. He believed that he had reduced the system to calculation, and to axioms of irresistible evidence; and as he was collecting a school, he gave himself the trouble to explain to me his new doctrine, in order to make me one of his proselytes. I applied all my force of comprehension to understand those truths which he told me were self-evident; but I found in them only vagueness and obscurity. To make him believe that I understood that which I really did not understand was beyond my power; but I listened with patient docility, and left him the hope that in the end he would enlighten me and make me believe his doctrine. I did more; I applauded his work, which I really thought very useful, for he tried to recommend agriculture in a country where it was too much disdained, and to turn many excellent understandings towards the study of it. While political storms were forming and dissolving above the *entresol* of Quesnay, he perfected his calculations and his axioms of rural economy, as tranquil and as indifferent to the movements of the Court, as if he had been a hundred leagues off.   Below, in the *salon* of Madame de Pompadour, they deliberated on peace or war—on the choice of generals—on the recall of ministers ; while we in the *entresol* were reasoning on agriculture, calculating the *produit net*, or sometimes were dining gaily with Diderot, D'Alembert, Duclos, Helvetius, Turgot, Buffon ; and Madame de Pompadour, not being able to induce this troop of philosophers to come down to her *salon*, came herself to see them at table and to chat with them.'   An opposition philosophy has rarely been so petted and well treated.   Much as the reign of Louis XVI. differed in most respects from that of Louis XV., it was like it in this patronage of the *Économistes*.   Turgot was made Minister of Finance, to reform France by applying their doctrines.

The reason of this favour to the *Économistes* from the government was, that on the question in which the government took far the most interest the *Économistes* were on its side.   The daily want of the French government was more power ; though nominally a despotism, it was feeble in reality. But the *Économistes* were above all things anxious for a very strong government ; they held to the maxim, everything *for* the people—nothing *by* them ; they had a horror of checks and counterpoises and resistances ; they wished to do everything by the *fiat* of the sovereign.   They had, in fact, the natural wish of eager speculators, to have an irresistible despotism behind them and supporting them ; and with the simplicity which marks so much of the political speculation of the eighteenth century, but which now seems so childlike, they never seemed to think how they were to get their despot, or how they were to ensure that he should be on their side.   The painful experience of a hundred years has taught us that influential despotisms are not easy to make, and that good ones are still less so.   But in their own time nothing could be more advantageous to the *Économistes* than to have an eager zeal for a perfect despotism ; in consequence they were patronised by the greatest existing authority, instead of being discountenanced by it.

This account of the *Économistes* may seem to a reader who looks at Adam Smith exclusively by the light of modern political economy to be too long for their relation to him. But he would not have thought so himself. He so well knew how much his mind had been affected by them and by their teaching, that he at one time thought of dedicating the 'Wealth of Nations' to Quesnay, their founder ; and though he relinquished that intention, he always speaks of him with the gravest respect. If, indeed, we consider what Glasgow is now, still more what it must have been a hundred years ago, we shall comprehend the degree to which this French experience—this sight of a country so managed, and with such a political economy—must have excited the mind of Adam Smith. It was the passage from a world where there was no *spectacle* to one in which there was the best which the world has ever seen, and simultaneously the passage from the most Scotch of ideas to others the most un-Scotch. A feeble head would have been upset in the transit, but Adam Smith kept his.

From France he went home to Scotland, and stayed quietly with his mother at his native town of Kirkcaldy for a whole ten years. He lived on the annuity from the Duke of Buccleugh, and occupied himself in study only. What he was studying, if we considered the 'Wealth of Nations' as a book of political economy only, we might be somewhat puzzled to say. But the contents of that book are, as has been said, most miscellaneous, and in its author's mind it was but a fragment of an immensely larger whole. Much more than ten years' study would have been necessary for the entire book which he contemplated.

At last, in 1776, the 'Wealth of Nations' was published, and was, on the whole, well received. Dr. Carlyle, indeed, preserves

an impression that, in point of style, it was inferior to the
'Theory of Moral Sentiments.' But all competent readers were
agreed as to the great value of the substance. And almost
everybody will probably now think, in spite of Dr. Carlyle, that
the style is very much better than that of the 'Moral Sentiments.' There is about the latter a certain showiness and an
'air of the professor trying to be fascinating,' which are not
very agreeable; and, after all, there is a ponderous weight in
the words which seems to bear down the rather flimsy matter.
But the style of the 'Wealth of Nations' is entirely plain and
manly. The author had, in the interval, seen at least a little
of the living world and of society, and had learnt that the
greatest mistake is the trying to be more agreeable than you
can be, and that the surest way to spoil an important book is
to try to attract the attention of, to 'write down' to, a class of
readers too low to take a serious interest in the subject. A
really great style, indeed, Adam Smith's certainly is not. Lord
Mansfield is said to have told Boswell that he did not feel, in
reading either Hume or Adam Smith, that he was reading
English at all; and it was very natural that it should be so.
English was not the mother tongue of either. Adam Smith
had, no doubt, spoken somewhat broad Scotch for the first
fourteen or fifteen years of his life; probably he never spoke
anything that could quite be called English till he went to
Oxford. And nothing so much hampers the free use of the
pen in any language as the incessant remembrance of a kindred but different one; you are never sure the idioms nature
prompts are those of the tongue you would speak, or of the
tongue you would reject. Hume and Adam Smith exemplify
the difficulty in opposite ways. Hume is always idiomatic, but
his idioms are constantly wrong; many of his best passages are,
on that account, curiously grating and puzzling; you feel that
they are very like what an Englishman would say, but yet
that, after all, somehow or other, they are what he never
would say;—there is a minute seasoning of imperceptible dif-

ference which distracts your attention, and which you are for ever stopping to analyse. Adam Smith's habit was very different. His style is not colloquial in the least. He adheres to the heavy 'book' English which he had found in the works of others, and was sure that he could repeat in his own. And in that sort of style he has eminent merit. No one ever has to read him twice to gather his meaning; no one can bring much valid objection to his way of expressing that meaning; there is even a sort of appropriateness, though often a clumsy sort, in his way of saying it. But the style has no intrinsic happiness; no one would read it for its own sake; the words do not cleave to the meaning, so that you cannot think of them without it, or of it without them. This is only given to those who write in the speech of their childhood, and only to the very few of those —the five or six in every generation—who have from nature the best grace, who think by inborn feeling in words at once charming and accurate.

Of the ' Wealth of Nations ' as an economical treatise, I have nothing to say now; but it is not useless to say that it is a very amusing book about old times. As it is dropping out of immediate use from change of times, it is well to observe that this very change brings it a new sort of interest of its own. There are few books from which there may be gathered more curious particulars of the old world. I cull at random almost that ' a broad wheel waggon, attended by two men, and drawn by eight horses,' then 'in about six weeks' time carried and brought trade between London and Edinburgh ; '--that in Adam Smith's opinion, if there were such an effectual demand for grain as would require a million tons of shipping to import it, the ' navy of England,' the mercantile navy of course, would not be sufficient for it ;—that ' Holland was the great emporium of European goods ; ' that she was, in proportion to the land and the number of inhabitants, by far the richest country in Europe; that she had the greatest share of the ocean-carrying trade ; that her citizens possessed 40,000,000*l.* in the French

T

and English funds;—that in Sheffield no master cutler can have more than one apprentice, by a by-law of the corporation, and in Norfolk and Norwich no weaver more than two;—that, if Adam Smith's eyes served him right, 'the common people in Scotland, who are fed with oatmeal, are in general neither so strong nor so handsome as the same class of people in England, who are fed with wheaten bread, and that they do not look or work as well'; that—and this is odder still—' the porters and coal-heavers in London, and those unfortunate women who live by prostitution—the strongest men and the most beautiful women, perhaps, in the British dominions—are from the lowest rank of people in Ireland, and fed with the potato';—that 1,000*l.* share in India stock ' gave a share not in the plunder, but in the appointment of the plunderers of India';—that ' the expense of the establishment of Massachussetts Bay, before the commencement of the late disturbances,' that is, the American war, ' used to be about 18,000*l.* a year, and that of New York, 4,500*l.* ;' that all the civil establishments in America did not at the same date cost 67,000*l.* a year ;—that ' in consequence of the monopoly of the American colonial market,' the commerce of England, ' instead of running in a great number of small channels, has been taught to run principally in one great channel ;'—that ' the territorial acquisitions of the East India Company, the undoubted right of the Crown,' ' might be rendered another source of revenue more abundant, perhaps, than all' others from which much addition could be expected ; —that Great Britain is, perhaps, since ' the world began, the only state which has extended its empire' ' without augmenting the area of its resources ;'—that, and this is the final sentence of the book, ' If any of the provinces of the British empire cannot be made to contribute towards the support of the whole empire, it is surely time that Great Britain should free herself from the expense of defending those provinces in time of war, and of supporting any part of their civil or military establishments in time of peace, and endeavour to accommodate her future views and designs to the real mediocrity of her circumstances.' A strange passage, considering all that has happened since, and all the provinces which we have since taken. No one can justly estimate the ' Wealth of Nations ' who thinks of it as a book of mere political economy, such as Quesnay had then written, or as Ricardo afterwards wrote. It is really full both of the most various kinds of facts and of thoughts often as curious on the most various kinds of subjects.

The effect of the publication of the ' Wealth of Nations ' on the fortunes of its author was very remarkable. It gave the Duke of Buccleugh the power of relieving himself of his annuity, by performing the equivalent clause in the bargain ; he obtained for Adam Smith a commissionership of customs for Scotland— an appointment of which we do not know the precise income, but which was clearly, according to the notions of those times, a very good one indeed. A person less fitted to fill it could not indeed easily have been found. Adam Smith had, as we have seen, never been used to pecuniary business of any kind ; he had never even taken part in any sort of action out of such business ; he was an absent and meditative student. It was indeed during his tenure of this office that, as I have said, he startled a subordinate, who asked for his signature, by imitating the signature of the last commissioner, instead of giving his own—of course in pure absence of mind. He was no doubt better acquainted with the theory of taxation than any other man of his time ; he could have given a minister in the capital better advice than anyone else as to what taxes he should, or should not, impose. But a commissioner of customs, in a provincial city, has nothing to do with the imposition of taxes, or with giving advice about them. His business simply is to see that those which already exist are regularly collected and methodically transmitted, which involves an infinity of transactions requiring a trained man of detail. But a man of detail Adam Smith certainly was not—at least of detail in business. Nature had probably not well fitted him for it, and his mode of life had completed the result, and utterly unfitted him. The appointment that was given him was one in which the great abilities which he possessed were useless, and in which much smaller ones, which he had not, would have been of extreme value.

But in another respect this appointment has been more blamed than I think is just. However small may be the value of Adam Smith's work at the Custom House, the effect of performing it and the time which it occupied prevented him from writing anything more. And it has been thought that posterity has in consequence suffered much. But I own that I doubt this exceedingly. Adam Smith had no doubt made a vast accumulation of miscellaneous materials for his great design. But these materials were probably of very second-rate value. Neither for the history of law, nor of science, nor of art, had the preliminary work been finished, which is necessary before such a mind as Adam Smith's can usefully be applied to them. Before the theorising philosopher must come the accurate historian. To write the history either of law or science or art is enough for the life of any single man: neither have as yet been written with the least approach to completeness. The best of the fragments on these subjects, which we now have, did not exist in Adam Smith's time. There was, therefore, but little use in his thinking or writing at large about them. If he had set down for us some account of his residence in France, and the society which he saw there, posterity would have been most grateful to him. But this he had no idea of doing ; and nobody would now much care for a series of elaborate theories, founded upon facts insufficiently collected.

Adam Smith lived for fourteen years after the publication of the ' Wealth of Nations,' but he wrote nothing, and scarcely studied anything. The duties of his office, though of an easy and routine character, which would probably have enabled a man bred to business to spend much of his time and almost all his mind on other things, were, we are told, enough ' to waste his spirits and dissipate his attention.' And not unnaturally, for those who have ever been used to give all their days to literary work, rarely seem able to do that work when they are even in a slight degree struck and knocked against the world : only those who have scarcely ever known what it is to have unbroken calm are able to accomplish much without that calm. During these years Adam Smith's life passed easily and pleasantly in the Edinburgh society of that time—a very suitable one, for it was one to which professors and lawyers gave the tone, and of which intellectual exertion was the life and being. Adam Smith was, it is true, no easy talker—was full neither of ready replies nor of prepared replies. He rather liked to listen, but if he talked—and traps it is said were laid to make him do so—he could expound admirably on the subjects which he knew, and also (which is quite as characteristic of the man as we see him in his works) could run up rapid theories on such data as occurred to him, when, as Dugald Stewart tells us in his dignified dialect, ' he gave a loose to his genius upon the very few branches of knowledge of which he only possessed the outlines.'

He died calmly and quietly, leaving directions about his manuscripts and such other literary things, and saying, in a melancholy way, ' I meant to have done more.' The sort of fame which the ' Wealth of Nations ' has obtained, and its special influence, did not begin in his lifetime, and he had no notion of it. Nor would he perhaps have quite appreciated it, if he had. His mind was full of his great scheme of the origin and history of all cultivation. As happens to so many men, though scarcely ever on so great a scale, aiming at one sort of reputation, he attained another. To use Lord Bacon's perpetual illustration, like Saul, he ' went in search of his father's asses, and he found a kingdom.'

Adam Smith has been said to belong to the Macaulay type of Scotchmen, and the saying has been thought a paradox, particularly by those who, having misread Macaulay, think him a showy rhetorician, and not having at all read Adam Smith, think of him as a dry and dull political economist. But the saying is true, nevertheless. Macaulay is anything but a mere rhetorical writer—there is a very hard kernel of business in him ; and Adam Smith is not dry at all—the objection to him is that he is not enough so, and that the real truth in several parts of his subject cannot be made so interesting as his mode of treatment implies. And there is this fundamental likeness between Macaulay and Adam Smith, that they can both describe practical matters in such a way as to fasten them on the imagination, and not only get what they say read, but get it remembered and make it part of the substance of the reader's mind ever afterwards. Abstract theorists may say that such a style as that of Adam Smith is not suitable to an abstract science ; but then Adam Smith has carried political economy far beyond the bounds of those who care for abstract science, or who understand exactly what it means. He has popularised it in the only sense in which it can be popularised without being spoiled ; that is, he has put certain broad conclusions into the minds of hard-headed men, which are all which they need know, and all which they for the most part will ever care for, and he has put those conclusions there ineradicably. This, too, is what Macaulay does for us in history, at least what he does best ; he engraves indelibly the main outlines and the rough common sense of the matter. Other more refining, and perhaps in some respects more delicate, minds may add the nicer details, and explain those wavering, flickering, inconstant facts of human nature which are either above common sense or below it. Both these great Scotchmen excelled in the 'osteology of their subject,' a term invented by Dr. Chalmers, a third great Scotchman who excelled in it himself : perhaps, indeed, it is an idiosyncrasy of their race.

Like many other great Scotchmen—Macaulay is one of them—Adam Smith was so much repelled by the dominant Calvinism in which he was born, that he never voluntarily wrote of religious subjects, nor, as far as we know, spoke of them. Nothing, indeed, can repel a man more from such things than what Macaulay called the ' bray of Exeter Hall.' What can be worse for people than to hear in their youth arguments, alike clamorous and endless, founded on ignorant interpretations of inconclusive words? As soon as they come to years of discretion, all instructed persons cease to take part in such discussions, and often say nothing at all on the great problems of human life and destiny. Sometimes the effect goes farther; those subjected to this training become not only silent but careless. There is nothing like Calvinism for generating indifference. The saying goes that Scotchmen are those who believe most or least; and it is most natural that it should be so, for they have been so hurt and pestered with religious stimulants, that it is natural they should find total abstinence from them both pleasant and healthy. How far this indifference went in Adam Smith's case we do not exactly know; but there is no reason to think it extended to all religion. On the contrary, there are many traces of the complacent optimism of the eighteenth century—a doctrine the more agreeable to him perhaps, because it is the exact opposite of Calvinism—and one which was very popular in an easy-going age, though the storms and calamities of a later time dispelled it, and have made it seem to us thin and unreal. The only occasion when Adam Smith ever came near to theological discussion was in a letter on Hume's death, in which he said that Hume, one of his oldest friends, was the best man he had ever known—praise which perhaps was scarcely meant to be taken too literally, but which naturally caused a great storm. The obvious thing to say about it is, that it does not indicate any very lofty moral standard, for there certainly was no sublime excellence in Hume, who, as Carlyle long ago said, ' all his life through did not so much morally live, as critically investigate.' But though the bigots of his time misunderstood him, Adam Smith did not by so saying mean to identify himself with irreligion or even with scepticism.

Adam Smith's life, however, was not like Macaulay's—'a life without a lady.' There are vestiges of an early love affair, though but vague ones. Dugald Stewart, an estimable man in his way, but one of the most detestable of biographers, for he seems always thinking much more of his own words than of the facts he has to relate, says: 'In the early part of Mr. Smith's life, it is well known to his friends that he was for several years attached to a young lady of great beauty and accomplishment.' But he does not tell us who she was, and 'has not been able to learn' 'how far his addresses were favourably received,' or, in fact, anything about the matter. It seems, however, that the lady died unmarried, and in that case the unsentimental French novelists say that the gentleman is not often continuously in earnest, for that 'a lady cannot be always saying No!' But whether such was the case with Adam Smith or not, we cannot tell. He was a lonely, bookish man, but that may tell both ways. The books may be opposed to the lady, but the solitude will preserve her remembrance.

If Adam Smith did abandon sentiment and devote himself to study, he has at least the excuse of having succeeded. Scarcely any writer's work has had so much visible fruit. He has, at least, annexed his name to a great practical movement which is still in progress through the world. Free trade has become in the popular mind almost as much his subject as the war of Troy was Homer's: only curious inquirers think of teachers before the one any more than of poets before the other. If all the speeches made at our Anti-Corn Law League were examined, I doubt if any reference could be found to any preceding writer, though the name of Adam Smith was always on men's lips. And in other countries it is the same. Smith-ism is a name of reproach with all who reject such doctrines, and of respect with those who believe them; no other name is used equally or comparably by either. So long as the doctrines of protection exist—and they seem likely to do so, as human interests are what they are and human nature is what it is—

Adam Smith will always be quoted as the great authority of Anti-Protectionism—as the man who first told the world the truth so that the world could learn and believe it.

And besides this great practical movement, Adam Smith started a great theoretical one also. On one side his teaching created Mr. Cobden and Mr. Bright, on another it rendered possible Ricardo and Mr. Mill. He is the founder of that analysis of the ' great commerce' which in England we now call political economy, and which, dry, imperfect, and unfinished as it is, will be thought by posterity one of the most valuable and peculiar creations of English thought. As far as accuracy goes, Ricardo no doubt began this science ; but his whole train of thought was suggested by Adam Smith, and he could not have written without him. So much theory and so much practice have rarely, perhaps never, sprung from a single mind.

Fortunate in many things, Adam Smith was above all things fortunate in his age. Commerce had become far larger, far more striking, far more world-wide than it ever was before, and it needed an effectual explainer. A vigorous Scotchman, with the hard-headedness and the abstractions of his country, trained in England and familiar with France, was the species of man best fitted to explain it, and such a man was Adam Smith.

## LORD ALTHORP AND THE REFORM ACT OF 1832.[1]

### [1877.]

'ALTHORP carried the Bill,' such is the tradition of our fathers : 'the Bill,' of course, being the Bill to them—the great Reform Act of 1832, which was like a little revolution in that generation—which really changed so much, and which seemed to change so much more. To have been mainly concerned in passing so great a measure seems to many of the survivors of that generation, who remember the struggles of their youth and recall the enthusiasm of that time, almost the *acme* of fame. And in sober history such men will always be respectfully and gravely mentioned, but all romance has died away. *The* Bill is to us hardly more than other Bills; it is one of a great many Acts of Parliament which in this day, partly for good and partly for evil, have altered the ever-varying constitution of England. The special charm, the charm which to the last you may see that Macaulay always felt about it, is all gone. The very history of it is forgotten. Which of the younger generation can say what was General Gascoigne's amendment, or who were the 'waverers,' or even how many Reform 'Bills' in those years there were? The events for which one generation cares most, are often those of which the next knows least. They are too old to be matters of personal recollection, and they are too new to be subjects of study : they have passed out of memory, and they have not got into the books. Of the well-informed young people about us, there are very many who scarcely know who Lord Althorp was.

[1] *Memoir of John Charles, Viscount Althorp, third Earl Spencer.* By the late Sir Denis Le Marchant, Bart. London : Richard Bentley & Son, 1876.

And in another respect this biography has been unfortunate. It has been kept back too long. The Reform Act of 1867 has shed a painful light on the Reform Act of 1832, and has exhibited in real life what philosophers said were its characteristic defects. While these lingered in the books they were matters of dull teaching, and no one cared for them; but now Mr. Disraeli has embodied them, and they are living among us. The traditional sing-song of mere eulogy is broken by a sharp question. Those who study that time say, 'Althorp, you tell us, passed the Bill. It was his frankness and his high character and the rest of his great qualities which did it. But was it good that he should have passed it? Would it not have been better if he had not possessed those fine qualities? Was not some higher solution possible? Knowing this Bill by its fruits, largely good, but also largely evil, might we not have had a better Bill? At any rate, if it could not be so, show *why* it could not be so. Prove that the grave defects in the Act of 1832 were necessary defects. Explain how it was that Althorp had no choice, and then we will admire him as you wish us.' But to this biographer—a man of that time, then in the House of Commons on the Whig side, and almost, as it were, on the skirts of the Bill—such questions would have seemed impossible. To him, the Act of 1832 is still wonderful and perfect— the great measure which *we* carried in *my* youth; and as for explaining defects in it, he would have as soon thought of explaining defects in a revelation.

But if ever Lord Althorp's life is well written, it will, I think, go far to explain not only why the Reform Bill was carried, but why that Bill is what it was. He embodies all the characteristic virtues which enable Englishmen to effect well and easily great changes in politics: their essential fairness, their 'large roundabout common sense,' their courage, and their disposition rather to give up something than to take the uttermost farthing. But on the other hand also he has all the characteristic English defects: their want of intellectual and guiding principle, their

even completer want of the culture which would give that
principle, their absorption in the present difficulty, and their
hand-to-mouth readiness to take what solves it without thinking
of other consequences.   And I am afraid the moral of those
times is that these English qualities as a whole—merits and
defects together—are better suited to an early age of politics
than to a later.   As long as materials are deficient, these qualities
are most successful in hitting off simple expedients, in adapting old things to new uses, and in extending ancient customs;
they are fit for instantaneous little creations, and admirable at
bit-by-bit growth.   But when, by the incessant application of
centuries, these qualities have created an accumulated mass of
complex institutions, they are apt to fail, unless aided by others
very different.   The instantaneous origination of obvious expedients is of no use when the field is already covered with the
heterogeneous growth of complex past expedients; bit-by-bit
development is out of place unless you are sure which bit should,
and which bit should not, be developed; the extension of customs may easily mislead when there are so many customs; no
immense and involved subject can be set right except by faculties which can grasp what is immense and scrutinise what is
involved.   But mere common sense is here matched with more
than it can comprehend, like a schoolboy in the differential calculus;—and absorption in the present difficulty is an evil, not
a good, for what is wanted is that you should be able to see
many things at once, and take in their bearing, not fasten yourself on one thing.   The characteristic danger of great nations,
like the Romans, or the English, which have a long history of
continuous creation, is that they may at last fail from not
comprehending the great institutions which they have created.

No doubt it would be a great exaggeration to say that this
calamity happened in its fulness in the year 1832, and it would
be most unfair to Lord Althorp to cite him as a complete
example of the characteristics which may cause it; but there
was something in him of those qualities, and some trace in 1832

of that calamity—enough in both cases to be a warning.   Only
a complete history of the time can prove this ; but perhaps in
a few pages I may a little explain and illustrate it.

   Let us first get, both as more instructive and as less tedious
than analysis, a picture of the man as he stood in the principal
event of his life.   A good drawer has thus painted him.   Lord
Jeffrey, the great Edinburgh Reviewer, who was an able lawyer
and practical man of business in his day, though his criticism
on party has not stood the test of time, was Lord Advocate in
the Reform Ministry of 1830, and he is never tired of describing Lord Althorp.   'There is something,' he writes, 'to me
quite delightful in his calm, clumsy, courageous, immutable
probity, and it seems to have a charm for everybody.'   'I went
to Althorp,' he writes, 'again, and had a characteristic scene
with that most honest, frank, true, and stout-hearted of God's
creatures.   He had not come downstairs, and I was led up to
his dressing-room, with his arms (very rough and hairy) bare
above the elbows, and his beard half shaved and half staring
through the lather, with a desperate razor in one hand, and a
great soap-brush in the other.   He gave me the loose finger of
his brush hand, and with the usual twinkle of his bright eye
and radiant smile, he said, "You need not be anxious about
your Scotch Bills to-night, for we are no longer his Majesty's
ministers."'   And soon after he writes again, at a later stage
of the ministerial crisis, 'When they came to summon Lord
Althorp to a council on the Duke's giving in, he was found in
a shed with a groom, busy oiling the locks of his fowling-pieces,
and lamenting the decay into which they had fallen during his
ministry.'   And on another occasion he adds what may serve as
an intellectual accompaniment to these descriptions : 'Althorp,
with his usual frankness, gave us a pretended confession of his
political faith, and a sort of creed of his political morality, and
showed that though it was a very shocking doctrine to promulgate, he must say that he had never sacrificed his own inclinations to a sense of duty without repenting it, and always found

himself more substantially unhappy for having employed himself for the public good.' And someone else at the time said, 'The Government cannot be going out, for Althorp looks so very dismal.' He was made (as we learn from this volume) a principal minister, contrary to his expectation and in opposition to his wish. He was always wanting to resign ; he was always uncomfortable, if not wretched ; and the instant he could do so, he abandoned politics, and would never touch them again, though he lived for many years. And this, though in appearance he was most successful, and was almost idolized by his followers and friends.

At first this seems an exception to one of Nature's most usual rules. Almost always, if she gives a great faculty she gives also an enjoyment in the use of it. But here Nature had given a remarkable power of ruling and influencing men—one of the most remarkable (good observers seem to say) given to any Englishman of that generation ; and yet the possessor did not like, but, on the contrary, much disliked to use it. The explanation, however, is, that not only had Nature bestowed on Lord Althorp this happy and great gift of directing and guiding men, but, as if by some subtle compensation, had added what was, under the circumstances, a great pain to it. She had given him a most sluggish intellect—only moving with effort, and almost with suffering—generally moving clumsily, and usually following, not suggesting. If you put a man with a mind like this—especially a sensitive, conscientious man such as Lord Althorp was—to guide men quickly through complex problems of legislation and involved matters of science, no wonder that he will be restive and wish to give up. No doubt the multitude wish to follow him ; but where is he to tell the multitude to go ? His mind suggests nothing, and there is a pain and puzzle in his brain.

Fortune and education had combined in Lord Althorp's case to develop his defects. His father and mother were both persons of great cultivation, but they were also busy people of

the world, and so they left their son to pick up his education as
he could.   A Swiss footman, who did not know English very
well, taught him to read, and 'was his sole instructor and most
intimate associate till he went to Harrow.'   His father, too, being
a great fox-hunter, the son clearly cared more for, and was more
occupied with hounds and animals, as a young boy, than with
anything else ; and he lived mainly with servants and people
also so occupied, from which, as might be expected, he contracted
a shyness and awkwardness which stayed with him through life.
When he went to Harrow, the previous deficiencies of his education were, of course, against him, and he seems to have shown
no particular disposition to repair them.   As far as can now be
learnt, he was an ordinary strong-headed and strong-willed
English boy, equal to necessary lessons, but not caring for
them, and only distinguished from the rest by a certain suppressed sensibility and tenderness, which he also retained in
after years, which softened a manliness that would otherwise
have been rugged, and which saved him from being unrefined.

At Cambridge his mother, as it appears, suddenly, and for
the first time, took an interest in his studies, and told him she
should expect him to be high at his first college examination.
And this seems to have awakened him to industry.   The
examination was in mathematics, which suited him much better
than the Harrow classics, and he really came out high in it.
The second year it was the same, though he had good com-
petitors.   But there his studies ended.   His being a nobleman
at that time excluded him from the university examinations,
and he was far too apathetic to work at mathematics, except for
something of the sort, and his tutor seems to have discouraged
his doing so.   Then, as since, the bane of Cambridge has been
a certain incomplete and rather mean way of treating great
studies, which teaches implicitly, if not plainly, that it was as
absurd to learn the differential calculus in and for itself as it
would be to keep a ledger for its own sake.   On such a mind
as Lord Althorp's, which required as much as possible to be

awakened and kept awake to the interest of high studies, no external surroundings could have been more fatal. He threw up his reading and took to hounds, betting, and Newmarket, and to all which was then, even if not since, thought to be most natural, if not most proper, in a young nobleman.

As far as classical studies are concerned he probably lost nothing. He was through life very opaque to literary interests, and in his letters and speeches always used language in the clumsiest way. But he had—perhaps from his childish field sports—a keen taste for animals and natural history, which now-a-days would have been developed into a serious pursuit. And as it was, he had an odd craving for figures, which might have been made something of in mathematics. ' He kept,' we are told, ' an account of every shot he fired in the course of a year, whether he missed or killed, and made up the book periodically.' He would not pass the accounts of the Agricultural Society without hunting for a missing threepence ; and when Chancellor of the Exchequer he used, it is said, ' to do all his calculations, however complicated, alone in his closet,' which his biographer thinks very admirable, and contrasts with the habit of Mr. Pitt, ' who used to take a Treasury clerk into his confidence,' but which was really very absurd. It is not by such mechanical work that great budgets are framed ; and a great minister ought to know what *not* to do himself, and how to use, for everything possible, the minds of others. Still there is much straight-forward strength in this, if also some comic dulness.

If Lord Althorp's relatives did not give him a very good education, they did not make up for it by teaching him light accomplishments. They sent him the ' grand tour,' as it was then called ; but he was shy and awkward, seems to have had no previous preparation for foreign society, would not go into it, and returned boasting that he could not speak French. His mother—a woman of great fashion and high culture—must have sighed very much over so uncourtly and so ' English ' an eldest son.

Then, in the easy way of those times—it was in 1804—he was brought into Parliament for Okehampton, a nomination borough, some 'Mr. Strange,' a barrister, retiring in his favour, and his interest being strong, he was made a Lord of the Treasury.   But the same apathy to intellectual interests which showed itself at college clung to him here also.   He showed energy, but it was not the energy of a man of business.   He passed, we are told, 'the greatest part of his time in the country, and when he attended at the Treasury, which was very rarely, and only on particular occasions to make up a Board, he returned home immediately afterwards.   Indeed, he used to have horses posted on the road from London to Althorp, and often rode down at night, as soon as the House had risen, in order that he might hunt with the Pytchley the next morning.'   'On these occasions,' says another account, 'he had no sleep, and often the hacks which he rode would fall down on the road.'   And years afterwards the old clerks of the office used to tell of the rarity and brevity of his visits to the department, and of the difficulty of getting him to stay;—all which shows force and character, but still not the sort of character which would fit a man to be Chancellor of the Exchequer.   But though he had much of the want of culture, Lord Althorp had none of the unfeelingness which also the modern world is getting somehow to attach to the character of the systematic sportsman.   On the contrary, he was one of the many instances which prove that this character may be combined with an extreme sensibility to the sufferings of animals and man.   He belonged to the class of men in whom such feelings are far keener than usual, and his inner character approached to the 'Arnold type,' 'for to hear of cruelty or injustice pained him' almost 'like a blow.'

He, it seems, kept a hunting journal, which tells how his hounds found a fox at Parson's Hill, and 'ran over old Naseby field to Althorp in fifty minutes, and then, after a slight check, over the finest part of Leicestershire;' and all that sort of thing.   But probably it does not tell one the very natural conse-

U

quence which happened to him from such a life. Being a somewhat uncouth person, addicted to dogs and horses—a ' man's
man,' as Thackeray used to call it—he did not probably go much
into ladies' society, and was not very aggressive when he was
there. But men who do not make advances to women are apt
to become victims to women who make advances to them ; and
so it was with Lord Althorp. He married a Miss Acklom, a
' Diana Vernon ' sort of person, ' rather stout, and without pretension to regular beauty ; ' but nevertheless, it is said, ' with
something prepossessing about her—clever, well read, with a
quick insight into the character of others, and with much self-
dependence.' And this self-dependence and thought she showed
to her great advantage in the principal affair of her life. Lord
Althorp's biographer is sure, but does not say how, that the
first declaration of love was made by the lady ; he was, it seems,
too shy to think of such a thing. As a rule, marriages in which
a young nobleman is actively captured by an aggressive lady
are not domestically happy, though they may be socially useful,
but in this case the happiness seems to have been exceptionally
great ; and when she died, after a few years, he suffered a very
unusual grief. ' He went,' we are told, ' at once to Winton, the
place where he had lived with her, and passed several months in
complete retirement, finding his chief occupation in reading the
Bible,' in which he found, at first, many grave difficulties, such
as the mention of the constellation ' Orion ' by the prophet
Amos, and the high place (an equality with Job and David)
given by Ezekiel to the prophet Daniel when still a young man,
' and before he had proved himself to be a man of so great a
calibre as he certainly did afterwards.' On these questions, he
adds, ' I have consulted a Mr. Shepherd, the clergyman here,
but his answers are not satisfactory.' Happily, however, such a
man is not at the mercy of clergymen's answers, nor dependent
on the petty details of ancient prophets. The same sensibility
which made him keenly alive to justice and injustice in things
of this world, went further, and told him of a moral government

in things not of this world. No man of or near the Arnold species was ever a sceptic as to, far less an unbeliever in, ultimate religion. New philosophies are not wanted or appreciated by such men, nor are book arguments of any real use, though these men often plod over them as if they were; for in truth an inner teaching supersedes everything, and for good or evil closes the controversy; no discussion is of any effect or force; the court of appeal, fixed by nature in such minds, is peremptory in belief, and will not hear of any doubt. And so it was in this case. Through life Lord Althorp continued to be a man strong, though perhaps a little crude, in religious belief; and thus gained at the back of his mind a solid seriousness which went well with all the rest of it. And his grief for his wife was almost equally durable. He gave up not only society, which perhaps was no great trial, but also hunting—not because he believed it to be wrong, but because he did not think it seemly or suitable that a man after such a loss should be so very happy as he knew that hunting would make him.

Soon after his marriage he had begun to take an interest in politics, especially on their moral side, and of course the increased seriousness of his character greatly augmented it. Without this change, though he might have thought himself likely to be occasionally useful in outlying political questions, probably he would have had no grave political career, and his life never would have been written. But the sort of interest which he took in politics requires some explanation, for though his time was not very long ago, the change of feeling since then is vast.

'If any person,' said Sir Samuel Romilly, the best of judges, for he lived through the times and was mixed up, heart and soul, in the matters he speaks of,—' if any person be desirous of having an adequate idea of the mischievous effects which have been produced in this country by the French Revolution and all its attendant horrors, he should attempt some reforms on humane and liberal principles. He will then find not only what a stupid spirit of conservation, but what a savage spirit, it has infused into the minds of his countrymen.' And very naturally, for nothing is so cruel as fear. A whole generation in England, and indeed in Europe, was so frightened by the Reign of Terror, that they thought it could only be prevented by another Reign of Terror. The Holy Alliances, as they were then called, meant this and worked for this. Though we had not in name such an alliance in England, we had a state of opinion which did the work of one without one. Nine-tenths of the English people were above all things determined to put down ' French principles ; ' and unhappily ' French principles ' included what we should all now consider obvious improvements and rational reforms. They would not allow the most cruel penal code which any nation ever had to be mitigated ; they did not wish justice to be questioned ; they would not let the mass of the people be educated, or at least only so that it came to nothing ; they would not alter anything which came down from their ancestors, for in their terror they did not know but there might be some charmed value even in the most insignificant thing ; and after what they had seen happen in France, they feared that if they changed a single iota all else would collapse.

Upon this generation, too, came the war passion. They waged, and in the main—though with many errors—waged with power and spirit, the war with Napoleon ; and they connected this with their horror of liberal principles in a way which is now very strange to us, but which was very powerful then. We know now that Napoleon was the head of a conservative reaction, a bitter and unfeeling reaction, just like that of the contemporary English ; but the contemporary English did not know this. To the masses of them he was *Robespierre à cheval,* as some one called him—a sort of Jacobin waging war, in some occult way, for liberty and revolution, though he called himself Emperor. Of course, the educated few gradually got more or less to know that Napoleon hated Jacobins and revolution, and liberty too, as much as it is possible to hate them ; but the ordinary multitude, up to the end of the struggle, never dreamed of it.   Thus, in an odd way, the war passion of the time strengthened its conservative feeling; and in a much more usual way it did so too, for it absorbed men's minds in the story of battles and the glory of victories, and left no unoccupied thought for gradual improvement and dull reform at home.   A war time, also, is naturally a harsh time; for the tale of conflicts which sometimes raises men above pain, also tends to make men indifferent to it: the familiarity of the idea ennobles but also hardens.

This savageness of spirit was the more important because, from deep and powerful economical agencies, there was an incessant distress running through society, sometimes less and sometimes more, but always, as we should now reckon, very great.   The greatest cause of this was that we were carrying on, or trying to carry on, a system of free trade under a restrictive tariff: we would not take foreign products, and yet we wished to sell foreigners ours.   And our home market was incessantly disordered.   First the war, and then the corn-laws confined us chiefly to our own soil for our food; but that soil was of course liable to fail in particular years, and then the price of food rose rapidly, which threw all other markets into confusion—for people must live first, and can only spend the surplus, after paying the cost of living, upon anything else. The fluctuations in the demand for our manufactures at home were ruinously great, though we were doing all we could to keep them out of foreign markets, and the combined effect was terrible.   And the next great cause was that we were daily extending an unprecedented system of credit without providing a basis for it, and without knowing how to manage it.   There was no clear notion that credit, being a promise to pay cash, must be supported by proportionate reserves of cash held in store; and that as bullion is the international cash, all international credit must be sustained by a store of bullion.   In consequence, all changes for the worse in trade, whether brought on by law or nature, caused a destruction of confidence, and diffused an uneasy moral feeling which made them far worse than they would have been otherwise. The immense fluctuations in our commerce, caused by protection, were aggravated by immense fluctuations in our credit, and the combined result was unspeakably disastrous.

During the French war these causes were not so much felt. Trade was better, because we were creating a foreign market for ourselves. Just as lately, by lending to a miscellaneous mass of foreign countries, we enabled those countries to buy of us, so in the great war, by large subsidies and huge foreign expenditure, we created a 'purchasing power' which was ultimately settled by our manufactures. We had nothing else to settle it with; if we did not send them direct, we must use them to buy the bullion, or whatever else it might be which we did send indirectly. This 'war demand,' of which so much is said in the economical literature of those years, of course ceased at the peace; and as we declined to take foreign products in exchange for ours, no substitute for it could be found, and trade languished in consequence. Agriculture, too, was worse after the peace, for the natural protection given by the war was far more effective than the artificial protection given by the corn-laws. The war kept out corn almost equally whatever was the price, but the corn-laws were based on the 'sliding scale,' which let in the corn when it became dear. Our farmers, therefore, were encouraged to grow more corn than was enough for the country in good years, which they could not sell; and they did not get a full price in bad years, for the foreign corn came in more and more as the price rose and rose. Though the protection availed to hurt the manufacturer, it was not effectual in helping the farmer. And the constant adversity of other interests, by a reflex action, also hurt him. Committees on agricultural distress, and motions as to the relief of trading distress, alternate in the parliamentary debates of those years. Our credit system, too, was in greater momentary danger after the peace than before; for during the war it was aided by a currency of inconvertible paper, which absolved us from the necessity of paying our promises in solid cash, though at very heavy cost in other ways, both at the instant and afterwards.

These fluctuations in trade and agriculture of course told on the condition of the working classes. They were constantly suffering, and then the 'savage spirit' of which Sir Samuel has spoken showed itself at its worst. Suffering, as usual, caused complaint, and this complaint was called sedition. The Habeas Corpus Act was suspended, harsh laws were passed, and a harsher administration incited to put it down. It could not be put down. It incessantly smouldered and incessantly broke out, and for years England was filled with the fear of violence, first by the breakers of the law and then by the enforcers of it.

Resistance to such a policy as this was most congenial to a nature half unhinged by misfortune, and always in itself most sensitive and opposed to injustice. Even before his wife's death, Lord Althorp had begun to exert himself against it, and afterwards he threw the whole vigour not only of his mind but of his body into it. So far from running away perpetually to hunt, as in old times, he was so constant in his attendance in Parliament that tradition says hardly anyone, except the clerks at the table, was more constantly to be seen there. He opposed all the Acts by which the Tory Government of the day tried to put down disaffection instead of curing it, and his manly energy soon made him a sort of power in Parliament. He was always there, always saying what was clear, strong, and manly; and therefore the loosely-knit opposition of that day was often guided by him; and the ministers, though strong in numerical majority, feared him, for he said things that the best of that majority understood in a rugged English way, which changed feelings, even if it did not alter votes. He was a man whom everyone in the House respected, and who therefore spoke to prepossessed hearers. No doubt, too, the peculiar tinge which grief had given to his character added to his influence. He took no share in the pleasures of other men.

Though a nobleman of the highest place, still young, as we should now reckon (he was only thirty-six when Lady Althorp died), he stood aloof from society, which courted him, and lived for public business only ; and therefore he had great weight in it, for the English very much value obviously conscientious service, and the sobered foxhunter was a somewhat interesting character.

He had not indeed any clear ideas of the cause of the difficulties of the time, or of the remedies for them. He did no doubt attend much to economical questions ; and his taste for figures, shown before in calculating the ratio of his good shots to his bad, made statistical tables even pleasing to him. His strong sense, though without culture and without originality, struggled dimly and sluggishly with the necessary problems. But considering that he lived in the days of Huskisson and Ricardo, his commercial ideas are crude and heavy. He got as far as the notion that the substitution of direct taxes for the bad tariff of those days would be ' a good measure ;' but when he came to apply the principle he failed from inability to work it out. Nor did years of discussion effectually teach him. In his great budget of 1832—the first which the Whigs had made for many years, and at which therefore everyone looked with unusual expectation—he proposed to take off a duty on tobacco and to replace it by a tax on the transfer of real and funded property, together with a tax on the import of raw cotton ; and it was the necessity of having to withdraw the larger part of this plan, that more than anything else first gave the Whigs that character for financial incapacity which clung to them so long. A crude good sense goes no way in such problems, and it is useless to apply it to them. The other economical problem of the time, how to lay a satisfactory basis for our credit, Lord Althorp was still less able to solve, and excusably so ; for the experience which has since taught us so much did not exist, and the best theories then known were very imperfect. The whole subject was then encumbered with what was called the 'currency question,' and on this Lord Althorp's views were fairly sensible, but no more.

I have said what may seem too much of the distresses of the country fifty or sixty years ago, not only because the mode in which he dealt with them is the best possible illustration of Lord Althorp's character, but also because some knowledge of them is necessary to an understanding of 'parliamentary reform,' as it was in his time, on account of which alone any-one now cares for him. The 'bill,' if I may say so, for these miseries of the country was sent in to the old system of par-liamentary representation; and very naturally. The defenders of that system of necessity conceded that it was anomalous, complex, and such as it would have been impossible to set up *de novo.* But they argued that it was practically successful, worked well, and promoted the happiness of the people better than any other probably would. And to this the inevitable rejoinder at the time was: 'The system does not work well; the country is not happy; if your system is as you say to be judged by its fruits, that system is a bad system, for its fruits are bad, and the consequences everywhere to be seen in the misery around us.' Upon many English minds which would have cared nothing for an apparent work of theoretical com-pleteness, this 'practical' way of arguing, as it was called, pressed with irresistible strength.

The unpopularity was greater because a new generation was growing up with 'other thoughts' and 'other minds' than that which had preceded it. Between 1828 and 1830 a new race came to influence public affairs, who did not remember the horrors of the French Revolution, and who had been teased to death by hearing their parents talk about them. The harsh and cruel spirit which those horrors had awakened in their contemporaries became itself, by the natural law of reaction, an object of disgust and almost of horror to the next generation. When it was said that the old structure of Parliament worked well, this new race looked not only at the evident evils amid

which they lived, but at the oppressive laws and administration
by which their fathers had tried to cure those evils; and they
'debited' both to the account of the old Parliament. It was
made responsible for the mistaken treatment as well as for the
deep-rooted disease, and so the gravest clouds hung over it.

The Duke of Wellington, too (the most unsuccessful of
premiers as well as the most successful of generals), broke the
Tory party—the natural party to support this system—into
fragments. With a wise renunciation both of his old principles and of his fixed prejudices he had granted 'Catholic
Emancipation,' and so offended the older and stricter part of
his followers. They accused him of treachery, and hated him
with a hatred of which in this quiet age, when political passion
is feeble, we can hardly form an idea. And he then quarrelled,
also, with the best of the moderate right—Mr. Huskisson and
the Canningites. He had disliked Mr. Canning personally
when alive, he hated still more the liberal principles which he
had begun to introduce into our foreign policy, and he was an
eager, despotic man, who disliked difference of opinion; so
just when he had broken with the most irrational section of
his party, he broke with its most rational members too, and
left himself very weak. No one so much, though without
meaning it, aided the cause of parliamentary change, for he
divided and enfeebled the supporters of the old system; he
took away the question of Catholic Emancipation which before
filled the public mind ; and he intensified the unpopularity of
all he touched by the idea of a 'military premier,' for which
we should not care now, but which was odious and terrible
then, when men still feared oppression from the Government.

Upon minds thus predisposed, the French Revolution of
1830 broke with magical power. To the young generation it
seemed like the fulfilment of their dreams.

> The meagre, stale, forbidding ways
> Of custom, law, and statute took at once
> The attraction of a country in Romance,

> And lively thought that they might be
> Called upon to exercise their skill,
> Not in Utopia, subterranean fields,
> Or some secluded island, heaven knows where,
> But in the very world, which is the world
> Of all of us.

And even to soberer persons this new revolution seemed to prove that change, even great change, was not so mischievous as had been said—that the good of 1789 might be gained without the evil, and that it was absurd not to try reform when the unreformed world contained so much which was miserable and so much which was difficult to bear.   Even a strong Tory ministry might have been overthrown, so great was the force of this sudden sentiment: the feeble ministry of the Duke of Wellington fell at once before it, and the Whigs were called to power.

Their first act was to frame a plan of parliamentary reform, and that which they constructed was many times larger than anything which anyone expected from them.   All those who remember those times say that when they heard what was proposed they could hardly believe their ears.   And when it was explained to the House of Commons, the confusion, the perplexity, and the consternation were very great.   Reform naturally was much less popular in the assembly to be reformed than it was elsewhere.   The general opinion was that if Sir Robert Peel had risen at once and denounced the Bill as destructive and revolutionary he might have prevented its being brought in.   Another common opinion in the House was that the 'Whigs would go out next morning.'   But the Bill had been framed by one who, with whatever other shortcomings and defects, has ever had a shrewd eye for the probable course of public opinion.   'I told Lord Grey,' says Lord Russell, 'that none but a large measure would be a safe measure.'   And accordingly, as soon as its provisions came to be comprehended by the country, there was perhaps the greatest burst of enthusiasm which England has ever seen (certainly the greatest enthusiasn for a law, though that for a favourite person may sometimes have risen as high or higher). A later satirist has spoken of it as the 'Great Bill for giving everybody everything,' and everybody almost seems to have been as much in favour of it as if they were to gain everything by it. Agricultural counties were as eager as manufacturing towns; men who had always been Tories before were as warm as Liberals. The country would have 'the Bill, the whole Bill, and nothing but the Bill.'

But this enthusiasm did not of itself secure the passing of the Bill. There were many obstacles in the way which it took months to overcome, and which often made many despair. First, the Bill was not one of which the political world itself strongly approved; on the contrary, if left to itself, that world would probably have altogether rejected it. It was imposed by the uninitiated on the initiated, by the many on the few; and inevitably those who were compelled to take it did not like it. Then, the vast proposals of the ministry deeply affected many private interests. In 1858 I heard an able politician say, 'The best way for a Government to turn itself out is to bring in a Reform Bill; the number of persons whom every such Bill must offend is very great, and they are sure to combine together, not on Reform, but on something else, and so turn out the Government.' And if there was serious danger to a ministry which ventured to propose such petty reforms as were thought of in 1858, we can imagine the magnitude of the danger which the ministry of 1832 incurred from the great measure they then brought in. One member, indeed, rose and said, 'I am the proprietor of Ludgershall, I am the member for Ludgershall, I am the constituency of Ludgershall, and in all three capacities I assent to the disfranchisement of Ludgershall.' But the number of persons who were so disinterested was rare. The Bill of 1832 affected the franchise of every constituency, and, therefore, the seat of every member; it

abolished the seats of many, and destroyed the right of nomination to seats also possessed by many; and nothing could
be more repugnant to the inclinations of most. A House of
Commons with such a Bill before it was inevitably captious,
unruly, and difficult to guide. And even if there had been or
could have been a House of Commons which at heart liked the
Bill, there would still have been the difficulty that many other
people then most influential did not much like it. A great
many members of the Cabinet which proposed it, though they
believed it to be necessary, did not think it to be desirable.
The country would have some such measure, and therefore they
proposed this. 'Lord Palmerston and Mr. Grant,' says Lord
Russell, 'had followed Mr. Canning in his opposition to Parliamentary Reform. Lord Lansdowne and Lord Holland had
never been very eager on the subject.' Lord Brougham did
not approve of the disfranchisement of nearly so many boroughs,
and others of the Cabinet were much of the same mind. Their
opinion was always dubious, their action often reluctant, and,
according to Mr. Greville, some of the most influential of them,
being very sensitive to the public opinion of select political
society, were soon 'heartily ashamed of the whole thing.'

The House of Lords, too, was adverse, not only as an
assembly of men mostly rich and past middle age is ever
adverse to great political change, or as a privileged assembly is
always hostile to any movement which may destroy it, but for
a reason peculiar to itself. The English House of Lords, as we
all know, is not a rigid body of fixed number like the upper
chambers of book constitutions, but an elastic body of unfixed
number. The Crown can add to its members when it pleases
and as it pleases. And in various ways which I need not
enumerate now, this elasticity of structure has been of much
use, but in one way it does much harm. The Crown for this
purpose means the ministry; the ministry is appointed by a
party, and is the agent of that party, and therefore it makes
peers from its own friends all but exclusively. Under a Tory

Government more than nine-tenths of the new peers will be Tory; under a Whig Government more than nine-tenths will be Whig; and if for a long course of years either party has been continuously, or nearly so, in power, the House of Lords will be filled with new members belonging to it. And this is a serious inconvenience, because the longer any party has been thus in power, the more likely it is to have to go out and lose power; and the new ministry which comes in, and the new mode of thought which that ministry embodies, finds itself face to face with a House of Peers embodying an antagonistic mode of thought, and one formed by its enemies. In 1831 this was so, for the Tories had been in office almost without a break since 1784, had created peers profusely, who were all Tories, and added the Irish elective peers, who, from the mode of election, were all Tories too. In consequence, the reform movement of 1831 and 1832 found itself obstinately opposed to a hostile House of Lords, whose antagonism aided the reluctance diffused through the House of Commons, and fostered the fainthearted-ness common in the Cabinet. The King, too, who had begun by being much in favour of reform, gradually grew frightened. His correspondence with Lord Grey gives a vivid picture of a well-meaning, but irresolute man, who is much in the power of the last speaker, who at last can be securely relied on by no one, and who gives incessant (and as it seems unnecessary) trouble to those about him. The rising republicanism of the day will find in these letters much to serve it; for, however convinced one may be, on general grounds, that English royalty was necessary to English freedom at that time, it is impossible not to be impatient at seeing how, month after month in a great crisis, when there was so much else to cause anxiety and create confusion, one stupid old man should have been able to add so much to both.

And all through the struggle the two effects of the new French Revolution were contending with one another. Just as it aroused in young and sanguine minds (and the majority of the country was just then disposed to be sanguine) the warmest hopes, in minds oppositely predisposed it aroused every kind of fear.   Old and timid people thought we should soon have in England 'Robespierre and the guillotine.'   Indeed, in a way that it is rather amusing now to consider, the French horrors of 1793 are turned into a kind of intellectual shuttlecock by two disputants.   One says, 'See what comes of making rash changes, how many crimes they engender, and how many lives they lose!' 'No,' replies the other; 'see what comes of not making changes till too late, for it was delay of change, and resistance to change, which caused those crimes and horrors.' Nor were these unreal words of mere rhetoric.   They told much on many minds, for what France had done and would do then naturally filled an immense space in men's attention, as for so many years not long since, Europe had been divided into France and anti-France.

With all these obstacles in its way, the ministry of 1831 had the greatest difficulty in carrying the Reform Bill.   I have not space to narrate, even in the briefest way, the troubled history of their doing so.   Parliamentary debates are generally dull in the narration; but so great was the excitement, and so many were the relieving circumstances, that an accomplished historian will be able to make posterity take some sort of exceptional interest in these.   The credit of the victory, such as it is, must be divided between many persons.   Lord Grey managed the King, and stood first in the eye of the country; Lord Russell contributed the first sketch of the Bill, containing all its essential features, both good and bad, and he introduced the first Bill into the House of Commons; the late Lord Derby then first showed his powers as a great debater.   But the best observers say that Lord Althorp carried the Bill: he was leader of the House at the time, and the main strain of ruling one of the most troubled of Parliaments was on him.   His biographer, Sir Denis Le Marchant, who was present at the debates, says :—

'Lord Althorp's capacity as a leader had been severely tested throughout this tremendous struggle, and it extorted the praise even of his political opponents. I recollect Sir Henry Hardinge saying, "It was Althorpe carried the Bill. His fine temper did it. And in answer to a most able and argumentative speech of Crocker, he rose and merely said 'that he had made some calculations which he considered as entirely conclusive in refutation of the right honourable gentleman's arguments which he had mislaid, but if the House would be guided by his advice they would reject the amendment'—which they accordingly did. There is no standing against such influence as this. The Whigs ascribed Lord Althorp's influence not to his temper alone, but to the confidence felt by the House in his integrity and sound judgment, an opinion so universal that Lord Grey was induced by it to press upon him a peerage, that he might take charge of the Bill in the committee of the Lords; and the design was abandoned not from any hesitation or unwillingness on the part of Lord Althorp, but from the difficulty of finding a successor to him in the Commons." So bad a speaker, with so slow a mind, has never received so great a compliment in a scene where quickness and oratory seem at first sight to be the most absolutely requisite of qualities.'

But it is no doubt a great mistake to imagine that these qualities are the true essentials to success of this kind. A very shrewd living judge says, after careful reflection, that they are even hurtful. 'A man,' says Mr. Massey in his history, 'who speaks seldom, and who speaks ill, is the best leader of the House of Commons.' And no doubt the slow-speeched English gentlemen rather sympathize with slow speech in others. Besides, a quick and brilliant leader is apt to be always speaking, whereas a leader should interfere only when necessary, and be therefore felt as a higher force when he does so. His mind ought to be like a reserve fund—not invested in showy securities, but sure to be come at when wanted, and always of staple value. And this Lord Althorp's mind was; there was not an epigram in the whole of it; everything was solid and ordinary. Men seem to have trusted him much as they trust a faithful animal, entirely believing that he would not deceive if he could, and that he could not if he would.

And what, then, was this great ' Bill '—which it was so great an achievement to pass? Unfortunately this is not an easy question to answer shortly. The ' Bill ' destroyed many old things and altered many old things, and we cannot understand its effects except in so far as we know what these old things were.

' A variety of rights of suffrage,' said Sir James Mackintosh, ' is the principle of the English representation.' How that variety began is not at all to the present purpose ; it grew as all English things grow—by day-by-day alterations from small beginnings; and the final product was very different from the first beginning, as well as from any design which ever at any one time entered anyone's mind. There always was a great contrast between the mode of representation in boroughs and in counties, because there was a great contrast in social structure between them. The ' knight of the shire ' was differently chosen from the ' burgess of the town,' because the ' shire ' was a different sort of place from the town, and the same people could not have chosen for the two—the same people not existing in the two. The borough representations of England, too, ' struggled up '—there is hardly any other word to describe it—in a most irregular manner. The number of towns which sent representatives is scarcely ever the same in any two of our oldest Parliaments. The sheriff had a certain discretion, for the writ only told him to convene ' de quolibet burgo duos bur- genses,' and did not name any towns in particular. Most towns then disliked the duty and evaded it, if possible, which seems to have augmented the sheriff's power, for he could permit or prevent the evasion as much as he chose. And at a very early period great differences grew up between the ways of election in the towns which were always represented. There seems to have been a kind of ' natural selection ; ' the most powerful class in each borough chose if it could at each election, and if any class long continued the most powerful, it then acquired customary rights of election which came to be unalterable.

x

Nor was there any good deciding authority to regulate this confusion. The judge of elections was the 'House of Commons' itself, and it often decided not according to law or evidence, but as political or personal influence dictated. And rights of election thus capriciously recognised became binding on the borough for ever. As might be expected, the total result was excessively miscellaneous. The following are the franchises of the boroughs in two counties as legislators of 1832 found them.

### SOMERSETSHIRE.

| | |
|---|---|
| BRISTOL . . . | Freeholders of 40*s*., and free burgesses. |
| BATH . . . . | Mayor, aldermen, and common councilmen only. |
| WELLS . . . . | Mayor, masters, burgesses, and freemen of the seven trading companies of the said city. |
| TAUNTON . . . | Potwallers not receiving alms or charity. |
| BRIDGEWATER . | Mayor, aldermen, and twenty-four capital burgesses of the borough paying scot and lot. |
| ILCHESTER . . | Alleged to be the inhabitants of the said town paying scot and lot, which the town called potwallers. |
| MINEHEAD . . | The parishioners of Dunster and Minehead, being housekeepers in the borough of Minehead, and not receiving alms. |
| MILBORN PORT . | The capital bailiffs and their deputies, the number of bailiffs being nine, and their deputies being two ; in the commonalty, stewards, their number being two ; and the inhabitants thereof paying scot and lot. |

### LANCASHIRE.

| | |
|---|---|
| LANCASTER . . | Freemen only |
| WIGAN . . . | Free burgesses. |
| CLITHEROE . . | Freeholders resident and nonresident. |
| LIVERPOOL . . | Mayor, bailiffs, and freemen not receiving alms. |
| PRESTON . . . | All the inhabitants. |

Nothing could be more certain than that a system which was constructed in this manner must sooner or later need great alteration. Institutions which have grown from the beginning by adaptation may last as long as any, if they continue to possess the power of adaptation. The force which created them still exists to preserve them. But in this case the power of adaptation was gone. A system of representation made without design was fixed as eternal upon a changing nation, and somehow or other it was sure to become unsuitable. Nothing could be more false in essence than the old anti-reform arguments as far as they affected the ' wisdom of our ancestors ; ' for the characteristic method of our ancestors had been departed from. Our ancestors changed what they wanted bit by bit, just when and just as they wanted. But their descendants were forbidden to do so ; they were asked to be content not only with old clothes, but with much-patched old clothes, which they were denied the power to patch again. And this sooner or later they were sure to refuse.

In 1832 a grave necessity existed for changing it. The rude principle of natural selection by which it had been made, insured that, at least approximately, the classes most influential in the nation would have a proportionate power in the legislation ; no great class was likely to be denied anything approaching to its just weight. But now that a system framed in one age was to be made to continue unchanged through after ages, there was no such security. On the contrary, the longer the system went on without change the more sure it was to need change. Some new class was sure in course of time to grow up for which the fixed system provided no adequate representatives ; and the longer that system continued fixed, the surer was this to happen, and the stronger was it likely that this class would be. In 1832, such a class had arisen of the first magnitude. The trading wealth of the country had created a new world which had no voice in Parliament comparable to that which it had in the country. Not only were some of the greatest towns, like Birmingham and Manchester, left without any members at all, but in most other towns the best of the middle class felt that they had no adequate power ; they were either extinguished by a franchise too exclusive, or swamped by one too diffused; either way, they were powerless.

There was equal reason to believe that, by the same inevitable course of events, some class would come to have more power in Parliament than it should. The influences which gave the various classes their authority at the time in which the machinery of our representation was framed, would be sure in time to ebb away, wholly or in part, from some of them. And in matter of fact they did so. The richer nobility and the richer commoners had come to have much more power than they ought. The process of letting the most influential people in a borough choose its members, amounted in time to letting the great nobleman or great commoner to whom the property of the town belonged, choose them. And many counties had fallen into the direction of the same hands also, so that it was calculated, if not with truth, at any rate with an approach to it, that one hundred and seventy-seven lords and gentlemen chose as many as three hundred and fifty-five English members of Parliament. The parliamentary power of these few rich peers and squires was much too great when compared with their share in the life of the nation, just as that of the trading class was too weak; the excess of the one made the deficiency of the other additionally difficult to bear; and the contrast was more than ever galling in the years from 1830 to 1832, because just then the new French Revolution had revived the feud between the privileged classes and the non-privileged. The excessive parliamentary power of these few persons had before been a yoke daily becoming heavier and heavier, and now it could be endured no longer.

The 'Reform Bill' amended all this. It abolished a multitude of nomination boroughs, gave members to large towns and cities, and changed the franchise, so that in all boroughs, at any rate, the middle classes obtained predominant power. And no one can deny that the good so done was immense; indeed, no one does now deny it, for the generation of Tories that did so has passed away.  No doubt the Reform Act did not produce of itself at once the new heaven and new earth which its more ardent supporters expected of it.  It did nothing to remove the worst evils from which the country suffered, for those evils were not political but economical ; and the classes whom it enfranchised were not more economically instructed than those whom they superseded.  The doctrine of protection then reigned all through the nation, and while it did so no real cure for those evils was possible.  But this Act, coming as it did when a new political generation was prepared to make use of it, got rid entirely of the ' cruel spirit ' by which our distresses had been repressed before, and which was as great an evil as those distresses themselves, introduced many improvements—municipal reform, tithe reform, and such like—in which the business-like habit of mind due to the greater power of the working classes mainly helped and diffused a sweeter and better spirit through society.

But these benefits were purchased at a price of the first magnitude, though, from the nature of it, its payment was long deferred.  The reformers of 1832 dealt with the evils of their time, as they would have said, in an English way, and without much thinking of anything else.  And exactly in that English way, as they had under their hands a most curious political machine which had grown without design, and which produced many very valuable, though not very visible effects, they, without thought, injured and destroyed some of the best parts of it.

First, the old system of representation, as we have seen, was based on a variety of franchises.  But, in order to augment the influence of the middle class, the reformers of 1832 destroyed that variety; they introduced into every borough the 10*l.* household franchise, and with a slight exception, which we need not take account of, made that franchise the only one in all boroughs.  They raised the standard in the boroughs in which it was lower than 10*l.*, and lowered it in those where it was higher; and in this way they changed the cardinal principle of the system which they found established for uniformity as the rule instead of variety.

And this worked well enough at first, for there was not for some years after 1832 much wish for any more change in our constituencies. But in our own time we have seen the harm of it. If you establish any uniform franchise in a country, then it at once becomes a question, What sort of franchise is it to be? Those under it will say that they are most unjustly excluded; they will deny that there is any real difference between themselves and those above; they will show without difficulty that some whom the chosen line leaves out, are even better than those whom it takes in. And they will raise the cry so familiar in our ears—the cry of class legislation. They will say, Who are these ten-pound householders, these arbitrarily chosen middle-class men, that they should be sole electors? Why should they be alone enfranchised and all others practically disfranchised, either by being swamped by their more numerous votes or by not having votes at all? The case is the stronger because one of the most ancient functions of Parliament, and especially the Commons House of Parliament, is the reformation of grievances. This suited very well with the old system of variety; in that miscellaneous collection of constituencies every class was sure to have some members who represented it. There were then working-class constituencies sending members to speak for them—'men,' says Mackintosh, 'of popular talents, principles, and feelings; quick in suspecting oppression, bold in resisting it, not thinking favourably of the powerful; listening almost with credulity to the complaints of the humble and the feeble, and impelled by ambition when they are not prompted by generosity to be defenders of the defenceless.' And in cases of popular excitement, especially of erroneous excitement, this plan insured that it should have adequate expression, and so soon made it calm. But the legislation of 1832 destroyed these working-men's constituencies; 'they put the country,' as it was said afterwards, 'under ten-pounders only.' And in consequence there are in our boroughs now nothing but working-class constituencies; there are no longer any ten-pound householders at all. There is throughout our boroughs a uniform sort of franchise, and that the worst sort— a franchise which gives the predominance to the most ignorant and the least competent, if they choose to use it. The middle classes have as little power as they had before 1832, and the only difference is, that before 1832 they were ruled by those who were richer than themselves, and now they are ruled by those who are poorer.

No doubt there is still an inequality in the franchise between counties and boroughs—the sole remnant of the variety of our ancient system. But that inequality is much more difficult to defend now when it stands alone, than it was in old times when it was one of many. And the 'ugly rush' of the lower orders, which has effaced the 'hard and fast' line established in 1832, threatens to destroy this remnant of variety. In a few years probably there will be but one sort of franchise throughout all England, and the characteristic work of 1832 will be completely undone; the middle classes, whose intelligence Macaulay praised, and to whom he helped to give so much power, will have had all that power taken away from them.

No doubt, too, there is still a real inequality of influence, though there is a legal equality of franchise. The difference of size between different boroughs gives more power to those in the small boroughs than to those in the large. And this is very valuable, for elections for large boroughs are costly, and entail much labour that is most disagreeable. But here, again, the vicious precedent of establishing uniformity set in 1832 is becoming excessively dangerous. Being so much used to it people expect to see it everywhere. There is much risk that before long there may be only one sort of vote and only one size of constituency all over England, and then the reign of monotony will be complete.

And, secondly, the reformers of 1832 committed an almost worse error in destroying one kind of select constituency without creating an intellectual equivalent.  We are not used now-a-days to think of nomination boroughs as select constituencies, but such, in truth, they were, and such they proved themselves to be at, perhaps, the most critical period of English history. Lord Russell, no favourable judge, tells us ' that it enabled Sir Robert Walpole to consolidate the throne of the House of Hanover amid external and internal dangers.'  No democratic suffrage would then have been relied on for that purpose, for the mass of Englishmen were then more or less attached to their hereditary king, and they might easily have been induced to restore him.  They had not, indeed, a fanatical passion of loyalty towards him, nor any sentiment which would make them brave many dangers on his behalf; but there was much sluggish and sullen prejudice which might have been easily aroused to see that he had his rights, and there were many relics of ancient loyal zeal which might have combined with that prejudice and ennobled it.  Nor did the people of that day much care for what we should now call parliamentary government.  The educated opinion of that day was strongly in favour of the House of Hanover; but the numerical majority of the nation was not equally so; perhaps it would have preferred the House of Stuart.  But the higher nobility and the richer gentry possessed a great power over the opinions of Parliament because many boroughs were subject to their control, and by exerting that power they, in conjunction with the trading classes, who were then much too weak to have moved by themselves, fixed the House of Hanover on the throne, and so settled the freedom of England.  These boroughs at that time, for this purpose being select constituencies, were of inestimable value, because they enabled the most competent opinion in England to rule without dispute, when, under any system of diffused suffrage, that opinion would either have been out-voted or almost so.

And to the last these boroughs retained much of this peculiar merit.   They were an organ for what may be called
specialized political thought, for trained intelligence busy with
public affairs.   Not only did they bring into parliament men
of genius and ability, but they kept together a higher political
world capable of appreciating that genius and ability when
young, and of learning from it when old.   The Whig party,
such as it was in those days especially, rested on this parliamentary power.   In them was a combination of more or less
intelligent noblemen of liberal ideas and aims, who chose
such men as Burke, and Brougham, and Hume, and at last
Macaulay, to develop those ideas and to help to attain those
aims.   If they had not possessed this peculiar power, they
would have had no such intellectual influence; they would
have simply been gentlemen of what we now think good ideas,
with no special means of advancing them.   And they would not
have been so closely combined together as they were; they
would have been scattered persons of political intelligence.
But having this power they combined together, lived together,
thought together; and the society thus formed was enriched
and educated by the men of genius whom it selected as instruments, and in whom in fact it found teachers.   And there was
something like it on the Government side, though the long
possession of power, and perhaps the nature of Toryism, somewhat modified its characteristics.

The effect is to be read in the parliamentary debates of those
times.   Probably they are absolutely better than our own.
They are intrinsically a better discussion of the subjects of their
day than ours are of our subjects.   But however this may be,
they are beyond question relatively better.   General knowledge
of politics has greatly improved in the last fifty years, and the
best political thought of the present day is much superior to
any which there was then.   So that, even if our present parliamentary debates retained the level of their former excellence
they would still not bear the same relation to the best thought

of the present, that the old ones bear to the best thought of the past. And if the debates have really fallen off much (as I am sure they have), this conclusion will be stronger and more certain.

Nor is this to be wondered at. If you lessen the cause you will lessen the effect too. Not only are the men whom these select constituencies brought into Parliament not now to be found there, but the society which formed those constituencies, and which chose those men, no longer exists. The old parties were combinations partly aristocratic, partly intellectual, cemented by the common possession and the common use of political power. But now that the power is gone the combinations are dissolved. The place which once knew them knows them no more. Anyone who looks for them in our present London and our present politics will scarcely find much that is like them.

This society sought for those whom it thought would be useful to it in all quarters. There was a regular connection between the ' Unions '—the great debating societies of Oxford and Cambridge—and Parliament. Young men who seemed promising had even a chance of being competed for by both parties. We all know the line which the wit of Brookes's made upon Mr. Canning—

> The turning of coats so common is grown,
>   That no one would think to attack it ;
> But no case until now was so flagrantly known
>   Of a schoolboy's turning his jacket.

This meant that it having been said and believed that Mr. Canning, who had just left Oxford, was to be brought into Parliament by the Whig Opposition, he went over to Mr. Pitt, and was brought in by the Tory ministry. The Oxford Liberals of our generation are quite exempt from similar temptations. So far from their support in Parliament being craved by both sides, they cannot enter Parliament at all. When many of these tried to enter Parliament in the autumn of 1867, their egregious failure was one of the most striking events of that remarkable time.

There was a connection, too, then between the two parts of the public service now most completely divided—the permanent and the parliamentary civil services.   Now, as we all know, the chief clerks in the Treasury and permanent heads of departments never think of going into Parliament; they regard the parliamentary statesmen who are set to rule over them much as the Bengalees regard the English—as persons who are less intelligent and less instructed than themselves, but who nevertheless are to be obeyed.   They never think of changing places any more than a Hindoo thinks of becoming an Englishman.   But in old times, men like Lord Liverpool, Sir George Rose, and Mr. Huskisson were found eminent in the public offices, and in consequence of that eminence were brought into Parliament.   The party in office were then, as now, anxious to obtain competent help in passing measures of finance and detail, and they then obtained it thus, whereas now their successors do not obtain it at all.

There was then, too, a sort of romantic element in the lives of clever young men which is wholly wanting now.   Some one said that Macaulay's was like a life in a fairy tale;—he opens a letter which looks like any other letter, and finds that it contains a seat in Parliament.   Gibbon says that just as he was destroying an army of barbarians, Sir Gilbert Elliot called and offered him a seat for Liskeard.   Great historians will never probably again be similarly interrupted.   The effect of all this was to raise the intellectual tone of Parliament.   At present the political conversation of members of Parliament;—a few of the greatest excepted—is less able and less striking than that of other persons of fair capacity.   There is a certain kind of ideas which you hardly ever hear from any other educated person, but which they have to talk to their constituents, and which, if you will let them, they will talk to you too.   Some of

316 Lord Althorp and the Reform Act of 1832.

the middle-aged men of business, the 'soap-boilers,' as the London world disrespectfully calls them, whom local influence raises to Parliament, really do not seem to know any better; they repeat the words of the hustings as if they were parts of their creed. And as for the more intellectual members who know better, no one of good manners likes to press them too closely in argument on politics any more than he likes to press a clergyman too strictly on religion. In both cases the *status* in the world depends on the belief in certain opinions, and therefore it is thought rather ill-bred, except for some great reason, to try to injure that belief. Intellectual deference used to be paid to members of Parliament, but now, at least in London, where the species is known, the remains of that deference are rare.

The other side of the same phenomenon is the increased power of the provinces, and especially of the constituencies. Any gust of popular excitement runs through them instantly, grows greater and greater as it goes, till it gains such huge influence that for a moment the central educated world is powerless. No doubt, if only time can be gained, the excitement passes away; something new succeeds, and the ordinary authority of trained and practised intelligence revives. But if an election were now to happen at an instant of popular fury, that fury would have little or nothing to withstand it. And, even in ordinary times, the power of the constituencies is too great. They are fast reducing the members, especially the weaker sort of them, to delegates. There is already, in many places, a committee which often telegraphs to London, hoping that their member will vote this way or that, and the member is unwilling not to do so, because at the next election, if offended, the committee may, perchance, turn the scale against him. And this dependence weakens the intellectual influence of Parliament, and of that higher kind of mind of which Parliament ought to be the organ.

We must remember that if now we feel these evils we must

expect ere long to feel them much more. The Reform Act of 1867 followed in the main the precedent of 1832; and year by year we shall feel its consequences more and more. The two precedents which have been set will of necessity, in the English world, which is so much guided by precedent, determine the character of future Reform Acts. And if they do, the supremacy of the central group of trained and educated men which our old system of parliamentary choice created, will be completely destroyed, for it is already half gone.

I know it is thought that we can revive this intellectual influence. Many thoughtful reformers believe that by means of Mr. Hare's system of voting, by the cumulative suffrage, the limited suffrage, or by some others like them, we may be able to replace that which the legislation of 1832 began to destroy, and that which those who follow them are destroying. And I do not wish to say a word against this hope. On the contrary, I think that it is one of the most important duties of English politicians to frame these plans into the best form of which they are capable, and to try to obtain the assent of the country to them. But the difficulty is immense. The reformers of 1832 destroyed intellectual constituencies in great numbers without creating any new ones, and without saying, indeed without thinking, that it was desirable to create any. They thus by conspicuous action, which is the most influential mode of political instruction, taught mankind that an increase in the power of numbers was the change most to be desired in England. And of course the mass of mankind are only too ready to think so. They are always prone to believe their own knowledge to be 'for all practical purposes' sufficient, and to wish to be emancipated from the authority of the higher culture. What we have now to do, therefore, is to induce this self-satisfied, stupid, inert mass of men to admit its own insufficiency, which is very hard; to understand fine schemes for supplying that insufficiency, which is harder; and to exert itself to get those ideas adopted, which is hardest of all. Such is the duty which the reformers of 1832 have cast upon us.

And this is what of necessity must happen if you set men like Lord Althorp to guide legislative changes in complex institutions. Being without culture, they do not know how these institutions grew; being without insight, they only see one half of their effect; being without foresight, they do not know what will happen if they are enlarged; being without originality, they cannot devise anything new to supply, if necessary, the place of what is old. Common sense no doubt they have, but common sense without instruction can no more wisely revise old institutions than it can write the Nautical Almanac. Probably they will do some present palpable good, but they will do so at a heavy cost; years after they have passed away, the bad effects of that which they did, and of the precedents which they set, will be hard to bear and difficult to change. Such men are admirably suited to early and simple times. English history is full of them, and England has been made mainly by them; but they fail in later times, when the work of the past is accumulated, and no question is any longer simple. The simplicity of their one-idead minds, which is suited to the common arithmetic and vulgar fractions of early societies, is not suited, indeed rather unfits them, for the involved analysis and complex 'problem papers' of later ages.

There is little that in a sketch like this need be said of Lord Althorp's life after the passing of the Reform Act. The other acts of Lord Grey's ministry have nothing so memorable or so characteristic of Lord Althorp that anything need be said about them. Nor does anyone in the least care now as to the once celebrated mistake of Mr. Littleton in dealing with O'Connell, or Lord Althorp's connection with it. Parliamentary history is only interesting when it is important constitutional history, or when it illustrates something in the character of some interesting man. But the end of Lord Althorp's public life was very curious. In the November of 1834 his brother,

Lord Spencer, died, and as he was then leader of the House of
Commons, a successor for him had to be found.   But William
IV., whose liberal partialities had long since died away, began
by objecting to everyone proposed, and ended by turning out
the ministry—another event in his reign which our coming re-
publicans will no doubt make the most of.   But I have nothing
to do with the King and the constitutional question now.   My
business is with Lord Althorp.   He acted very characteristically
—he said that a retirement from office was to him the ' cessation of acute pain,' and never afterwards would touch it again,
though he lived for many years.   Nor was this an idle affectation, far less indolence.   ' You must be aware,' he said once
before, in a letter to Lord Brougham, ' that my being in office
is nothing less than a source of misery to me.   I am perfectly
certain that no man ever disliked it to such a degree as I do ;
and, indeed, the first thing that usually comes into my head when
I wake is how to get rid of it.'   He retired into the country
and occupied himself with the rural pursuits which he loved
best, attended at quarter sessions, and was active as a farmer.
' Few persons,' said an old shepherd, ' could compete with my
lord in a knowledge of sheep.'   He delighted to watch a whole
flock pass, and seemed to know them as if he had lived with
them.   ' Of all my former pursuits,' he wrote, just after Lady
Althorp's death, and in the midst of his grief, 'the only one in
which I now take any interest is breeding stock ; it is the only
one in which I can build castles in the air.'   And as soon as he
could, among such castles in the air he lived and died.   No
doubt, too, much better for himself than for many of his friends,
who long wanted to lure him back to politics.   He was wise
with the solid wisdom of agricultural England ; popular and
useful ; sagacious in usual things ; a model in common duties ;
well able to advise men in the daily difficulties which are the
staple of human life.   But beyond this he could not go.
Having no call to decide on more intellectual questions, he was
distressed and pained when he had to do so.   He was a man so

picturesquely out of place in a great scene, that if a great describer gets hold of him he may be long remembered; and it was the misfortune of his life that the simplicity of his purposes and the trustworthiness of his character raised him at a great conjuncture to a high place for which Nature had not meant him, and for which he felt that she had not meant him.

# ADDENDA.

## THE PRINCE CONSORT.

[1861.]

So much has, ere this, been said upon the life and character of Prince Albert, that scarcely anything now remains except to join very simply and plainly in the regret and sympathy which have been everywhere expressed by all classes of the nation—the low as well as the high. A long narrative of a simple career would now be wholly needless, for our contemporaries have supplied many such; and any protracted eulogy would be unsuitable both to our business-like pages [1] and to the simple character of him whom we have lost.

If our loss is not—as has been extravagantly said—the greatest which the English nation could have sustained, it is among the most irreparable. Our parliamentary constitution, in some sense, renews itself, or tends to do so. As one old statesman leaves the scene, a younger one comes forward, in the vigour of hope and power, to fill his place. When one great orator dies, another commonly succeeds him. The opportunity of the new aspirant is the departure of his predecessor; on every vacancy some new claimant—many claimants probably—strive with eager emulation to win it and to retain it. Every loss is, in a brief period, easily and fully repaired. Even, too, in the hereditary part of our constitution, most calamities are soon forgotten. One monarch dies, and another

---

[1] The *Economist* of December 21, where this article first appeared.

Y

succeeds him.  A new court, a new family, new hopes and new interests, spring up and supersede those which have passed away.  What was, is forgotten; what is, is seen.  But now we have the old Court without one of its mainstays and principal supports.  The royal family of last week is still (and without change) the royal family of to-day; but the father of that family is removed.  For such a loss there is not, in this world, any adequate resource or any complete compensation.  In no rank of life can any one else be to the widow and children what the deceased husband and father would have been.  In the Court as in the cottage, such loss must not only be grief now, but perplexity, trouble, and perhaps mistake hereafter.

The present generation, at least the younger part of it, have lost the idea that the Court is a serious matter.  Everything for twenty years has seemed to go so easily and so well, that it has seemed to go of itself.  There is no such thing in this world.  Everything requires anxiety, and reflection, and patience.  And the function of the Court, though we easily forget it when it is well performed, keeps itself much in our remembrance when it is ill performed.  Old observers say that some of the half-revolutionary discontent in the times preceding the Reform Bill was attributable to the selfish apathy and decrepit profligacy of George the Fourth.  The Crown is of singular importance in a divided and contentious free state, because it is the sole object of attachment which is elevated above every contention and division.  But to maintain that importance, it must create attachment.  We know that the Crown now does so fully; but we do not adequately bear in mind how much rectitude of intention, how much judgment in conduct, how much power of doing right, how much power of doing nothing, are requisite to unite the loyalty and to retain the confidence of a free people.

Some cynical observers have contrasted the unlimited encomiums of the last week with the ' cold observance ' and very measured popularity of Prince Albert during his life.  They remember the public hisses of 1855, and perhaps recall many hints and whispers of politics that have passed away. But the most graphic of our contemporaries have found nothing to record of Prince Albert so truly characteristic as this change.

His circumstances, and perhaps his character, forbade him to attempt the visible achievements and the showy displays which attract momentary popularity. Discretion is a quality seldom appreciated till it is lost; and it was discretion which Prince Albert eminently possessed.

## WHAT LORD LYNDHURST REALLY WAS.

[1863.]

A GREAT phenomenon has passed away from English public life. Not long since, Lord Lyndhurst observed: 'My Lords,— I well remember the breaking out of the French Revolution in 1789, the death of Louis the Sixteenth, and the course of the consequent events.' There is not, perhaps, a conspicuous public man now in Europe who could say this; certainly there is none in England. The picturesque features of Lord Lyndhurst's mind and character made the phenomenon still more striking. The characteristic of his intellect was the combination of great force and great lucidity. Every sentence from him was full of light and energy. His face and brow were, perhaps, unrivalled in our time for the expression of pure intellect, and he preserved the physical aptitude for public oratory to an old age when most men are scarcely fit for mere conversation. To the very extremity of a protracted life—and this is very rare—he both looked, and was, a great man. The intellect was undimmed, and the power of expression hardly abated. There is no such man left.

It is very natural that such a man should have lived till his career should be half a myth or a legend. Few, indeed, of those who, during the last few years, gazed on that remarkable face, had any distinct conception of the life which had been led by the person they saw. The singular vigour of his conversation charmed those who resorted to him, and they were led to believe that a man who talked so very well could hardly have acted very ill. The lives which have been put forth in the newspapers, carefully prepared, like those of most old men, are merely panegyrics. For once the physical vigour of a long old age has redeemed, in public estimation, the errors and vices of a long life. But it is not so that history should be written ; it is in no strain of panegyric that an impartial observer can review the career of Lord Lyndhurst.

The beginning of the public life of Lord Lyndhurst was towards the end of the long reign of the Tory party. Sir George Lewis justly observed ' that the Tories in 1815 had an immense balance of popularity arising from the successful issue of the great war, and that they managed to spend it most completely before 1830.' They governed, as all Conservatives even would now admit, in precisely the wrong spirit.

They governed, not in the spirit of Mr. Pitt, but in the spirit of Lord Eldon. They maintained not only the main in- stitutions of the country which were acceptable and popular, but also the minutest abuses which, in the course of years, had clung to those institutions. They connected the name of the Tory party with every petty abuse and misdemeanour through- out the country. They would alter nothing, and they would let nothing be altered. When public meetings were convened to express public opinion, the organs of the Government cried out sedition, and talked as if a ' French Revolution ' were going to break out here. By this stupid—there is no milder epithet that is fitting—and narrow-minded policy, the Tories caused the outburst of public opinion which carried the Reform Bill. Their best organs have admitted as much of late years. ' A few more drops,' said the ' Quarterly Review ' not long since, ' of Eldonine, and we should have had the People's Charter.' The Tory party kept the nation in such tight and painful fet- ters, that it was driven wild, and rose and broke them. If the Tories will permit no improvement—so went the national idea —we must have an end of Toryism.

All this was excusable and natural in men like Lord Eldon. He had been a Tory from his youth, and he had been confirmed

in Toryism by the events of the French Revolution. When
the peace came, and a new generation sprang up, he was too
old to change his creed. He honestly believed that it was
necessary to resist every innovation, no matter of what sort,
and to maintain everything, no matter of what kind. In Lord
Eldon such conduct was natural and excusable. But it was
not natural in a young man of great intelligence in the next
generation. Able young men well knew that this illiberal
Toryism was out of place, and an anachronism. It was in 1818,
when the effects of this system were beginning to be plainly
visible, that Lord Lyndhurst chose to connect himself with it.

He did so under circumstances of great suspicion. He
had held—loosely, we apprehend—some sort of ultra-Liberal
opinions. He had been, at any rate, in the habit of talking in
that style at young men's parties and the circuit mess. He
was a Liberal, if he was anything; and charges continued to be
made against him for many years of having deserted his principles. It is, indeed, utterly inconceivable that Lord Lyndhurst should have believed in Toryism such as Toryism was in
1818. He would have no title to fame if he had believed in it.
His claim is an intellectual claim. He is said, and justly said,
to have had, when he chose to exert it, an intellect of the
highest cultivation, more fitted than almost any other in his
time for the perception of the truth ;—a first-rate judicial mind,
with culture and experience far transcending the ordinary judicial range.

It is inconsistent with this claim that he should really have
been on the wrong side in all the important questions of his
time. It is absurd to say that the greatest political intellect
of his time—and some such claim as this might be justly made
for Lord Lyndhurst—really believed that the Catholics should
not be emancipated; that the Corn Laws should be maintained ; that there should be no reform in Parliament ; that
the narrow system of 1818 was a perfect or even an endurable
system. We do not mean to charge him with acting contrary to

his principles—that charge was made years ago, but was the exaggerated charge of political opponents, who saw that there was something to blame, but who in their eagerness and haste overdid their accusation. The true charge is that he had no principles, that he did not care to have opinions. If he had applied his splendid judicial faculties to the arguments for Free-trade or for Catholic emancipation, he would soon enough have discovered the truth. But he never did apply them. There is a story of a clever young official ' who said it was inconvenient to keep opinions.' And this exactly expresses Lord Lyndhurst's life and sentiments. They tell a story which may be true or false, but is certainly characteristic of what he said as to the Act which bears his name forbidding a man to marry a deceased wife's sister. The real object of that Act was to please certain particular people who had married their sisters-in-law, and as it stands to this day it legalises all antecedent marriages. As it was originally brought in, it legalised subsequent marriages also. Persons conversant with the clergy, and other strict people represented to Lord Lyndhurst that there would be an outcry against this. He replied, ' Put it the other way, then, forbid the future marriages; I am sure I do not care which way it is.' He wanted to serve a temporary purpose, and he did so always. He regarded politics as a game; to be played first for himself, and then for his party. He did not act contrary to his opinion, but he did not care to form a true opinion.

This was the explanation of his joining the Tories. Not to join them was poverty then; to join them was wealth. They were firmly fixed in office. As the satirist then sang—

> Naught's constant in the human race,
> Except the Whigs not getting into place.

As was the pleasant habit of that time, the Government picked out Mr. Copley, a clever young lawyer, and gave him a seat in Parliament.

He accepted it, though he had no more formed opinion that

Toryism was true than he had that Mahometanism was true.
He took up the opinions of the existing Government and advocated them, and to the end of his life would have thought it
' nonsense and rubbish ' to act otherwise.

Probably, however, he would have acted more profitably if
he had acted more conscientiously. It really was a case when
honesty was the best policy. If he had paid a fair attention to
the subjects of his time, he would have been on what all
parties now admit to be the right side. If he had had a sincere
wish to improve and benefit mankind, he would have been forward in the ranks of the Liberal party, who were then employed
in doing so. The chances of life were various, but most likely
he would have had his reward. The Whigs wanted a first-rate
judge who was also a first-rate politician. During their long
period of power they have never possessed one. The Whigs
have been in power, roughly speaking, five-and-twenty years
out of the last thirty. If Lord Lyndhurst had been their
leader instead of the Tory leader, he would have had far more
of what he valued, more power and influence, more wealth, and
greater station. He would have been among the foremost of
the winners instead of being among the foremost of the losers.
There was nothing which he would have liked so much. There
was nothing which he appreciated so much as success in the
game of political life ; nothing that he despised and detested
like want of success.

It is pleasant to turn to a more favourable topic. Many
duties Lord Lyndhurst may have neglected, or despised, or dis-
owned ; but one duty, and a neglected one, he performed
better, perhaps, on the whole, than any man in his generation.
He had the most disciplined intellect of his time. There is
in every one of his productions evidence not only of natural
sinewy strength, but of careful culture and intellectual gymnastic. Lord Brougham tells a story of finding him occupied
over the integral calculus for amusement's sake, years ago.
Every line of his speeches tells how well he understood, and

how well he acted on, the manly principles of Greek oratory. Few men led a laxer life; few men, to the very end of their life, were looser in their conversation; but there was no laxity in his intellect. Everything there was braced and knit. Great oratory is but a transitory art; few turn even to the best speeches of the past, and even the best of these are so clogged with the detail of the time that they are dull and wearisome to a hasty posterity. Few will recur to Lord Lyndhurst's speeches, but those who do so will find some of the best, if not the very best, specimens in English, of the best manner in which a man of great intellect can address and influence the intellects of others. Their art, we might almost say their merit, is of the highest kind, for it is concealed. The words seem the simplest, clearest, and most natural that a man could use. It is only the instructed man who knows that he could not himself have used them, and that few men could.

Such was the great man whom we have just buried; great in power, but not great in the use of power; a politician, not a statesman; a man of small principle and few scruples. Of him, far more truly than of Burke, it may be said that 'to party he gave up what was meant for mankind.'

He played the game of life for low and selfish objects, and yet, by the intellectual power with which he played it, he redeemed that game from its intrinsic degradation.

## THE TRIBUTE AT HEREFORD TO SIR G. C. LEWIS.

[1864.]

NOTHING could be in more perfect taste than the proceedings at Hereford on the uncovering of the statue of Sir George Lewis. These local events are local casualties. It is impossible to fore-tell whether the principal local person is not a loquacious fool of good intentions who will say just what he should not, or whether he is a man of feeling and judgment, who will say what he should say with taste and propriety.

There is nothing which Sir George Lewis would so much have disliked as an exaggerated *éloge* over his grave: those who knew him would have had his quiet smile of utter contempt present to them while they read it. Happily nothing of this sort was attempted. The sober and modest nature of the man was duly honoured in the quiet and unobtrusive nature of the remembrance.

Both Mr. Clive and Lord Palmerston spoke of Sir George Lewis with guarded care, as English gentlemen wish to be spoken of, as one English gentleman, therefore, should speak of another. Sir George Lewis had no enemies, but, if he had, no enemy could have taken a just exception to the praises of his friends. He would have exactly desired this. He cared very little, perhaps nothing, for passing popularity; he would have been prepared with various classical quotations upon the mutability of the vulgar judgment, but he would deeply value a restrained expression of deep respect by neighbours and friends who knew him well; he would have believed that they were the legitimate 'authority,' the persons who ought to speak on that matter.

It is very curious that Lord Palmerston, who spoke, so to say, Sir George Lewis's epitaph, should have had the slowest, and that Sir George Lewis should have had the most rapid, political rise of our time. Unquestionably Lord Palmerston is in some sense a buoyant man, and Sir George Lewis was in some sense a heavy man, yet the latter came to the surface far quicker. Lord Palmerston was a quarter of a century in Parliament before he was anything at all—before he was any more than a subaltern official; Sir George Lewis was only thirteen years in Parliament altogether, and in that time he was Secretary of the Treasury, Chancellor of the Exchequer, Home Secretary, Secretary for War, and had acquired the perfect respect and confidence of the House of Commons. He finished his whole career as a statesman in about half the number of years that it took Lord Palmerston to become a statesman at all.

The causes which so much delayed Lord Palmerston's rise are not to the present purpose, but the cause which so much accelerated that of Sir George Lewis is very simple. He had, above every other statesman of the age, the gift of inspiring confidence. Coleridge said of Southey that he inspired every one with a confidence in his reliability, and this is an almost exact description of Sir George Lewis. Political opponents and political friends both felt that he had fairly applied a strong and unfettered mind to vast accumulated information, and that his measures were the result of that application. People thought twice before they opposed a grave and business-like measure, proposed by Sir George Lewis in that grave and business-like manner.

In one most important respect he was like Lord Palmerston, though in every other most unlike. His opinions were always plain and simple opinions. People who went to him with the notion that he was a great philosopher and scholar were often puzzled at his plainness. They expected something far-fetched

and recondite, and certainly they did not get it.   He held as a
principle that difficult schemes, fine calculations, unintelligible
policies, were, as such, beyond the range of popular government.   Perhaps too he hated them as if they were a kind of
mysticism.   At all events a person who could not understand
Sir George Lewis's conversation on political business, must
have been unfit for every kind of business.   It had exactly the
homely exactitude that English people like.   We have heard
it remarked of Sir Robert Peel's speeches that he generally
made a remark which seemed to have been left by every one
on purpose for him ;  it was so sensible, when made, that every
one believed he could have made it.   It was much the same
with Sir George Lewis.   What he said seemed so credible and
sensible that in an hour or two you were apt to believe that
you had always thought so.

     Possibly this distinctness of aim has been rather deficient
in our policy for a year past.   We certainly believe that Sir
George Lewis could have cross-examined Lord Russell on the
Danish policy rather acutely.   'What,' he would have said, 'is
the object you desire ?   When we are agreed on that, we will
discuss the *modus operandi* ;  but it is a mistake to deliberate
on expedients when there is a fundamental discrepancy respecting ends.'   At any rate we should like to hear Lord Russell
answer Sir George Lewis on this subject.   This need of a
definite aim ran through all his speculations.   To take an
example from the foreign politics now most interesting to us—
American politics :  'I have never,' said Sir George Lewis in a
letter of March 1861, now lying before us, 'been able, either
in conversation or by reading, to obtain an answer to the question, What will the North do if they beat the South ?   To
restore the old Union would be an absurdity.   What other state
of things does that village lawyer, Lincoln, contemplate as the
fruit of victory ?   It seems to me that the men now in powe
at Washington are much such persons as in this country get
possession of a disreputable joint-stock company.   There is

almost the same amount of ability and honesty.' After nearly three years of experience it would be difficult to describe Washington more justly.

But we do not cite the instance to prove Sir George Lewis's power of prediction, so much as to prove his unfailing desire for a distinct aim.

The political precision of Sir George Lewis is peculiarly English, but it is not at all more English than his scholarship. Persons who do not read such books may fancy that 'scholars' books' are much the same in all countries. But such is not the case. Mr. Grote's History, to take an instance, could no more have been written in Germany than Bacon's 'Novum Organon' could have been written by Socrates. That history belongs to the intellectual atmosphere of England as plainly as our parliamentary debates. There is in it the constant sense of evidence, the habitual perception of tested probability, which the atmosphere of a free country produces and must produce. Sir George Lewis's books have this instinctive sense of the real value of evidence even more than Mr. Grote's. He could not help feeling it; he did not wish to forget it, and he could not have forgotten it if he had wished.

Sir George Lewis is gone, but he has left a remembrance in many minds which will not grow cold while they are still warm. For many years it will to many be much to have known one who was learned and yet wise, just but yet kind; considerate and observing, and yet never in the least severe.

# MR. COBDEN.

TWENTY-THREE years ago—and it is very strange that it should be so many years—when Mr. Cobden first began to hold Free-trade meetings in the agricultural districts, people there were much confused. They could not believe the Mr. Cobden they saw to be the ' Mr. Cobden that was in the papers.' They expected a burly demagogue from the North, ignorant of rural matters, absorbed in manufacturing ideas, appealing to class prejudices—hostile and exciting hostility. They saw ' a sensitive and almost slender man, of shrinking nerve, full of rural ideas, who proclaimed himself the son of a farmer, who understood and could state the facts of agricultural life far better than most agriculturists, who was most anxious to convince every one of what he thought the truth, and who was almost more anxious not to offend any one.' The tradition is dying out, but Mr. Cobden acquired, even in those days of Free-trade agitation, a sort of agricultural popularity. He excited a personal interest, he left what may be called a *sense* of himself among his professed enemies. They were surprised at finding that he was not what they thought; they were charmed to find that he was not what they expected; they were fascinated to find what he was. The same feeling has been evident at his sudden death—a death at least which was to the mass of occupied men sudden. Over political Belgravia—the last part of English society Mr. Cobden ever cultivated—there was a sadness. Every one felt that England had lost an individuality which it could never have again, which was of the highest value, which was in its own kind altogether unequalled.

What used to strike the agricultural mind, as different from what they fancied, and most opposite to a Northern agitator, was a sort of playfulness. They could hardly believe that the lurking smile, the perfectly magical humour which they were so much struck by, could be that of a 'Manchester man.' Mr. Cobden used to say, 'I have as much right as any man to call myself the representative of the tenant farmer, for I am a farmer's son, and the son of a Sussex farmer.' But agriculturists keenly felt that this was not the explanation of the man they saw. Perhaps they could not have thoroughly explained, but they perfectly knew that they were hearing a man of singular and most peculiar genius, fitted as if by 'natural selection' for the work he had to do, and not wasting a word on any other work or anything else, least of all upon himself.

Mr. Cobden was very anomalous in two respects. He was a sensitive agitator. Generally, an agitator is a rough man of the O'Connell type, who says anything himself, and lets others say anything. You 'peg into me and I will peg into you, and let us see which will win,' is his motto. But Mr. Cobden's habit and feeling were utterly different. He never spoke ill of any one. He arraigned principles, but not persons. We fearlessly say that after a career of agitation of thirty years, not one single individual has—we do not say a valid charge, but a producible charge—a charge which he would wish to bring forward against Mr. Cobden. You cannot find the man who says, 'Mr. Cobden said this of me, and it was not true.' This may seem trivial praise, and on paper it looks easy. But to those who know the great temptations of actual life it means very much. How would any other great agitator, O'Connell or Hunt or Cobbett look, if tried by such a test? Very rarely, if even ever in history, has a man achieved so much by his words—been victor in what was thought at the time to be a class struggle—and yet spoken so little evil as Mr. Cobden. There is hardly a word to be found, perhaps, even now, which the recording angel would wish to blot out. We may on other grounds object to an agitator who lacerates no one, but no watchful man of the world will deny that such an agitator has vanquished one of life's most imperious and difficult temptations.

Perhaps some of our readers may remember as vividly as we do a curious instance of Mr. Cobden's sensitiveness. He said at Drury Lane Theatre, in tones of feeling, almost of passion, curiously contrasting with the ordinary coolness of his nature, ' I could not serve with Sir Robert Peel.' After more than twenty years, the curiously thrilling tones of that phrase still live in our ears. Mr. Cobden alluded to the charge which Sir Robert Peel had made, or half made, that the Anti-Corn Law League and Mr. Cobden had, by their action and agitation, conduced to the actual assassination of Mr. Drummond, his secretary, and the intended assassination of himself—Sir Robert Peel. No excuse or palliation could be made for such an assertion except the most important one, that Peel's nerves were as susceptible and sensitive as Mr. Cobden's. But the profound feeling with which Mr. Cobden spoke of it is certain. He felt it as a man feels an unjust calumny, an unfounded stain on his honour.

Mr. Disraeli said on Monday night (and he has made many extraordinary assertions, but this is about the queerest), ' Mr. Cobden had a profound reverence for tradition.' If there is any single quality which Mr. Cobden had not, it was traditional reverence. But probably Mr. Disraeli meant what was most true, that Mr. Cobden had a delicate dislike of offending other men's opinions. He dealt with them tenderly. He did not like to have his own creed coarsely attacked, and he did—he could not help doing—as he would be done by; he never attacked any man's creed coarsely or roughly, or in any way except by what he in his best conscience thought the fairest and justest argument.

This sensitive nature is one marked peculiarity in Mr. Cobden's career as an agitator, and another is, that he was an agitator for men of business.

Generally speaking, occupied men charged with the respon-
sibilities and laden with the labour of grave affairs are jealous of
agitation. They know how much may be said against any one
who is responsible for anything. They know how unanswerable
such charges nearly always are, and how false they easily may
be. A capitalist can hardly help thinking, ' Suppose a man was to
make a speech against my mode of conducting my own business,
how much he would have to say!' Now it is an exact description of Mr. Cobden, that by the personal magic of a single-
minded practicability he made men of business abandon this
objection. He made them rather like the new form of agitation.
He made them say, 'How business-like, how wise, just what it
would have been right to do.'

Mr. Cobden of course was not the discoverer of the Free-
trade principle. He did not first find out that the Corn Laws
were bad laws. But he was the most effectual of those who
discovered how the Corn Laws were to be repealed, how
Freetrade was to change from a doctrine of the 'Wealth
of Nations' into a principle of tariffs and a fact of real life.
If a thing was right, to Mr. Cobden's mind it ought to
be done; and as Adam Smith's doctrines were admitted on
theory, he could not believe that they ought to lie idle, that
they ought to be 'bedridden in the dormitory of the understanding.'

Lord Houghton once said, 'In my time political economy
books used to begin, "Suppose a man on an island."' Mr.
Cobden's speeches never began so. He was altogether a man of
business speaking to men of business. Some of us may remember
the almost arch smile with which he said 'the House of Commons
does not seem quite to understand the difference between a
cotton mill and a print work.' It was almost amusing to him
to think that the first assembly of the first mercantile nation
could be, as they were and are, very dim in their notions of the
most material divisions of their largest industry. It was this
evident and first-hand familiarity with real facts and actual

z

life which enabled Mr. Cobden to inspire a curiously diffused
confidence in all matter-of-fact men. He diffused a kind
of 'economical faith.' People in those days had only to say,
'Mr. Cobden said so,' and other people went and 'believed it.'

Mr. Cobden had nothing in the received sense classical
about his oratory, but it is quite certain that Aristotle, the
greatest teacher of the classical art of rhetoric, would very
keenly have appreciated his oratory. This sort of economical
faith is exactly what he would most have valued, what he
most prescribed. He said: 'A speaker should convince his
audience that he was a likely person to know.' This was
exactly what Mr. Cobden did. And the matter-of-fact philosopher would have much liked Mr. Cobden's habit of ' coming to
the point.' It would have been thoroughly agreeable to his
positive mind to see so much of clear, obvious argument. He
would not, indeed, have been able to conceive a ' League Meeting.' There has never, perhaps, been another time in the
history of the world when excited masses of men and women
hung on the words of one talking political economy. The
excitement of these meetings was keener than any political
excitement of the last twenty years, keener infinitely than
any which there is now. It may be said, and truly, that the
interest of the subject was Mr. Cobden's felicity, not his mind ;
but it may be said with equal truth that the excitement
was much greater when he was speaking than when any one
else was speaking. By a kind of keenness of nerve, he said the
exact word most fitted to touch, not the bare abstract understanding, but the quick individual perceptions of his hearers.

We do not wish to make this article a mere panegyric. Mr.
Cobden was far too manly to like such folly. His mind was
very peculiar, and like all peculiar minds had its sharp limits.
He had what we may call a supplementary understanding, that
is, a bold, original intellect, acting on a special experience, and
striking out views and principles not known to or neglected by
ordinary men. He did not possess the traditional education of

his country, and did not understand it. The solid heritage of transmitted knowledge has more value, we believe, than he would have accorded to it. There was too a defect in business faculty not identical, but perhaps not altogether without analogy. The late Mr. James Wilson used to say, 'Cobden's administrative power I do not think much of, but he is most valuable in counsel, always original, always shrewd, and not at all extreme.' He was not altogether equal to meaner men in some beaten tracks and pathways of life, though he was far their superior in all matters requiring an original stress of speculation, an innate energy of thought.

It may be said, and truly said, that he has been cut off before his time. A youth and manhood so spent as his well deserved a green old age. But so it was not to be. He has left us, quite independently of his positive works, of the repeal of the Corn Laws, of the French treaty, a rare gift—the gift of a unique character. There has been nothing before Richard Cobden like him in English history, and perhaps there will not be anything like him. And his character is of the simple, emphatic, picturesque sort which most easily, when opportunities are given as they were to him, goes down to posterity. May posterity learn from him! Only last week we hoped to have learned something ourselves.

> 'But what is before us we know not,
> And we know not what shall succeed.'

## LORD PALMERSTON.

[1865.]

LORD PALMERSTON only died on Wednesday, and already the world is full of sketches and biographies of him. It is very natural that it should be so, for he counted for much in English politics: his personality was a power, and it is natural that every one should, at his death, seek to analyse what we used to have, and what we have now lost. We will do so, but, remembering how often the tale has been told, we will be as brief as possible.

Lord Derby happily said that he was born in the 'pre-scientific' period, and Lord Palmerston was so born, or even more. He was, it is true, a boarder at Dugald Stewart's, and we believe transcribed at least a part of the lectures on political economy of that philosopher, lately published. But the combined influence of interior nature and the surrounding situation was too strong. His real culture was that of living languages and the actual world. He was the best French scholar among his contemporaries—so much so that when he went to Paris in 1859, the whole society, which fancied he was an imperious and ignorant Englishman, was charmed by the grace of his expression. His English in all his speeches was sound and pure, and in his greater efforts almost fastidiously correct. The feeling for language, which is one characteristic of a great man of the world, was very nice in Lord Palmerston, and very characteristic.

It was from the actual knowledge of men—from close specific contact—that Lord Palmerston derived his data. We have heard grave men say with surprise, 'He always has an anecdote to cap his argument. He begins, " I knew a man once," ' and the anecdotes had no trace of the garrulity of age : they were real illustrations of the matter in hand. They were the chosen instances of a man who thought in instances. Some think, as the philosophers say, by ' definition,' others by ' type.' Lord Palmerston, like an animated man used to the animated world, thought in examples, and hardly realised abstract words.

It was because of this that in international matters—the only ones for which in youth he cared—he was a great practical lawyer. He knew what hardly any one knows, the subject-matter. He knew the cases with which during a long life he had to deal. To most men international law is a matter of precedent and words; to him it was a matter of personal adventure and reality. Some people not unqualified to judge have said that his opinion on such matters was as good as any law officer's. He might not have studied Vattel or Wheaton so closely as some, but he had, what is far better, followed with a keen interest the actual and necessary practice of present nations.

It was this sort of worldly sympathy and worldly education which gave Lord Palmerston his intelligibility. He was not a common man, but a common man might have been cut out of him. He had in him all that a common man has, and something more. And he did not at all despise, as some philosophers teach people to do, the common part of his mind. He was profoundly aware that the common mass of plain sense is the great administrative agency of the world ; and that if you keep yourself in sympathy with this you win, and if not you fail. Sir George Lewis used to say that just as Demosthenes declared action to be the first, second, and third thing in a statesman, so intelligibility is the first, second, and third thing in a constitutional statesman. It is to us certainly the first, second, and third thing in Lord Palmerston. This is not absolutely eulogistic. No one resembled less than Lord

Palmerston the fancied portrait of an ideal statesman laying down in his closet plans to be worked out twenty years
hence. He was a statesman for the moment. Whatever was
not wanted now, whatever was not practicable now, whatever
would not take now, he drove quite out of his mind. The
pre-requisites of a constitutional statesman have been defined as
the 'powers of a first-rate man, and the creed of a second-rate
man.' The saying is harsh, but it is expressive. Lord Palmerston's creed was never the creed of the far-seeing philosopher ;
it was the creed of a sensible and sagacious but still commonplace man. His objects were common objects : what was uncommon was the will with which he pursued them.

No man was better in action, but no man was more free
from the pedantry of business. People, he has been heard to
say, have different minds. 'When I was a young man, the
Duke of Wellington made an appointment with me at half-
past seven in the morning, and some one asked me, Why,
Palmerston, how will you keep that engagement ? Oh, I said,
of course, the easiest thing in the world. I shall keep it the
last thing before I go to bed.' He knew that the real essence
of work is concentrated energy, and that people who really have
that in a superior degree by nature, are independent of the
forms and habits and artifices by which less able and active
people are kept up to their labours.

Lord Palmerston prided himself on his foreign policy, on
which we cannot now pronounce a judgment. But it is not
upon this that his fame will rest. He had a great difficulty as
a Foreign Minister. He had no real conception of any mode of
life except that with which he was familiar. His idea, his
fixed idea, was that the Turks were a highly improving and
civilised race, and it was impossible to beat into him their
essentially barbaric and unindustrial character. He would
hear anything patiently, but no corresponding ideas were
raised in his mind. A man of the world is not an imaginative
animal, and Lord Palmerston was by incurable nature a man of

the world: keenly detective in what he could realise by experience—utterly blind, dark, and impervious to what he could
not so realise. Even the best part of his foreign policy was
alloyed with this defect. The mantle of Canning had descended
on him, and the creed and interests of Canning. He was most
eager to use the strong influence of England to support free
institutions—to aid ' the Liberal party ' was the phrase in those
days everywhere on the Continent. And no aim could be juster
and better—it was the best way in which English strength
could be used. But he failed in the instructed imagination
and delicate perception necessary to its best attainment. He
supported the Liberal party when it was bad, and the country
unfit for it, as much as when it was good and the nation eager
for it. He did not define the degree of his sympathy, or ap-
portion its amount to the comparative merits of the different
claims made on it. According to the notions of the present age,
too, foreign policy should be regulated by abstract, or at least
comprehensive, principles, but Lord Palmerston had no such
principles. He prided himself on his exploits in Europe, but
it is by his instincts in England that he will be remembered.

It was made a matter of wonder that Lord Palmerston
should begin to rule the House of Commons at seventy, and
there is no doubt that he was very awkward at first in so ruling
it. Sir James Graham, and other judges of business management, predicted that ' the thing would fail,' and that a new
Government would have to be formed. But the truth is, that
though he had been fifty years in the House of Commons, Lord
Palmerston had never regularly attended it, and even still less
attended to it. His person had not been there very much, and
his mind had been there very little. He answered a question
on his own policy, or made a speech, and then went away.
Debate was not to him, as to Mr. Pitt or Mr. Gladstone, a
matter of life and pleasure. Mr. Canning used to complain, ' I
can't get that three-decker Palmerston to bear down.' And
when he was made leader of the House, it came out that he

hardly knew, if he did know, the forms of the House. But it was a defect of past interest, not a defect of present capacity. He soon mastered the necessary knowledge, and as soon as he had done so the sure sagacity of his masculine instincts secured him an unconquerable strength.

Something we wished to say more on these great gifts, and something, too, might be said as to the defects by which they were alloyed. But it is needless. Brevity is as necessary in a memorial article as in an epitaph. So much is certain, we shall never look upon his like again. We may look on others of newer race, but his race is departed. The merits of the new race were not his merits; their defects are not his. England will never want statesmen, but she will never see in our time such a statesman as Viscount Palmerston.

## THE EARL OF CLARENDON.

[1870]

THE late Lord Clarendon belonged to a very small and very remarkable class of peers. There are many peers, as the lawyers, who have no birth, but who worked hard in their youth ; and there are also many who have the highest birth, and have never worked the least. There are many who have earned rank, and many who have inherited rank. But it is rare to find a peer who inherits his rank, and yet who has known what it is to earn his bread. Of eminent peers there is perhaps hardly more than one now living of whom this is true. Lord Salisbury has indeed a right to feel that circumstances cannot ruin him, that a revolution may come, that the House of Lords may perish, that estates may be confiscated, but that his abilities as a popular writer will earn him his living as they did before. Though in a different way Lord Clarendon was of this class also. When he was in the Excise office in Dublin, and all through his younger life, there was but a distant probability of his coming to the title ; and he had to work really for his bread. And the training of his youth was probably of use to him always. To the last week of his death he was a curiously unremitting worker. With somewhat peculiar hours and times, he got through more work probably in the twenty-four hours than most administrators of his time, and finished it all with care and accuracy. There were none of the gratuitous blunders and hurried errors which mostly characterise the work of one who is much praised for great activity ; everthing was carefully considered and carefully executed.

Perhaps it is not unconnected with this praise, that there was an indescribable repose about Lord Clarendon's manner and appearance. No one who saw him, in his later years at least, would have ever thought him a specially active man. He seemed a very calm, sensible, and singularly courteous old gentleman; and it would scarcely have occurred to a casual observer that he was an exceedingly indefatigable worker. But those who have watched the habits of men of business in politics and out of it will have seen many cases in which a still and quiet man who does not seem to be doing much, and probably is talking of something quite different, has in matter of fact and at the week's end accomplished much more than the ' rushing mighty wind ; '—the very energetic man who is never idle or at rest and who has no thought but his office business. A still man like Lord Clarendon has time to think what he will do, and most incessant men are apt to act before they have thought, and therefore land where they should not, or else lose half their time in sailing back again.

It was, perhaps, the result of Lord Clarendon's early training that he always took great interest in commerce, and whenever he had the power, steadily used the agency of the Foreign Office for its advantage. He was much too thoroughly on a level with his time to do this by an aggressive foreign policy. The old notion of fighting for foreign markets, or of intriguing for their exclusive use, had so completely died out that he cannot be praised for being exempt from it. Lord Clarendon used only the legitimate functions for trade purposes. He was especially eager for the collection of actual statistical information by our foreign consuls and embassies. The commencement of their reports on these subjects, and the establishment of the statistical department of the Board of Trade, were largely owing to his great interest in these objects.

That Lord Clarendon showed great originality as a Foreign Minister will hardly be contended, and some, among whom the present writer is to be counted, have grave doubts whether extreme originality in such an office is either possible or desirable. Examples of great inventiveness are rare in all business, but they are particularly rare in those kinds of business which require the constant consent of many persons—and of these the English foreign policy is one. Not, indeed, that at the moment of taking his decision, the Foreign Minister is particularly trammelled. In great cases he must consult the Prime Minister and perhaps the Cabinet. But if these stood by themselves, having the power of peculiar information, he could probably mostly carry with him the minds of men occupied with near and pressing questions, and not in general ready to master disagreeable and uncertain detail as to remote topics and strange events. But the great obstacle to originality is the English nation. In a free country a minister can only do that which the nation is prepared for, and if he tries to do more the nation will disown him. Within special limits, and on minor questions, he can give an effectual guidance and control the decision, but beyond those limits, and on vital matters, he has no power at all. The subtle power which we call ' opinion,' which is the product of so long a history and the offspring of so many causes, hems him in, and he cannot do as he would ; but if he stays, he must act as he would not. An irritable, far-seeing originality is commonly a vice in business, and in a Foreign Minister it would be an intolerable nuisance. It was exactly because Lord Clarendon had a delicate instinct of the limits of his power, that he was so truly useful and so really influential.

In one respect we are not inclined to join in the universal praise which within the last few days Lord Clarendon has received. He has been greatly praised as a writer, and no doubt he wrote not only with great facility but with much elegance. But there is one great difficulty about almost all his despatches. Each sentence is clear, and no word brings you to a stop; but yet after a few paragraphs a careful reader suddenly pauses to think where he is and what he has assented to. And even when he reads the paragraphs over again he will not always find it easy to be sure that he sees the limits of what was meant and the limits of what was not meant. The limpid flow of delicate words takes him steadily on; but where at any precise instant he is, he cannot be very confident. For the former intercourse of foreign Courts this sort of style had immense advantages ; it gave no offence, and, having no marked sentences, left no barbed words for after irritation. And in Lord Russell we had a warning of the evils of the opposite style. He wrote as he used to speak in the House of Commons. With a certain cold acumen he ' pitched' (there is no less familiar word adequate) ' into ' the foreign Courts, as he used to ' pitch into ' Sir Robert Peel ; and not being used to Parliamentary plainness, the foreign Courts did not like it. Lord Russell hardly conducted a foreign controversy in which the extreme intelligibility of his words did not leave a sting behind them. Of Lord Clarendon the very contrary may be said—he scarcely ever left a sting, never an unnecessary one. But, on the other hand, Lord Russell's despatches, hard and unpleasant as they often are, never left anyone in doubt as to their precise meaning. If they did mislead some foreign Courts it was because they could not understand that a Minister would blurt out all his meaning in that *gauche* manner ; but to a common reader they are as plain as words can make them. And, as in the present day, great despatches, being published, are really addressed to whole nations of common readers as well as to small Courts of special training, they ought to be so written as to combine the gentle suavity that suits the one with the unmistakeable plainness which is essential to the other. It was exactly the gliding urbanity of Lord Clarendon's style which pleased the Courts while it perplexed the common people.

But we do not need now to dwell at length on a point so subordinate. It is much for a man of Lord Clarendon's standing to have written nearly perfectly in the old style ; it is no ground for serious blame to him that he did not invent a new style. He will be remembered by posterity as a Minister singularly suited to the transition age in which he lived, and, as possessing both the courtly manners which are going out and also the commercial tastes and the business knowledge which are coming in. Some critics will, as we have said, find fault with his want of special designs and of a far-reaching policy. But to this generation of Englishmen this was no fault at all. We wish that foreign nations should, as far as may be, solve their own problems; we wish them to gain all the good they can by their own exertions, and to remove all the evil. But we do not wish to take part in their struggles. We fear that we might mistake as to what was best; we fear that in so shifting a scene we might find, years hence, when the truth is known, that we had in fact done exactly the reverse of what we meant, and had really injured what we meant to aid. We fear that, amid the confusion, our good might turn to evil, and that our help would be a calamity and not a blessing. And for an age like this Lord Clarendon was a fitting Minister, for he had a wise sagacity which taught him to interfere as little, and to refrain from acting as much, as prudence rendered possible.

## MR. LOWE AS CHANCELLOR OF THE EXCHEQUER.

### [1871]

'AN oak,' said a great Irish orator, who did not succeed so well
as he expected in England, 'an oak should not be transplanted
at fifty.' And we believe that to be the reason why Mr. Lowe
—though in many respects he has shown great ability as
Finance Minister—upon the whole has not, as yet, succeeded
better than many much stupider men, nor as well as his genius
deserved. Mr. Lowe, before he began his finance studies, had
already 'invested' so much mind that most men would have
had no more left. His career at Oxford was unusually long ;
he was not a mere student who took high honours. After that
he stayed several years as a working tutor, and has described
to a Royal Commission how steadily he worked for ten hours a
day as a 'coach,' and how little in consequence he accepts the
'romance' of tuition. And the inevitable result has been that
Mr. Lowe has become a scholar, not only as young students
become such, but as men of maturer years, who mean to earn
money by it, become scholars. A certain part of the substance
of his mind is embarked in that pursuit, and cannot now be
transferred to any other. After leaving Oxford, Mr. Lowe made
himself not only an excellent English lawyer, but an admirable
general jurist. He is acquainted not only with the technicalities of English law, but with the structure of other systems
of law, and with the principles of scientific jurisprudence. He
has studied what Bentham said law 'ought' to be, and what

Austin said law 'must' be. And this too is a very exhausting study, requiring, if the knowledge is really to be acquired as Mr. Lowe has acquired it, and retained as he retains it, a great 'capital' of mind. No one can wonder that, when on the verge of threescore, he was suddenly made Finance Minister, he should not possess or display so much free and applicable mind as some younger men. Great mind he must always display. But he has not displayed proportionate mind—proportioned, we mean, to the immense abilities which everyone knows he has. After all, there is only room in even the largest head for a certain number of thoughts, and Mr. Lowe had crowded his, long before he had tried finance, with many dissimilar and occupying ideas.

It is true that under our Parliamentary system, Ministers of as mature an age as Mr. Lowe are not unfrequently transferred from post to post, and are placed in charge of offices with whose subjects they have no knowledge. No one supposes that Mr. Cardwell knew much of military business before he was made Secretary for War; and yet unquestionably he has pulled the Army Regulation Bill better through Parliament than the planners who contrived it, or the soldiers who will act on it. But these transferable statesmen commonly belong to a different class from Mr. Lowe. Like Mr. Cardwell, they are trained Parliamentary advocates. They have learned to know the House of Commons, and the way of putting an argument so as to suit the House of Commons, as a long-practised advocate knows the sort of arguments which suit a jury, and the most telling way in which to state them to a jury. Sir Robert Peel was once said to know how to 'dress up a case for Parliament' better than anyone else. And in this art there are two secrets, of which Mr. Cardwell is an eminent master. The first is always to content yourself with the minimum of general maxims which will suit your purpose and prove what you want. By so doing, you offend as few people as possible, you startle as few people as possible, and you expose yourself to as few retorts as possible. And the second secret is to make the wohle discussion very uninteresting—to leave an impression that the subject is very dry, that it is very difficult, that the department had attended to the dreary detail of it, and that on the whole it is safer to leave it to the department, and a dangerous responsibility to interfere with the department. The faculty of disheartening adversaries by diffusing on occasion an oppressive atmosphere of business-like dulness is invaluable to a Parliamentary statesman.

But these arts Mr. Lowe does not possess. He cannot help being brilliant. The quality of his mind is to put everything in the most lively, most exciting, and most startling form. He cannot talk that monotonous humdrum which men scarcely listen to, which lulls them to sleep, but which seems to them the 'sort of thing you would expect,' which they suppose is 'all right.' And Mr. Lowe's mode of using general principles not only is not that which a Parliamentary tactician would recommend, but is the very reverse of what he would advise. Mr. Lowe always ascends to the widest generalities. The *axiomata media,* as logicians have called them—the middle principles, in which most minds feel most reality and on which they find it most easy to rest—have no charms for him. He likes to go back to the bone, to the abstract, to the attenuated, and if he left these remote principles in their remote unintelligibility, he would not suffer so much. But he makes the dry bones live. He wraps them in illustrations which Macaulay might envy. And he is all the more effective, because he uses our vernacular tongue. The phrases that 'the money market must take care of itself,' and that 'it was not the business of the Treasury to cocker up the Bank of England,' will long be remembered, and will longer impair his influence with grave, quiet, and influential persons. Mr. Lowe startles those who do not like to be startled, and does not compose those who wish to be composed—those who need a little commonplace to assure them that they are acting on safe principles

—that they are not, according to the saying, 'lighting the streets with fireworks.'

These defects would be felt in any new office; but besides these, Mr. Lowe has one—a physical one—to which he has often himself alluded, and which hampers him beyond expression. In our younger days he would have been cited in books of 'entertaining knowledge' as a conspicuous instance of the 'pursuit of knowledge under difficulties.' Being almost unable to read books with his own eyes, he knows more about books than almost anyone who has eyes. A wonderful memory, and an intense wish to know the truth, have filled his head with knowledge; but though great powers may compensate for inherent defects, none, not even the greatest, can annihilate those defects. They are ineradicable, and the consequences of them will come back again to lessen every victory, and to enhance every disaster. It is so with Mr. Lowe in this case. A man who cannot easily read figures for himself, who cannot manipulate them for himself, who cannot throw them into various shapes, as it were, on trial for himself, cannot be a great financier. Our greatest financiers, Pitt, Peel, and Gladstone, have all of them been men who did not take their figures from others, but who spent a great—almost an excessive—labour on the *minutiæ* of them for themselves. It is from no lack of labour, and no lack of mind, that Mr. Lowe does not do this. By physical constitution he is incapable of it.

Something of this is at the bottom of Mr. Lowe's occasionally defective dealing with small financial forms, which was the only point that Mr. Disraeli made against him in criticising his Budget. It is hardly possible that a man with such immense disadvantages for business can have his tackle quite as ready and quite as perfect as those who are more fortunate. And Mr. Disraeli is scarcely the man who ought to have made the taunt. No one regards these legal forms with more sublime indifference than he does when it suits his object. 'Gentlemen of the long robe,' he used to say when in office, 'will attend to

these details;' and he would have deemed it absurd that a
Minister, charged with the fate of Cabinets and the policy of
measures, should even consider them. And perhaps he was
right; perhaps it would have been absurd. But what is unnecessary for one Minister cannot be incumbent on another
similar Minister. It was not for Mr. Disraeli, who has scarcely
seemed to be able to see details and technicalities (so exclusively did he look on them from the most elevated heights of
policy), to reproach Mr. Lowe with a few trivial, innocuous, and
excusable deficiencies in them.

The result of all this is very plain. It is that Mr. Lowe is
under peculiar difficulties in finance—that it is not a region in
which his great powers can ever show to the best advantage—
that, on the contrary, it is a region in which they will frequently
be seen to the greatest disadvantage. But there is a profound
truth in the saying that 'men of pre-eminent ability are
always safe;' not of course that so wide a phrase is to be taken
exactly to the letter, but that there is a 'reserve fund' in the
highest ability which will enable it to pull through scrapes, to
remedy errors, to surmount disasters, which would ruin and
bury common men. Mr. Lowe will certainly not have an un-
chequered reign at the Exchequer; but he may reign long,
he may do much good, and notwithstanding many failures and
defects, may leave the special stamp and impress of his mind
on many great Budgets and important measures.

## MONSIEUR GUIZOT.

[1874]

THE announcement of the death of M. Guizot will take the minds of many back to the cold February evenings in 1848, when London, long used to political calm, was convulsed by a new excitement, when we heard cried in rapid succession, 'Resignation of Guizot,' 'Flight of Louis Philippe,' 'Proclamation of the Republic,' and when the present chapter of European politics began. M. Guizot lived to see many events and many changes, but none which restored him to pre-eminence, or which made him once more a European personage. His name was never cried in the London streets again. M. Guizot was in most respects exactly the opposite of the common English notion of a Frenchman. There floats in this country an idea that a Frenchman is a light, changeable, sceptical being, who is fond of amusement, who is taken with childish shows, who always wants some new thing, who is incapable of fixed belief on any subject, and on religion especially. But Guizot was, on the contrary, a man of fixed and intense belief in religion, who was wholly devoted to serious study, who probably cared as little for the frivolous side of life as any human being who ever lived, who was stiff in manner and sedate in politics to a fault. A Puritan born in France by mistake, is the description which will most nearly describe him to an ordinary Englishman, for he had all the solidity, the solemnity, and the energy of Puritanism, as well as some of its shortcomings. And it is very natural that such should be his character, for he came of a Huguenot family, who really were French Puritans.

The French national character is much more various than it is supposed to be according to common English ideas, and the stern variety which M. Guizot represents is one of the most remarkable.

Indeed, in the special peculiarity which coloured his political life, he was a most characteristic Frenchman. He represented their excessive propensity to political fear. As we all know, a principal obstacle to good Government in France is a deficiency in political courage. At the present moment a very considerable part of the nation are inclined to return to the Empire—not that they are attached to the Empire, not that they do not see its defects, not that they are not ashamed of its end, but because they are so impressed by the difficulties of making any other strong Government that their heart fails them. They want something which will save them from the *Commune,* and they are disposed to run back to what saved them from the Commune before, without any sufficient inquiry whether a better safeguard cannot be found, or whether this one will be effectual. The excess of their apprehension dims their eyes and distorts their judgment. Guizot had no partiality for the Empire, or for anything like the Empire, but nevertheless his whole political life rested on a similar feeling and aimed at a similar end. He, too, was frightened at revolutionary excess; his father perished in the first revolution. He was born in 1787, and consequently began his intellectual life about 1800, just when the reaction against the revolution was the strongest, when its evil was most exaggerated, and when its good was most depreciated. A strong, serious, unoriginal mind—and such was M. Guizot's—which receives such penetrating impressions early in life generally holds them on, in one shape or another, till the end. And so it was in this case. Guizot was devoted through life to what he called the ' Conservative' policy; he was always endeavouring to avert revolution; he was incessantly in dread of tumult: he saw attack and commotion everywhere. But he had no notion what was the real counterforce in France to the revolutionary force. We now know from experience that that force, though it calls itself the force of numbers, can be controlled by appealing to numbers; that the peasant proprietors, who are the majority in France, hate nothing so much and fear nothing so much; that they think revolution may take from them their property, their speck of land, their ' all ; ' and, therefore, they will resist revolution at any time and on any pretence, and will support any power which they think can prevail against it. But Guizot did not perceive this great force. His great *recipe* for preventing revolution was not by extending the suffrage, but by restricting it. He did not see that the masses in France, having property of their own, were only too likely to be timid about property. His scheme was to resist revolution by keeping the suffrage so high that it included only a few in the towns, that it scarcely included any of the masses in the country. He proposed to found the throne of constitutional liberty on a select *bourgeoisie*—few in number, moderate in disposition, easily conciliated by their interests. The revolution of 1848 might have been avoided if he had been willing a little to extend the suffrage, but he would not extend it. The proposals then made for so doing seem now trivial and unimportant, but Guizot sincerely believed that they would ruin the country; sooner than grant them he incurred a revolution. He was so perturbed by the excessive dread of revolution that he could not see what was the true power with which to oppose it—that he threw away a mighty power—that he relied solely on a weak one—that he caused the calamity he was always fearing.

It is this great misfortune which will always colour any retrospect of M. Guizot's career, and render it a melancholy one. In many minor ways he accomplished much good. As a minister of public instruction he did much—much, perhaps, which no other man at that time could have done—for education in France. When ambassador in England he did much to prevent a war which was then imminent, and which M. Thiers would have hurried on; through his whole career, by

a lofty scrupulosity, he did much to raise the low level of
morality in French public life. As an orator he had great
triumphs at the tribune, though his eloquence is too little
business-like and too academical for our English taste. But
notwithstanding these triumphs and these services, his political
career must ever be held to be a complete failure, for he failed
in the work of his life—in the aim he had specially chosen as
his own. His mission—he would have accepted the word—was
to avert revolution, and he caused revolution. Nor is the
failure one which was slight in its effects, or which history can
forget. On the contrary, every page of present French politics bears witness to its importance. No French Republic and
no French Monarchy can now have nearly as much strength or
nearly as much chance of living as the Monarchy of July which
Guizot destroyed.

Of his literary productions, this is not the place to speak.
Nothing can be more unlike ordinary Parisian literature than
they are. That literature generally reminds its readers of the
old saying, 'That the French would be the best cooks in Europe
if they had got any butcher's meat.' Of French cookery nothing
can be more libellous; but of much French literature it would
be quite true to say that the writers would be the first in Europe
if they only knew anything about their subject. The power of
expression has been cultivated to an extreme perfection, but
unfortunately the writers have neglected the further task of
finding anything true and important to say. But M. Guizot's
works are the reverse of all this. A work of more solid erudition
than the 'History of French Civilisation' was never written by
a German professor, and few Germans have ever written anything so accurately matured, and so perfectly mastered. In
this respect he contrasts admirably with his great rival. There
used to be a story—a just story in the main we believe—of a
critic who betted that he would find five errors in any five pages
of Thiers' great history of the Revolution. Even his warmest
admirers indeed have never contended that M. Thiers had a

scrupulous love of truth, was a careful collector of evidence, or
a fine judge of it when collected. But M. Guizot was all three.
The labour expended on his books must have been very great,
and much more than it would be now, for he has himself
helped his successors—certainly to arrive at his own conclusions with greater ease, and perhaps also to arrive at improved
conclusions.

From our peculiar view, as an economical statesman, M.
Guizot has, we are sorry to say, no title to respect. He and
his fellow-ministers under Louis Philippe left it to the Empire
to improve the material condition of the French people. He
did little to promote railways, and he objected to the English
treaty of 1860 because it was an approach to Free-trade, because
it would enable 'the English manufacturers, after an English
commercial crisis, to export their goods to France and to swamp
the French manufacturers.' The real principles of Free-trade
had never penetrated into his mind, any more than into the
minds of Louis Philippe's other ministers, and partly on that
account France now looks back to the time of the Empir as to
the 'golden age' of wealth and industry, and not to the time
of the free Monarchy.

We are sorry to have to write so much of blame of one
whose character all Europe respected, and some of whose virtues
were so valuable to France. But it is one perhaps painful consequence of prolonged old age that a man's character at death is
estimated with perfect partiality. Those who most hated him
and those who most loved him are mostly passed away or superseded in the scene of affairs. And if, as in M. Guizot's case,
the good which he did was mostly one of temporary moral impression, and the evil which he caused one of lasting political
result, there will be always more blame than praise to say.
The impalpable virtues can hardly be described and are mostly
forgotten, but the indelible consequences of the political errors
are fixed on the face of the world; they cannot be overlooked,
and they must be spoken of.

# PROFESSOR CAIRNES.

[1875]

WE cannot attempt at this moment to give anything like a full estimate of Mr. Cairnes's character, either as a political economist or a political writer. The first few days after the death of one so eminent and so peculiar, are never favourable to such a task ; and the difficulty is always greater when, as in this case, he wrote much on topics on which public opinion is still divided. We can only attempt a few descriptive words.

The characteristic of Mr. Cairnes's mind was a tenacious grasp of abstract principle. He applied to the subjects of his life exactly the sort of mind with which a great judge applies the principles of law to the facts before him ; and he applied it under more difficult circumstances, for, in the principles of positive law, a judge can absolutely be guided by previous precedent, whereas a thinker in the moral sciences has to make his principles, as well as to apply them—'to find,' at least often, 'the dream as well as the interpretation.' This quality is not common in any age, but it is particularly uncommon now. The habit of popular writing—a habit which is apt to grow on all who deal with political and moral subjects, for it is only by being in some degree popular that you will be read or can be influential—has a contrary influence. It generates a habit of leaving out difficulties, of saying that which is easy rather than that which is true, that which is clear rather than that which is exact. There are a great many parts of political and economical truth which are in their nature very complex, just as many parts of science are so, and, in these cases, extreme easiness of comprehension in a writer is a quality to be suspected; for, probably, it arises from his leaving out a part—frequently the most difficult part—of the subject. Mr. Cairnes never does this; he takes his readers through the subject, just as it seemed to him to be. He did not make it artificially easy, or attempt to please them by lessening its intricacies. And he showed himself even more careless of popularity in another way. The curiosity on such subjects is now far greater than the capacity for gratifying it; severe and abstract reasoning is necessary before they can be mastered, and there are many who dislike severe and abstract reasoning. Accordingly, something else is often put forward, as if it would do as well. 'Figures' are used instead of reasoning. But, as Mr. Cairnes always contended, the figures of an instance do not of themselves prove anything beyond that instance. They are most valuable in illustrating a distinct argument, but that argument must accompany them. But, as the argument is often more difficult than the illustration, it is apt not to be used, and 'political economy' is in danger of dissolving into 'statistics,' which is much as if anecdotes of animals were substituted for the science of biology.

The constant rigour with which Mr. Cairnes withstood these temptations, has given his writings a very peculiar character. There is a Euclidian precision about them which fits them for a tonic for the mind, and which makes much other writing seem but 'soft stuff' after we have been reading them;—at any rate, you feel that you have seen, in all likelihood, the worst of the subject. You have been in company with one who did not spare himself anything, and who despised readers that wished to be spared anything. Reading his works is like living on high ground; the 'thin air of abstract truth' which they give you, braces the mind just as fine material air does the body.

The wonder that this incessant intellectual vigour was displayed for years by a wasting invalid, hardly able to move, and often in the most intense pain, has long been familiar to his friends, and has now been published to the world. Much as those who read his writings valued his life, they felt almost forbidden to grieve when they heard of his death; for it seemed selfish to wish that their instruction should be purchased at the cost of such pain as his. Why a mind like his should have been created, and then the power to use it at all fully withheld, is one of the mysteries of which in this world we have no solution.

By far the most remarkable of Mr. Cairnes's writings, in our judgment, are his 'Logic of Political Economy' and his essays on some of the 'Unsettled Questions,' recently published. In the first he defines better, as we think, than any previous writer, the exact sort of science which political economy is, the kind of reasoning which it uses, and the nature of the relation which it, as an abstract science, bears to the concrete world. Those who know how many different opinions have been held on this, and how difficult a part of the subject it is as a rule, prize, we think, most highly what Mr. Cairnes has said on it. In his recent essays on 'Unsettled Questions' in political economy, Mr. Cairnes takes up the hardest parts of the subject and discusses them with a consistent power—it might almost be said with an enjoyment—which is scarcely given to any one who now remains to us. As the questions with which he deals are 'unsettled,' it would be premature to assume the truth of his conclusions; but this may be said, that all who hereafter write on these problems, not only ought to study what he has said, but also to reply to it, if they do not agree with it, a process which—if we may speak from some experience—they will not find at all easy.

We do not mean that Mr. Cairnes has conclusively solved these problems; there are several on which our opinions are not his. And all will agree that the recluse life which his health compelled him to lead, deprived him of information, and especially of a sort of easy familiarity with the course of business, which the greatest ability could not wholly make up for. But under such circumstances the wonder is, not that what he did was sometimes imperfect, but that he was able to do anything.

We have spoken of Mr. Cairnes principally as an economist, partly because that is more especially our own province, but partly also because we think that was the capacity in which his powers were best fitted to work, and by which he will be most remembered. But his other writings have much and characteristic merit, though this is not the time to attempt an estimate of them. In the presence of great difficulties, silence is ' better than many words; ' and there are few greater difficulties than that a mind so strong and pure should have been so thrust aside from life and subjected to so much pain.

# MR. DISRAELI AS A MEMBER OF THE HOUSE OF COMMONS.

[1876]

NOTHING could be more out of place or premature than to review as yet Mr. Disraeli's career. That career is not yet ended. But some remarks may be made on him as a member of the House of Commons, in which he has sat for forty years, and where he obtained his political eminence and power. That part of his career is certainly over, for he has chosen to leave its peculiar scene.

During this long period Mr. Disraeli has filled four parts. First—that of a political free-lance or outsider. And it was in this that he first obtained fame. The best opportunity for such a man is, when parties are breaking up ; when secret feelings are in many minds ; when cautious men do not know what to say. The latter part of Sir Robert Peel's ministry was such a period. From the time when he became conspicuously and obviously a Free-trader, there was always a secret anger in the Conservative ranks which craved for an outlet, but which no 'regular man' could express. This Mr. Disraeli spoke out. From the time of Mr. Milne's sugar amendment, in 1844, till the completion of the disruption of the Tories, in 1846, Mr. Disraeli poured epigram upon epigram and innuendo on innuendo on the 'organised hypocrisy' of his professed leader; and there is no doubt that Sir Robert Peel suffered exceedingly under the smart. He was, in every way, a most sensitive man, and he was especially sensitive in all that related to the House of Commons, which was the scene

of his life, and to his position there. But now he was, for
the first time in his life, exposed to a style of attack to which
he had not the sort of power to reply, but which was for the
moment the most effective style of any; and he was pained
accordingly. No 'free-lance,' perhaps, has ever achieved so
much and so suddenly as Mr. Disraeli then did. Upon this
part of his career an historical examiner would give him
first-rate marks—much greater than he would give to any
competitor.

The next, and far the longest, of Mr. Disraeli's Parliamentary parts is that of Leader of Opposition. And in this he
showed eminent mind—not equal to that of his free-lance
period, but still very great. His powers of epigram and
amusing nonsense gave infinite aid, year after year, to a party
that was to be beaten. And, after his fashion, he showed a
high magnanimity and conscience in not opposing or hamper-
ing the Ministry on great questions—say of foreign policy,
when his so doing would hurt the country. But this praise
must end here. On all minor Parliamentary questions, Mr.
Disraeli has simply no conscience at all. He regards them as
a game—as an old special pleader regarded litigation, to be
played so as to show your skill, and so as to win, but without any regard to the consequences. Indeed, Mr. Disraeli, at
bottom, believes that they have no consequences—that all is
settled by questions of race, 'Caucasian or Semitic,' and that it
is simple pedantry in such things to be scrupulous. And still
worse than this, which is an amusing defect after all, and
excusable—(for there *are* many deeper issues and causes than
are dreamed of in Parliamentary philosophy)—Mr. Disraeli
often showed in Opposition a turn for nonsense, which was *not*
amusing. He has many gifts, but he has not the gift of thinking out a subject, and when he tries to produce grave thought
he only makes platitudes. And some of his 'mares' nests,'
like his difficulty in the Franco-German War, arising out of
our guarantee to the Saxon provinces of Prussia, have been

almost incredible, and could only have been discovered by a mind
which, with many elements of genius, has also an element of
hare-brained recklessness. Drearier hearing, or drearier reading, than Mr. Disraeli's Opposition harangues, when they were
philosophical, can hardly anywhere be found. But still, though,
with these and other defects, he *did* lead the Tory Opposition
through long melancholy years, when one did not know who
else *could* have or who *would* have led it.

The next of Mr. Disraeli's Parliamentary parts was that of
Leader of a Ministry in a minority, where again he was first-
rate. He showed sometimes—in 1852, in 1858, and in 1866
—a nimbleness, a tact, and dexterity far surpassing, probably,
anything that Parliament has ever seen of a similar kind. He
'hit the House'—to use a phrase which Burke used of a like
but very inferior person—he 'hit the House between the wind
and the water,' and cut with a light witticism knots insoluble
by solemn argument. If, by a series of 'selections,' nature had
made a man so fit for this kind of work, it would have been a
marvel. But Mr. Disraeli drifted into it, as if by chance, from
quite another calling and another sphere.

Lastly, Mr. Disraeli has been lately, and was but yesterday, Leader of a Ministry in a majority. And here there was a
wonderful contrast. So far from being first-rate, he was ninth-
rate. He seemed to resemble those guerilla commanders who,
having achieved great exploits with scanty and ill-trained
troops, nevertheless are utterly at a loss and fail when they are
placed at the head of a first-rate army. In 1867 he made a
minority achieve wonderful things, but in 1876, when he had
the best majority—the most numerous and obedient—since
Mr. Pitt, he did nothing with it. So far from being able to
pass great enactments, he could not even despatch ordinary
business at decent hours. The gravest and sincerest of Tory
members—men who hardly murmur at anything—have been
heard to complain that it *was* hard that, after voting so well
and doing so little, they should be kept up so very late. The

Session just closed will be known in Parliamentary annals as one of the least effective or memorable on record, and yet one of the most fatiguing. And this collapse is no accident in Mr. Disraeli's career, but a thing essentially characteristic of the man, and which might have been predicted by any one who had analysed the traits which he had shown before. If we may be pardoned the metaphor—though his chaff is exquisite, his wheat is poor stuff. The solid part of his mind—the part fit for regulating bills and clauses—is as inferior to that of an ordinary man of decent ability, as the light and imaginative part is superior. An incessant and almost avowed inaccuracy pervades him. And if you ask such a man to regulate the stupendous business of Parliament—to arrange, and if possible effect, the most complex *agenda* that ever was in the world—failure is inevitable. It is like entering a light hack for a ploughing-match. In the last Parliamentary situation, Mr. Disraeli has scarcely seemed to be what he used to be, and this because that situation was the one for which he was the least suited, and the last in which he should have been placed. As so often happens, having obtained the ambition of his life —to be a Minister with power—he found he had only got where he ought not to be—he found that he could not wield the power.

And two things have been common to Mr. Disraeli all through these positions. In them all he has charmed the House, and has given debates in which he took part a kind of nice literary flavour which other debates had not, and which there is no one left to give to them. He was the best representative whom the 'Republic of Letters' ever had in Parliament, for he made his way by talents—especially by a fascination of words—essentially literary. And on the other hand, though he charmed Parliament, he never did anything more. He had no influence with the country. Such a vast power over Englishmen as has been possessed by Lord Palmerston and by Mr. Gladstone was out of his way altogether. Between

Mr. Disraeli and common Englishmen there was too broad a gulf—too great a difference. He was simply unintelligible to them. 'Ten miles from London,' to use the old phrase, there is scarcely any real conception of him. His mode of regarding Parliamentary proceedings as a play and a game, is incomprehensible to the simple and earnest English nature. Perhaps he has gained more than he has lost by the English not understanding him. At any rate, the fact remains that the special influence of this great gladiator never passed the walls of the amphitheatre: he has ruled the country by ruling Parliament, but has never had any influence in Parliament reverberating from the nation itself.

THE END.